# The Common Core Approach
# to Building Literacy in Boys

# THE COMMON CORE APPROACH TO BUILDING LITERACY IN BOYS

Liz Knowles, EdD, and Martha Smith

 LIBRARIES UNLIMITED

AN IMPRINT OF ABC-CLIO, LLC
Santa Barbara, California • Denver, Colorado • Oxford, England

**Library of Congress Cataloging-in-Publication Data**

Knowles, Elizabeth, 1946–
    The common core approach to building literacy in boys / Liz Knowles and Martha Smith.
        pages cm
    Includes bibliographical references and index.
        ISBN 978–1–61069–635–7 (pbk : acid-free paper) — ISBN 978–1–61069–636–4 (ebook)
    1. Boys—Books and reading—United States. 2. Reading—Sex differences. 3. Children's literature, American—Bibliography. 4. Young adult literature, American—Bibliography. 5. Boys—Education—United States. 6. Language arts (Elementary)—Curricula—United States. 7. Language arts (Elementary)—Standards—United States. 8. Language arts (Secondary)—Curricula—United States. 9. Language arts (Secondary)—Standards—United States. I. Smith, Martha. II. Title.
    Z1039.B67K585   2014
    028.5'5083—dc23           2014000500

ISBN: 978–1–61069–635–7
EISBN: 978–1–61069–636–4

18  17  16  15  14     1  2  3  4  5

This book is also available on the World Wide Web as an eBook.
Visit www.abc-clio.com for details.

Libraries Unlimited
An Imprint of ABC-CLIO, LLC

ABC-CLIO, LLC
130 Cremona Drive, P.O. Box 1911
Santa Barbara, California 93116-1911

This book is printed on acid-free paper ∞

Manufactured in the United States of America

# CONTENTS

Contents

# FOREWORD

"What are we to do with Derek?" We asked ourselves that question frequently, and that particular day, as we met around the kidney-shaped reading table, was no different. We were a group of seasoned educators with the best of intentions, an arsenal of strategies from our years of collective experience, and the highest of hopes; yet Derek continued to stump us.

Derek was a third-grader then. He was, without question, as smart as a whip. Motivation and engagement in learning activities? Marginal at best. In fact, when he did his work, it was always rushed and typically incomplete. During group lessons, Derek was constantly poking (and provoking) his neighbors and making random (and often inappropriate) noises at critical junctures of the teacher's lesson. The parents and school were united in their concern and desire to help Derek—as well as in their confusion about what to do. We just could not seem to get Derek "on board" with classroom learning.

If you are an educator, you have probably met a child like Derek. In fact, think back on your most challenging students—those who get lower grades, don't turn in their homework reliably, or just seem disinterested or unmotivated in general. Are those students mostly boys? If your answer is yes, your experience parallels that of most U.S. teachers, and it aligns with international findings as well.

Boys are more likely to be kicked out or drop out of school. They are less likely to do their homework and they earn most of the Ds and Fs. And this isn't just a problem in the United States. According to the OECD (Organisation for Economic Co-operation and Development), the 2012 Programme for International Assessment results show that there is a significant gap between boys and girls both in their levels of achievement *and* in their levels of engagement. Specifically, reading achievement—which underpins success in all academic areas, and increasingly so with the arrival of the Common Core—is lagging significantly in almost every country of the world, and to the greatest extent in the most highly ranked countries. This information is not new. Unfortunately, it reflects a persistent pattern of boys' underperformance in many areas of school and life. This achievement gap crosses nationalities, language backgrounds, and socioeconomics.

Now, with this vexing achievement gap as yet unresolved, the era of the Common Core State Standards is dawning and, with it, increasingly complex requirements for the area where boys struggle most—English language arts. How do we get those boys—like Derek—to do deep and sometimes painstaking analysis of informational text when frequently their modus operandi is "one and done"? How do boys demonstrate proficiency on a Common Core Standard when they are inclined to breeze through a passage and bubble in the first thing that looks remotely correct, just so they can be done with it? Given the reality that engagement precedes achievement, how might we increase boys' enthusiasm for close reading?

The trouble we have here is not with the boys themselves. The trouble is that we don't fully understand our boys, that most schools are a better "fit" for girl learners, and that we don't consistently teach to boys' strengths and passions. With the arrival of the Common Core, we are called to deeply and intimately know two things—the Common Core Standards themselves and the learning needs of our students. But let's take that one step further and use the lens of gender. Does your school have an intentional plan for understanding and targeting the unique literacy needs of underachieving boys? If not, be prepared for the gulf to widen between boys and girls with the first release of the Common Core English language arts assessment results in 2015.

Fortunately, the Common Core Standards are not a curriculum. They simply provide the "bar" that all students should reach at each grade level, as well as apples-to-apples comparisons of student performance. School districts are charged with determining the best ways to get their students across that bar. Now is the time, if there was ever a time, for schools to take seriously the underperformance of their boys and to ask themselves, "How do boys learn?", "What are boys passionate about?", and "How do we help boys clear an even higher bar set by the Common Core English language arts standards?"

This is where *The Common Core Approach to Building Literacy in Boys* comes in. Both one-of-a-kind and timely, this book is a valuable resource for developing a literacy program that focuses on boys and embraces the English Language Arts Common Core Standards. Knowles and Smith hit on the very topics that spark high levels of interest and engagement in boys, and then they identify the best teaching and learning resources across multiple platforms to specifically target the Common Core Standards at every grade level, preschool through twelfth grade. As an experienced teacher and school principal, this is a resource that I welcome— the right tool to help boys, put into the hands of teachers, is the key to reversing this stubborn trend. I know with great certainty that it works.

For Derek, that meant identifying what captured his mind and his heart and then tying everything that we possibly could into those themes. *The Common Core Approach to Building Literacy in Boys* is a resource that helps teachers do just that.

This is a book that belongs in the hands of every educator who is asking, "What are we to do with Derek?"

Kelley King

Kelley King is a twenty-seven-year veteran educator. As a school administrator, Kelley led her staff to close the gender gap in reading and writing in just one year and, in doing so, gained national media attention. Kelley's work has been featured on *The Today Show*, National Public Radio, and *National Health Journal*, as well as in *Newsweek* magazine and in *Educational Leadership*. Kelley is the author of *Writing the Playbook: A Practitioner's Guide to Creating a Boy-Friendly School*, published by Corwin Press in 2013. Kelley has also co-authored (with Michael Gurian and Kathy Stevens) two previous books in the education field: *Strategies for Teaching Boys and Girls: Elementary Level* and *Strategies for Teaching Boys and Girls: Secondary Level*. For more information and resources on boy-friendly school, go to www.boyfriendlyschools.com.

# INTRODUCTION

As far back as the year 2000, there has been an interest in the fact that boys in general were not doing well in school. In the mid-1980s there was a push for more support for girls in the areas of science and math. That was a success because the gender gap in math and science has grown smaller. Shortly after that, the focus turned to boys. We published a book in 2005 with Libraries Unlimited called *Boys and Literacy: Practical Strategies for Librarians, Teachers, and Parents* and annotated many newspaper, journal, and magazine articles about this dilemma. We also annotated a variety of professional books about boys from authors such as Gurian, Booth, Brozo, Kindlon, Newkirk, Odean, Sullivan, and Thompson. Most all of these works were proclaiming the sad state of affairs with regard to boys and school.

In our book we offered many suggestions with regard to titles and authors that would be appealing to boys and suggestions about changes at home, in the classroom, and in schools that would help to promote boys and reading and make a positive change for the future.

As we revisit this topic in 2014 we find that surprisingly not much has changed. The statistics are still pretty alarming, there have been many suggested reasons and changes but it seems that not much has actually been accomplished regarding the plight of boys. In 2009, neuroscientist Lise Eliot's book, *Pink Brain Blue Brain,* was a bit of a deviation from the norm with regard to the reasons boys have difficulty. She determined through thorough research that the differences between boys and girls starting at birth are not that significant. However, the way parents and then teachers treat boys and girls makes the difference.

We have read the work of Kelley King, *Writing the Playbook: A Practitioner's Guide to Creating a Boy-Friendly School* (2013). She had some excellent results in a school in Boulder, Colorado, in 2005, with her approach that teachers need to change their attitude toward boys and eliminate the preconceived ideas of how boys act in the classroom. The playbook has some excellent ideas but it seems that despite the success in the Colorado school this approach has not been widely embraced.

So we again focus on boys and literacy, this time with the background of the new English Language Arts Common Core Standards. The fact that the standards emphasize nonfiction texts leads us to a possibly stereotyped idea that boys like nonfiction/informational texts more than fiction, so therefore they might thrive in this kind of environment. We have endeavored to include every possible topic that might be of interest to boys, including a complete bibliography and annotated titles for each. We have provided a long list of strategies for change, including the area of technology. We have included: Strategies for Change, Apps, Authors—Just for Boys, Books Made into Film, Magazines—Just for Boys, Web Sites, and Annotated Professional Resources. We share many annotated articles from magazines, newspapers, journals, and professional books about boys as well as the English Language Arts Common Core Standards.

The book has 20 chapters that cover Action and Adventure; Arts and Music; Comics and Graphic Novels; Exceptionalities; Explorations and Journeys; Fantasy and Science Fiction; History and Historical Fiction; Humor and Poetry; LGBT; Math and Numbers; Mechanics and Technology; Nature, Environment, and Animals; Realistic and Social Issues; Science and Space; Sports; and Thrillers and Mystery. Each chapter includes an Introduction, two Featured Authors, Annotated Titles, a Bibliography, and an Annotated Professional Title.

In light of the fact that within the English Language Arts Common Core, questioning has changed because of text complexity, close reading and new expectations are in place for writing, there is a section called Read Like a Detective and Write Like a Journalist.

The titles for the chapter bibliographies were selected using Amazon, The Hornbook Guide Online, *Best Books for Children: Preschool through Grade 8* (Libraries Unlimited, 2013), *Best Books for Boys: A Resource for Educators* (Libraries Unlimited, 2008), *School Library Journal*, http://www.next reads.com and School Library Journal's Curriculum Connections.

In reviewing the research for both the *Boys and Literacy: The Research* and *Common Core English Language Arts: The Research* chapter, we provided the highlights of the articles and a few books so that readers could get the essence of the information accurately and then decide if they wanted to locate the information to read in more detail. This was done because I know teachers do not like to or have time to do research and read multiple journals. No thoughts in those review/summary paragraphs are mine. We have quoted or paraphrased the essence so that it would read exactly or very close. So—for each—I gave the bibliographical information right at the beginning of the paragraph(s), to facilitate the location of the complete work, if desired.

# Chapter 1

# BOYS AND LITERACY: THE RESEARCH

In June 2013 *The Atlantic* featured an article by Jessica Lahey ("Stop Penalizing Boys for Not Being Able to Sit Still at School") who began with some frightening statistics about what is happening to boys in schools today in comparison to girls. Boys are more often kept back or expelled, and they are more often diagnosed with learning disorders or attention problems. Boys do less homework, make lower grades, and are more likely to drop out of school. They currently make up only 43 percent of college students. Lahey takes her information from *Teaching Boys Reaching Boys: Strategies That Work and Why*. She also states that behavior plays a role in the way teachers grade and consequently boys receive lower grades from their teachers than standardized test scores predict. Effective lessons that hold boys' attention include more interesting end products, competitive games, lessons that include competition and teamwork, independent exploration, and drama and novelty.

Michael Kimmel ("Solving the Boy Crisis in School"), April 2013, Huffington Post Parents, decries the fact that the National Council of Teachers of English announced winners of their Promising Young Writers Competition—only six boys in the entire country won. Kimmel claims that the evidence tells us that boys' underachievement is caused by their desire to be masculine. Their culture forces them to feel that it is not manly to be smart or to succeed in school. "Reading is lame, sitting down and looking at words is a pathetic way to spend your time."

Claiborne and Siegel, March 2010 ("New Study Shows Boys Lagging Behind Girls in Reading: Boys Are Struggling With Reading in All 50 States"), state that in the past boys did not do better during the first couple of years of school: girls did better. But boys eventually caught up. Now they are seeing that boys are no longer catching up. They explore various theories for this gender gap—including the differences between the brains of boys and girls and the fact that boys are more physically active than girls and have a more difficult time sitting in a classroom situation.

Brett Smith, January 2013 ("Study Examines Why Girls Do Better than Boys in School"), reviews a study done by researchers at the University of Georgia and Columbia University. The findings indicate gender differences in teachers' grading and evaluation of students. Girls' good behavior in class for the most part seems to result in better overall grades. Boys' grades seem to be lower than aptitude and intelligence tests indicate, which are probably influenced by their overall behavior.

Lori Day, an educational consultant and writer for Huffington Post Education, June 2011 ("Why Boys Are Failing in an Educational System Stacked Against Them"), states that statistics show some pretty frightening numbers with regard to boys and education: their grades, their discipline, problems as dropouts, and low numbers attending college. The fact that "kindergarten is the new first-grade" makes it difficult for many boys to keep up. The overfocus on standardized test scores is also not a good thing for boys, especially when physical education and recess may be shortened or eliminated. Day states that it is necessary for boys to move in physical education, recess, and hands-on activities to harness some of their natural restlessness and channel their energy in positive ways.

Peg Tyre, February 2013 ("It's Time to Worry: Boys are Rapidly Falling Behind Girls in School"), reviews the evidence that has been piling up for nearly a decade now that boys are doing less well in school than girls. It seems that slowly teachers, parents, and school administrators are waking up to this fact. In the previously mentioned study from the University of Georgia and Columbia University, "boys who scored well on tests indicating mastery of the material being taught, did not get grades from teachers that reflected their abilities in three central subjects: reading, math, and science." It seems that teachers were more partial to girls. The research states that grades were influenced by discipline. Boys complain about being criticized more unfairly and after reading the results of this study—it seems as though that is accurate.

Reichert and Hawley ("Relationships Play a Primary Role in Boys Learning") in *Phi Delta Kappan*, May 2013, talk about the fact that relationships with teachers are key to adolescent boys' success in school. The teacher needs to identify the students' needs and to set high goals for the students. The teacher needs to know and like their subject area. They need to understand students' passions or talents, and take an interest. Teachers need to make every effort not to take boys' sometimes crazy behavior personally.

At the American Library Association's Annual Conference in June 2013, a session called *Attracting Reluctant Male Readers* presented by Binns and Klise brought to light some important ways to improve boys' attitudes toward reading. They state that boys need books with "fast moving action, frequent danger, high-stakes, and straight forward, unfussy narratives." It is important to be aware of what boys like to read and why those types of books appeal to them. It is equally important to talk to boys who won't or don't read and find out the reasons why. Binns and Klise believe it is important to highlight a variety of titles that are attractive to guys, and it is a good idea to organize a middle school/high school library in a subject-organized way, like a bookstore. They also share the importance of book clubs for boys and provide Web sites and information about creating book clubs. John Klise provides a list called *After Percy Jackson: 10 Irresistible Novels for Teen Boys at My Library* and another list called *Popular Nonfiction for Teen Boys at My Library.*

Judy Kleinfeld, from Fairbanks, Alaska ("Schools Find Ways to Help Boys Learn"), in April 2013, reviews *Writing the Playbook: a Practitioner's Guide to Creating a Boy-Friendly School* written by Kelley King. According to Kleinfeld, the book offers many good strategies and documented results that prove that the strategies actually worked in a school in Colorado. She states that to help boys with assignments, it's appropriate to emphasize high interest activities and challenging real-world projects.

In an article posted on the University of Georgia Web site, Matt Weeks and Christopher Cornwell give a summary of the previously mentioned research done by the University of Georgia in cooperation with Columbia University. Their research concludes that some of the difficulties that boys have in school comes from their behavior in class, which sometimes results in teachers lowering their grades. According to one of the researchers, Christopher Cornwell, "it seems that gender disparities in teacher grades start early and uniformly favor girls. Girls don't all of a sudden become more engaged and boys don't suddenly become more rambunctious."

John Sellers in June 2013 ("The Boy Readers Are All Right"), reported on a panel discussion about boys and reading, which included reference to the importance of humor in reading for boys.

In an article in the *Reading Teacher*, May 2013 ("Combating 'I Hate This Stupid Book!' Black Males and Critical Literacy"), Wood and Jocius share these three ways to combat negative attitudes of African-American male students toward reading: provide ethnically appropriate books, allow teamwork, and academic dialogue. It is important to have these male students' voices heard.

Julie Anderson, *World-Herald*, May 2013 ("To Encourage Boys Reading, Look To Book Clubs"), wrote about the importance of book clubs for boys in middle and high school. The article lists resources for finding books that will be appealing to boys and suggests that reading can be a social activity for boys. It is important to find ways to get boys involved in reading—they need to have a reason to read. A book club should provide a wide variety of different reading materials for boys such as: newspapers, magazines, nonfiction, comics, and graphic novels. Another important factor is male role models in reading both at school and in the home. It is a good idea to provide time to read in class and to also require some sort of independent reading time at home—perhaps as part of homework. Anderson pointed out that Jon Scieszka, founder of Guys Read, offers lists of book-picks for boys and even a template for creating book clubs, which he calls "field offices." The article also suggests organizing middle and high school libraries like a bookstore. The article also provides many resources for encouraging boys to read.

Shannon Firth, June 2011 ("Five Ways to Get Boys to Read"), tells us "to expand our definition of reading to include nonfiction, humor, graphic novels, comic books, wordless books, fantasy, science fiction, magazines, online audio books, and comic strips." Teachers and librarians need to focus on books that boys like and share them. They should also have boys keep book trackers to list the books they have read with some sort of a symbol as to how they rate them. She also recommends "a student story hour during lunch where a male teacher reads to boys as they eat, taking one week to finish a book. On Friday celebrate with cupcakes for dessert."

In an article in *Educational Leadership*, November 2010 ("Gender Friendly Schools"), King, Gurian, and Stevens discuss the crisis that boys are in with regard to their education and how school improvement must really focus on gender equality. The authors provide strategies for teaching boys and girls effectively.

Daryl Nelson, *Consumer Affairs*, April 2013 ("Girls Are Thrashing Boys in Academic Achievement. How Come?"), asked the question, "Are girls smarter than boys?" Girls are enrolling in college in higher numbers these days and boys are falling behind. Nelson shares that in a new book by Claudia Buchmann, *The Rise of Women: The Growing Gender Gap in Education and What It Means for American Schools,* "It's not about ability; it's about effort and engagement. Success in academics, like success in sports, requires time and effort. Because boys put forth less effort and are less engaged, they get lower grades and are less likely to get through college." Buchmann says that years ago when a boy didn't do well in school there were many well-paying technical or blue-collar jobs available for boys.

In August 2011, an article featured in the online *New York Times* by Robert Lipsyte, who interviewed Donald Gallo, a retired English professor, states that boys gravitate toward nonfiction but schools favor classics over contemporary fiction. Very often boys do not have enough positive male role models for literacy. "Today's books for boys seem to be supernatural space and sword epics that read like video game manuals and sports novels with moral messages. Many of the edgy books that boys might like to read are either not taught or banned."

In May 2013, Glenn Sacks wrote about boys as the "new underclass in American schools." Sacks states that boys at all levels are far more likely than girls to be disciplined, suspended, held back, or expelled. Children, especially boys, need physically connected activities because they learn best by doing.

In May 2012, Zimbardo and Duncan wrote a TED e-book, *The Demise of Guys: Why Boys Are Struggling and What We Can Do About It.* The authors state that "young men's addiction to video games and online porn have created a generation of shy, socially awkward, emotionally removed, and risk-adverse young men who are unable and unwilling to navigate the complexities and risks inherent to real-life relationships, school, and employment." The authors say that things can change but it's going to take a lot of determination and definitely a good deal of support and understanding from parents.

In an interview with Ralph Fletcher by Mike McQueen, Fletcher says that teachers limit the topics for creative writing to such an extent that boys really can't write about anything that they like. Blood, guts, battles, and murders are all off-limits. The advice he gives to boys is to read everything they can get their hands on and to keep a writer's notebook. It is also good to draw instead of trying to write a story—illustrate first and then write it. It is important to make sure that the school library has the kind of books that boys like: graphic novels, humor, war, nonfiction, action, survival, fantasy, and so on. His Web site, http://www.ralphfletcher.com/, is loaded with great tips for young writers.

Frank Serafini, in the *Reading Teacher*, September 2013 ("Supporting Boys as Readers"), reiterates the most popular reasons why boys are poor readers. He claims that the novels selected for use in schools are much more interesting for girls; therefore, boys are bored and never given novels that interest them. Serafini makes suggestions regarding the kinds of books boys like and also advises librarians and teachers to encourage browsing, use shorter texts, give boys plenty of opportunities to read, give them choices, and to limit the required abundance of before, during, and after reading activities. "All the access to books in the world will not make boys pick up a book if being a reader is not something they aspire to become or isn't an identity their peers would approve of. In other words, we have to find ways to make reading cool both in and out of school," says Serafini.

In the *Best of Educational Leadership 2010–2011* (*The Myth of Pink and Blue Brains*), Lise Eliot says that to make changes with regard to gender gaps in education we first need to eliminate the distinction of male and female brains. Boys and girls differ in many ways such as activity levels, self-control, and math and reading attitudes and interests. Eliot says that boys' brains are bigger than girls and boys finish growing a year or so later than girls. Girls show better ability to sit still and pay attention and to organize. These are about the only clear-cut differences. Eliot has shown that "the range of performance within each gender is wider than the difference between the average boy and girl." No mental ability is hardwired into the brain. The actual differences are magnified by a culture that sees boys and girls as different and encourages these stereotyped differences. Parents tend to encourage different playthings and physical actions for boys and girls. Eliot says that all this can be changed if we stop stereotyping from birth, if we recognize the scope of ability in either gender, and encourage boys to participate in nonathletic activities, and encourage more men to be teachers. "There are still teachers who believe that girls are good at reading and boys are good at math. There are teachers who cannot tolerate exuberance or coloring outside the lines. We must train teachers about potential bias and evaluate them with respect to it," says Eliot. She states that there are really no hardwired differences between boys and girls and that the "viral propagation" of these claims continues to hurt boys in school.

The following is information about the 2013 National Assessment of Educational Progress (NAEP) for boys and girls in the fourth and the eighth grade in reading.

### Achievement-level results in fourth- and eighth-grade NAEP reading: 1992, 2011, and 2013

### Reading Scores by Gender
Reading in Fourth Grade:

|      | Male | Female |
|------|------|--------|
| 2013 | 219  | 225    |
| 2011 | 218  | 225    |
| 1992 | 213  | 221    |

Reading in Eighth Grade:

|       | Male | Female |
|-------|------|--------|
| 2013  | 263  | 273    |
| 2011  | 261  | 270    |
| 1992  | 254  | 267    |

*Source:* U.S. Department of Education, Institute of Education Sciences, National Center for Education Statistics, National Assessment of Educational Progress (NAEP), 1992, 2011, and 2013 Reading Assessments.

## More Information—Reading Scores—Grade 4—by Gender

Subject, Grade: Reading, Grade 4
**Jurisdiction:** National
**Measure:** Composite scale
**Variables:** Gender
**Years:** 2013, 2011, 2009

Percentages for reading, grade 4 by gender [GENDER], year and jurisdiction: 2013, 2011, 2009

|       |              | Male       |                | Female     |                |
|-------|--------------|------------|----------------|------------|----------------|
| Year  | Jurisdiction | Percentage | Standard Error | Percentage | Standard Error |
| 2013  | National     | 51         | (0.2)          | 49         | (0.2)          |
| 2011  | National     | 51         | (0.1)          | 49         | (0.1)          |
| 2009  | National     | 50         | (0.1)          | 50         | (0.1)          |

*Note*: Detail may not sum to totals because of rounding. Some apparent differences between estimates may not be statistically significant.
*Source*: U.S. Department of Education, Institute of Education Sciences, National Center for Education Statistics, National Assessment of Educational Progress (NAEP), 2009, 2011, and 2013 Reading Assessments.

## More Information—Reading Scores—Grade 8—by Gender

Subject, Grade: Reading, Grade 8
**Jurisdiction:** National
**Measure:** Composite scale
**Variable:** Gender
**Years:** 2013, 2011, 2009

(*continued*)

Percentages for reading, grade 8 by gender [GENDER], year and jurisdiction: 2013, 2011, 2009

| Year | Jurisdiction | Male | | Female | |
|------|--------------|------|--|--------|--|
| | | Percentage | Standard Error | Percentage | Standard Error |
| 2013 | National | 51 | (0.2) | 49 | (0.2) |
| 2011 | National | 50 | (0.1) | 50 | (0.1) |
| 2009 | National | 50 | (0.1) | 50 | (0.1) |

*Note*: Detail may not sum to totals because of rounding. Some apparent differences between estimates may not be statistically significant.

*Source*: U.S. Department of Education, Institute of Education Sciences, National Center for Education Statistics, National Assessment of Educational Progress (NAEP), 2009, 2011, and 2013 Reading Assessments.

## SUMMARY OF RESEARCH

After reading through all this information it appears to me that there are some general points that are repeated by many. The statistics that show boys' educational decline have been available for more than ten years. Things are not improving for boys. Another issue is the boy code—the stereotyped culture that boys do not like to read, they are noisy and rowdy, and they do not like to pay attention in class, do homework, or study. That is just the way it is. Another factor is the overwhelming number of female teachers and the general perception that as a group they have trouble dealing with boys' humor, inattentiveness, and penchant for disruption and misbehavior. There seems to be proof that with some teachers this actually has a negative impact on some boys' grades.

Suggestions for change have been offered and based on the points just mentioned; we know what needs to be done. Teachers need to be trained and coached about their attitudes toward boys. We need to help boys with their impulses and issues, and we need to make attempts to change the culture that exists from the cradle and encourage boys to be happy with themselves the way they are. Perhaps the most difficult task will be to change these long-entrenched views in the parents.

# Chapter 2

# COMMON CORE ENGLISH LANGUAGE ARTS: THE RESEARCH

Educators have known for a long time that it is important for teachers of all content areas to offer students support in reading the texts of their particular area. Reading is not the responsibility only of the reading teacher in the elementary grades. Far too many students need support in reading specific texts for subject areas. Content-specific vocabulary can be very challenging and a firm and thorough background in reading informational texts can be very helpful as students move through more difficult levels of content.

## CLASSROOM AND TEACHING

Daniels, Zemelman, and Arthur Hyde (*Best Practice: Bringing Standards to Life in America's Classrooms*) wrote, in 2012, that "we can effectively meet the new standards by using curiosity, rather than coercion, as instructional fuel." Teachers should model the process first and then let students work on their own to develop their skills and understandings. Teachers can provide ample opportunities for students to work together and become deeply involved in the learning process from every angle.

Lehman, Christopher (*Energize Research Reading and Writing: Fresh Strategies to Spark Interest, Develop Independence, and Meet Key Common Core Standards, Grades 4–8*) wrote, in 2012, that it is important for teachers to make the best use of time by finding out what the students know about a topic before they plan their lessons. This is the way for maximum learning to take place.

In *Education Week*, April, 2012, Catherine Gewertz ("Common Standards Ignite Debate Over Prereading") reported that common core authors say that they "did not intend to abolish pre-reading but to curtail and revamp it. The standards call for students to be able to read independently and proficiently without significant scaffolding or instructional supports by teachers." It is not appropriate for a teacher to spend large amounts of time preparing students for a reading—it would be better to just read and then react to the student response.

Robert Rothman, a senior fellow at the Alliance for Excellent Education (*Something in Common: The Common Core Standards and the Next Chapter in American Education*), in 2011, tells of ways common core will change classroom practice. Nonfiction will take the center spotlight and students will be expected to read very carefully to find evidence to answer text-based questions. Rothman states that the English Language Arts Common Core Standards include criteria for content areas such as history, social science, science, and technical subjects. "This means that the subject area teachers will need to spend time making sure that students are able to understand information from any document and make judgments about its credibility."

Phillips and Wong in *Phi Delta Kappa International*, April 2012, state that "history, social studies, science, and technical teachers, not just English teachers, will use their content expertise to help students read, write, speak, and listen using the language of their disciplines." In the past, success in reading has been the job of the elementary classroom teacher and then the English teacher. Regularly, content area teachers would state that they are *not* reading teachers. This has changed. The Common Core State Standards now see reading and vocabulary study as the job of all teachers. The standards expect all teachers to become involved in reading, writing, speaking, and listening.

Pearson and Hebert in "What Happens To The Basics?" (*Educational Leadership*, December 2012/January 2013) discuss the importance of the second and third grades in light of the increasing expectations for text complexity. Because of the "disappointing comprehension results from the No Child Left Behind era," it is necessary to develop new and different reading strategies at a young age. By the end of the third grade, students must be proficient readers—it has been stated that reading ability in the third grade is a predictor of success in high school. We need to realize that starting early with quality informational texts helps to build students' knowledge, vocabulary and expands their interests. High-quality narrative texts need to replace "highly decodable text with nonsensical content." Students in second and third grades need to be given more time to read rather than spending time doing worksheets; it is suggested that students read a minimum of seven minutes more each day.

Meghan Everette, a blogger on the www.scholastic.com Web site, wrote (February 2013) that there are three key shifts with the Common Core English Language Arts standards. The focus now becomes "building knowledge through content rich nonfiction, reading, writing, and speaking grounded in evidence from the text, both literary and informational and there must be regular practice with complex text and its academic language." She also points out how important it is to provide ample time in class for students to read.

McTighe and Wiggins, September 2012 ("Common Core Standards to Curriculum: Five Big Ideas") conclude that the standards need to be read and thoroughly understood. We need to create: "long-term transfer goals, overarching understandings, overarching essential questions, and a set of reoccurring corner-stone tasks." In typical backward design style they say the curriculum built from the standards needs to be mapped backward from the desired results.

Jonathan Hunt writes in *Hornbook* in May 2013 ("The Amorphous Genre") that students like the style of nonfiction texts because they are nonlinear and visually stimulating. Students see nothing wrong with skimming or browsing as long as they are not doing that because they can't read the text. "Students have insatiable appetites to learn about particular topics as well as the uncanny ability to absorb that information like sponges." Hunt reminds us that "there are no books that all young nonfiction readers have read, no books that bond them together the way that Tolkien, Pullman, Rowling, or Lewis do for young fantasy readers." He says that nonfiction authors need to get busy and start producing bestseller quality series and titles.

In the area of the classroom and teaching, the common core focus may be good for boys in the sense that nonfiction will take a much more prominent role in reading choices. If teachers take a more proactive approach with regard to nonfiction, with book talks and author studies, this will help boys to make good nonfiction choices. Because all content area teachers will be expected to teach reading, this may help boys to get through some difficult subject area texts and give them the opportunity to do more "research" on topics that interest them.

## LEXILES

Sarah Brown Wessling, www.theteachingchannel.com, has recently written about her experiences in working with the English Language Arts Common Core Standards. Lexile scores have been confusing to many teachers because often "less-sophisticated vocabulary or sentence structure does not necessarily make an easier read." Lexile scores are still important, but text complexity is telling us that there is much more to it than that.

Elfrieda Hiebert, of TextProject, Inc., wrote in a post ("Looking 'Within' the Lexile for More Guidance: Word Frequency and Sentence Length") in January 2011, that Lexile data on reading material is only one of the three factors of text complexity that is currently available. She discusses the wide discrepancy in Lexile numbers for various texts and reminds us that short sentences do not necessarily mean easy reading. In nonfiction texts, authors often use "infrequent" words that have a lower Lexile rating. Hiebert advises teachers to use Lexile ratings as an initial piece of information before evaluating a title on the other components of text complexity, with the knowledge of the possible variations and discrepancies.

Timothy Shanahan, in a post ("CCSS Allows More than Lexiles") on Shanahan on Literacy in September 2012, states that the use of Lexiles led to the assumption that readability levels could also be used to determine instructional level. Shanahan says that there is no evidence to support that and that students can actually be successful with and learn from a wide range of readability levels with teacher support. Common core does not support instructional levels. He says teachers can still use Lexile levels but as only one measure of evaluating texts.

Personally, I have always felt that if a student is interested in the topic that the difficulty of the text is not a hindrance because a way can be found to get the desired information. Common core wants students to read outside their readability levels to learn more. Teachers need to encourage that and provide scaffolds where needed. Boys should be allowed to choose texts that appeal to them and help them learn more about topics of interest.

## APPENDIX B—EXEMPLAR LIST—ENGLISH LANGUAGE ARTS COMMON CORE STATE STANDARDS

Sarah Brown Wessling (The Teaching Channel) also states that there has been some confusion regarding ELA Appendix B. It is not a reading list. It is simply meant as examples for us to use in finding "similarly complex texts that meet the needs of our learners."

In the December 2012/January 2013 online issue of *Reading Today* ("The CCSS Text Exemplars: Understanding Their Aims and Use in Text Selection"), Hiebert wrote about the common core text exemplars and how to understand them and use them. The texts as listed in Appendix B are "intended only as models or examples, not as mandates or prescriptions," according to Hiebert. Rather than relying only on quantitative indices (Lexiles), the three-part model of text complexity also includes qualitative dimensions and reader and task considerations. CCSS Exemplars are there to help—they are not intended to be the curriculum according to Hiebert.

Chester Finn in "Standards, Reading Lists, and Censorship" from *The Education Gadfly*, September 2013, says that Appendix B isn't really part of the standards and does not mean that any of the books listed there need to be read by anyone. The choice of books related to the curriculum remains in the hands of the state, district, school, teacher, and so on.

Fenice Boyd in *Reading Today*, December 2012/January 2013 ("Unpacking the Text Exemplars Presented in Appendix B"), reminds us that the exemplars in Appendix B are there for reminders of the variety of diverse texts we must include in reading curriculum. She suggests adding Clinton's and Obama's inaugural addresses and other texts that represent all cultures and societies because "children need to see themselves in the books they read."

Boys will fare better if the texts selected are geared to the content and to their interests. Although the Appendix B list seems all encompassing—it was created in 2009 and we need to remind one and all that it is simply a list of examples and not meant as a shopping list!

## QUESTIONING

In *Reading Today* ("Analyze This!"), McLaughlin and Fisher state that we have frequently used the verb "analyze" when expressing student expectations. "Analyzing requires a response that demonstrates an ability to see patterns and to classify information into component parts." They also share that analyzing is a level in Bloom's taxonomy, for thinking about parts and how they work in unison.

Focusing on analyzing brings us the opportunity to move to a different level of questioning about reading. McLaughlin and Fisher remind us that students are used to answering literal questions, but the new standards expect students to answer questions at four different levels: memory, convergent, divergent, and evaluative.

In another article in this issue of *Reading Today* ("Did You Ask a Good Common Core Question Today?"), Ciardiello reminds us about the importance of asking good questions. Good questioning should promote self-checking and understanding meaning. Good questions help the reader to realize exactly what the author means. Ciardiello tells us to "question an author's assumptions and premises and to assess the veracity of claims and the soundness of reasoning." Because text-based or evidence-based questioning has become an integral part of the common core, it is necessary to find a framework or strategies for creating good questions.

Rothstein and Santana, coordinators of The Right Question Institute wrote for Harvard Education Press (September 2011) about how to teach students to ask their own questions. The process is called the Question Formulation Technique (QFT). The process is as follows: teachers are asked to use statements taken from reading to generate questions. Students then ask and write down as many questions as they can without judgment. Students must be taught the difference between closed- and open-ended questions. The students must then organize the questions and select the three or four best ones. "An important part of this process is that it increases participation in the group and peer learning process."

Questioning, in general, has changed. Gone are so many feeling and opinion questions and in their place are text-based questions. Now it is very important to find out exactly what the author means and also what sources are used. In the past it was thought that fiction was false and nonfiction was true. Now students have to realize that nonfiction is the author's truth and, in that sense, still needs to be questioned and qualified. There are processes to be taught for creating good questions and perhaps this kind of questioning will "feel better" for boys!

## TEXT COMPLEXITY

In an article by Hiebert from www.textproject.org at the University of California, Santa Cruz ("Seven Actions That Teachers Can Take Right Now: Text Complexity"), she explains seven worthy actions: focus on knowledge, create connections, activate passions, develop vocabulary, increase volume, build stamina, and identify benchmarks. Hiebert says it is important to challenge students to spend more time reading each day and then emphasize that concept by giving them adequate time to read in class.

In the December 2012/January 2013 issue of *Reading Today* ("Determining the Complexity of Contemporary Texts"), McLaughlin and Overturf remind teachers that it is important to understand that text complexity includes qualitative and quantitative measures as well as a closer look at the reader and the task. "The reader and task include variables such as the readers' cognitive capabilities, motivation, purposes for reading, and the knowledge and experiences unique to each reader." It is up to us to find text that will be both engaging and motivational to our students.

Paige Jaeger, in "Balancing Readability and Reading Fluency: On Common Core," March 2013, states that the best definition of close reading is read with a pencil. Jaeger says, "Educators across America know that our transliterated learners have eyes that gravitate to pictures over text, skim and scan Web pages at warp speed, and lack determination to read difficult material." She also reminds us that reading for pleasure is still how we build lifelong readers and therefore we need to allow students to read what they want during independent reading time.

## CLOSE READING

Catherine Snow in *Reading Today*, June/July 2013 ("Cold Versus Warm Close Reading: Building Students' Stamina for Struggling with Text") says, "I would argue that middle and high schools students are not, on average, deeply motivated to learn and master academic skills." Teachers can entice them with interesting issues and engaging questions. The author claims that close reading without any support will result in frustration so it is necessary to provide some scaffolding in vocabulary, purpose, and background knowledge.

Nancy Boyles, in *Educational Leadership*, December 2012/January 2013, wrote about "Closing In On Close Reading." She says, "Close reading means reading to uncover layers of meaning that lead to deep comprehension." She suggests using shorter texts and to work toward students becoming successful independent readers. It is also important to teach students to ask questions. "The goal is for students to take what they learn from the study of one text and apply it to the next text they read." Boyles also tells of the importance of being able to summarize or paraphrase precisely and clearly.

In *Reading Today*, the June/July 2013 issue ("Authentic Reasons for Close Reading: How to Motivate Students to Take Another Look"), Elizabeth Dobler states that, "close reading entails returning to the text multiple times for multiple reasons. A suggestion for teachers is to select high-quality texts that make reading and rereading worthwhile and then plan for a multi-day commitment to the text with a focus each day on a specific reading mission to be accomplished." It is important to allow the student to become involved with the text and discover meaning without the teacher providing all the answers and details.

As we promote close reading and text complexity in reading choices it will be important to offer scaffolding so that students are not overly frustrated. For boys, the key might be to find topics of interest so that they want to dig into the evidence and information in the texts they choose.

## WRITING

Another important aspect of the common core standards is the teaching of writing. Smith, Wilhelm, and Fredricksen ("The Common Core: New Standards, New Teaching"), in the January 2012 *Kappan*, say about the standards, "they emphasize writing convincing arguments about issues that matter, clear and comprehensive informational texts that can do meaningful work in the world, and compelling narratives that foster an understanding of oneself, others, and the world." They also warned that, "Traditional, formulaic writing instruction won't prepare students for the new standards." They state that students must be given plenty of opportunities to practice, they have to gather evidence, they have to compose using several drafts, and they have to be able to apply their learning to new situations.

Sarah Brown Wessling, from the Teaching Channel, states that evidence-based reading and writing does not mean just writing reports, we must look outside of school for other forms such as a blog, a podcast, a critique, a proposal, a letter to the editor, and more.

Schmoker and Jago, in an article in *Kappa Delta Pi Record*, April-June 2013 ("Simplifying the ELA Common Core: Demystifying Curriculum"), state that there are three instructional shifts embedded in the new standards: "building knowledge through content rich nonfiction and informational text, reading and writing grounded in evidence from the text, and regular practice with complex text and its academic vocabulary."

Amy Benjamin (*Big Skills for the Common Core*, 2012) says there are three essential skills around which the standards are built: comprehending complex texts requires close attention to the texts, writing calls upon multiple sources to justify assertions, and academic vocabulary is necessary.

In a January 2013, *Middle School Journal* article ("RAFTing with Raptors: Connecting Science, English Language Arts, and the Common Core State Standards"), Senn, McMurtrie, and Coleman show "the RAFT strategy for getting students to write across the curriculum in ways that connect with the Common Core State Standards." Using Role, Audience, Format, and Topic as the template, the authors show how this process can be used for "analyzing a text, drawing inferences; analyzing interactions among individuals, events, and ideas; determining an author's point of view; writing informative text to examine the topic and convey ideas, concepts, and information through the selection, organization and analysis of relevant content." As an example, they use environmental sciences as the topic and write from the point of view of a concerned citizen, with the audience being the governor of the state, and the format being an invitation and with the topic being how a natural disaster changes the city.

Writing will more often be evidence-based and substantiated with information from the reading. Argument writing has taken an important place in the new standards and in order to prepare a good argument, information must be proven and supported. Multiple sources must be used and there must be a focus on academic vocabulary to be utilized in good writing. Writing can also take many forms and the choice of many different types of writing might appeal more to boys. It will, however, be very important for the teacher to teach how to create these types of writing and to provide appropriate, frequent, and meaningful practice.

## LIBRARIANS/MEDIA SPECIALISTS

There are a number of articles about the importance of the media specialist in helping teachers make good choices for students, especially in the area of informational text. Traditionally school libraries have not developed large collections of informational text because of the expense, the validity, and the timeliness of these books. But now, because of the confusion over text complexity and the focus on informational texts, the media specialist's advice becomes much more valuable.

Marc Aronson, May 2013, in *School Library Journal* ("The Road Ahead: Common Core Insights: Consider the Source") wrote, "School librarians have the tools and position to be key players in this change—they understand inquiry and are eager to help students engage in research that goes beyond fact-finding missions. But to be essential participants in The Common Core Initiative, librarians must know their nonfiction as well is their fiction." Now research reports are not just about the facts, they are about the sources.

In another *School Library Journal* article, this one by Paige Jaeger, June 2013 ("Vulcanizing Vocabulary: Librarians Lead Path to Achievement"), the importance of the librarian in helping students to develop an academically rich vocabulary is discussed. In the new English Language Arts Common Core Standards *everyone* should be focusing on academic terminology. Jaeger says, "the greater your vocabulary the better you read. The better you read the more you comprehend. The more you comprehend the broader your knowledge base and the broader your knowledge base, the more you can achieve."

In another *School Library Journal* article written in March 2012 by Rebecca Hill ("All Aboard!: Implementing Common Core Offers School Librarians an Opportunity to Take the Lead"), the importance of school librarians is again highlighted. Hill says, "with Common Core's emphasis on reading across the entire curriculum, including areas such as math, science, and social studies, many librarians believe that it's the perfect time to step up their involvement as text and inquiry specialists, using the information literacy and critical thinking skills that they've advocated all along."

In September 2012 in *Kids & Book News*, Julie Corsaro ("Common Core: It's Not Happening Without the Librarian") wrote about the importance of the librarian in her interview with Mark Aronson, founder of The Uncommon Corps, a resource to share information and expertise about nonfiction and the English Language Arts Common Core Standards. Aronson says that it is absolutely imperative that all faculty in the school collaborate about the reading range of titles across age levels and content areas. Aronson says, "Another huge problem is that most really good nonfiction is published only in hardcover, making it meaningless for a teacher who needs multiple copies." One way to get around this would be to find different nonfiction titles on the same topic. He strongly recommends that students do nonfiction author studies because "nonfiction authors have an approach, a voice, and a way of seeing things."

Catherine Gewertz says in *Education Week*, September 2012 ("Common Core Thrusts Librarians into Leadership Role"), "librarians say they view the common core, with its emphasis on explanation, complex text, and cross-disciplinary synthesis, as an unprecedented opportunity for them to really strut their stuff." Gewertz says, "The new standards have prompted school librarians to take a hard look at their collections to weed outdated material and bolster challenging fiction and nonfiction resources." Librarians also need to help teachers understand that the new standards' emphasis on nonfiction will not limit the role of literature in the curriculum.

Librarians will be greatly needed to help teachers and students make appropriate nonfiction choices and to help with the inquiry process. They will be expected to find up-to-date and appropriate material so that students can read multiple texts from different sources on the topics that correlate with their classes. Librarians need to call on boys to help select books for the library and to help to share their critiques on the books they read. Librarians need to offer book clubs, booktalks, trailers, and Web sites to match boys with good reads. Nonfiction author studies and displays will be relevant, and links to databases will be necessary for evidence and proof when students are preparing arguments or research reports.

## THE UNCOMMON CORE BLOG

"The Uncommon Core: Champions of Nonfiction Literature for Children and Young Adult" http://nonfictionandthecommoncore.blogspot.com. This blog with posts from leading educators such as Mark Aronson, Kathleen Odean, Myra Zarnowski, and Sue Bartle features a variety of information regarding the common core:

- The use of shelf talkers to feature nonfiction titles. Shelf talkers are colorful cards attached to the edge of the shelf that give some information or a recommendation about a certain title. The post includes a number of Web sites that feature free samples of shelf talkers.
- The importance of school libraries and the need for a greater focus on the reading—writing connection and the ways that librarians can help.
- What is happening with Lexiles, with the focus on text complexity indicating that on the common core Web site there is some additional information about expanded Lexiles and that no school should be using Lexile levels as the sole factor in choosing books.
- The misconceptions of Appendix B.
- Nonfiction author studies, suggested authors, and a Web site with an amazing author toolkit: http://www.readingrockets.org/content/pdfs/authortoolkit_rr.pdf.

## INFORMATIONAL READ ALOUDS

Research says that informational books definitely belong in early childhood classrooms. Children in early childhood can actually read to learn or in fact be read to and learn at a much earlier age than originally thought. Young children can interact well with informational text when given the opportunity to do so.

Duke and Bennett-Armistead ("Reading & Writing Informational Text in the Primary Grades: Research-Based Practices"), Scholastic, 2003, stated that teachers should be reading informational text with younger children. "We find that children even at an early age are curious about the world around them. So it is easy to refer to informational books to answer questions and develop interest. Early childhood educators, however, seem more eager to utilize narratives in read aloud selections for their students. Even with younger students, boys in general seem more likely to select informational texts and this can greatly enhance their reading development."

Linda Hoyt, in a 2013 article ("Igniting a Sense of Wonder: Helping Students Find Joy in Informational Texts") for Heinemann, draws from her professional development work on nonfiction writing and shares that students, "showed me that nonfiction books could be the books of their dreams—books that allow them free reign with their intrinsic sense of wonder about the world." Teachers and librarians need to help students develop methods for making the right informational book selections and looking at them critically. "They need to take a critical, analytical stance—reading numerous titles on the same topic to compare and contrast the quality of the visuals, to notice points of view, and to evaluate the quality of the information presented."

Cummins and Stallmeyer-Gerard ("Teaching for Synthesis of Informational Texts with Read-Alouds"), *The Reading Teacher*, March 2011, share the benefits of using informational texts to support and develop background knowledge and learning in science, social studies, math, and other subject areas. The article lists the benefits of reading informational texts aloud. As teachers "they were studying the influence of reading informational texts aloud to students on a regular basis and nurturing the synthesis of the content in these texts through written and sketched responses." They share the results of their efforts to teach their third-grade students how to synthesize.

In an article by Bradley and Donovan ("Information Book Read-Alouds as Models for Second-Grade Authors"), *The Reading Teacher*, December 2010–January 2011, the authors share the idea that focusing read alouds on information books helps children to be more aware of how to write information compositions. "Informational read alouds that include a discussion of genre elements, features, and organization give students good background ideas for informational compositions about topics that interest them."

On www.elementarymatters.com in September 2012, DeCost, a veteran teacher, posted a list of reasons for reading aloud to children. Some of those stated reasons are: creating a positive attitude toward reading and books, promoting longer attention spans, exposing children to complex language, teaching children about the world, modeling good reading habits, understanding story structure, and experiencing different characters and situations.

In March 2013, Hiebert posted an article, "Read-Aloud Favorites: A Source for Enriching Students' Knowledge of the World and of Language," on www.textproject.org. The Web site now has a link to Read Aloud Favorites, a collection of trade book recommendations for read aloud by grade level, genre, topic, and format. Hiebert discloses the principles for choosing read alouds: compelling language, clear message, extending background knowledge in content areas such as math, science, and social studies, and sharing books that students might not select on their own.

Read alouds are not only important for the primary student but also for all ages. Students like to be read to in the classroom, the library, in the lunchroom, and on a rainy day. Reading aloud helps to improve vocabulary, background knowledge, story grammar, and puts new and different titles in front of students who may not have made those choices on their own. It is also a way to introduce both new topics and new authors. For boys, this is especially noteworthy because hearing a story may spark an unrealized interest.

## A SUMMARY DOCUMENT

The International Reading Association has provided a four-page document: *Literacy Implementation Guidance for the ELA Common Core State Standards*. It was written by the *IRA* Common Core State Standards Committee with co-chairs—Brenda Overturf and Timothy Shanahan. The document discusses the use of challenging texts and reminds us that in kindergarten and first grade this is mostly accomplished through having the text read to the students. The article reminds us that foundational skills still need to be taught. It also gives details about comprehension with regard to close reading and the importance of being able to accurately summarize text. They also talk about the serious need for vocabulary instruction and development by all teachers of all subject areas. And lastly, the importance of writing and how it must be closely related to evidence from texts is discussed. The document is easily found at www.reading.org and is worth close inspection.

# Chapter 3

# READ LIKE A DETECTIVE AND WRITE LIKE A JOURNALIST

The Common Core State Standards have focused on an instructional shift in our classroom communities by asking students to read and analyze more complex texts than ever before. The standards also point out that the literacy focus has to extend to all subject areas, including science, social science, and technical fields.

There is now an emphasis on text complexity meaning that students are requested to read more complex text multiple times and discuss them with their peers as well as ask good quality questions. These questions need to be based on the evidence contained in the reading. There has been a focus on shorter pieces of text to be read more closely. At the same time students are being asked to read for longer periods of time and eventually to complete longer and more complex texts. Because this is a shift from the way reading was taught and the expectations for reading in the No Child Left Behind era, teachers will have to model the way this is to be done and help students change their approach to reading.

Readers will be asked to draw on experiences to validate the text they are reading. They have to look closely at the author's purpose, the credibility of the author, and to validate the evidence presented within the text by comparing it to other texts on the same topic. Efferent reading will become the focus—where the student pays close attention to facts and ideas that can be taken from the reading.

The teacher will be expected to provide scaffolding for text-based discussions, to point students in the right direction for evidence, and to provide the beginnings for thoughtful text-based conversations among the students.

A slightly new way of examining the text is presented in the concept of argumentation. This is a way of putting text together logically so that the reader can make accurate and appropriate conclusions. There is definitely a social part to argumentation and thorough analysis can be developed through good quality classroom discussions guided by the teacher. The student needs to look closely at the text to discern the arguments. Quite often, academic vocabulary is an important part of this because, to truly understand the information presented in the text, the student needs to interpret the meanings of the content-specific words.

There are multiple parts to an argument, and the reader needs to find out what the claim is and the background information that is presented to support that claim. Clarifying evidence must be found and presented in the form of a rebuttal. The reader also needs to be a bit skeptical about the information offered in a text and to participate in thoughtful discussion to evaluate the argument.

This same stance needs to be taken in analyzing and discussing narrative texts as well. Narrative texts offer readers various features such as character, dialogue, plot, setting, and various literary devices for the students to understand, analyze, and participate in thoughtful discussions about the text. It is also important for the reader to be critical, to evaluate the information presented, and to look for the author's purpose. Students must decipher the point of view of the text, and they should interpret what the other side of the story might be.

Because of a greater variety of texts being used not only in the English Language Arts class but also in other content area classes, it will be necessary to develop skills in thinking aloud, read alouds, book clubs, literature circles, inquiry, and writing a variety of journals to validate and support the reading in all content areas.

Expository texts focus more on the subject areas within the sciences and social sciences. For the most part expository texts are more difficult to comprehend than narrative texts. One of the biggest issues is a specialized vocabulary and possibly not knowing enough background knowledge to support understanding of the reading. With expository text it is important to look for specific structures such as a table of contents, glossary, index, graphs, charts, illustrations, and sidebar notes. Evaluating these additional features and using them effectively are necessary parts of reading like a detective. Again, mastering the specialized vocabulary of expository texts is the most critical element needed to understand the concepts. Reading informational texts at a young age becomes imperative not only in the task of learning to read but also in the task of building knowledge.

Another part of this is the increasing focus on digital texts and being able to read from the computer or from some sort of device. Students now more than ever can find information with ease, so part of reading like a detective is looking critically at information that might be found on the Internet. It is essential, therefore, that teachers understand the role played by technology in the lives of even our youngest students. Part of the responsibility of teaching them to read like a detective is to arm them with the tools that will help them analyze and evaluate what they find as they participate in a wide variety of types of reading outside the classroom.

The discussion questions of years ago that ask readers how they feel about their reading and for their opinion about their reading are no longer the focus. The tone of the questions has changed to text-dependency. Students still need to identify characters, plot, setting, and literary devices. The various levels of the twenty-first century version of Bloom's taxonomy (remember, understand, apply, analyze, evaluate, and create) are valid as question starters. The reader also needs to be questioned about the truth of the material and therefore be questioned about the author's purpose and background. The reader needs to realize that all stories are written through the perspective of the author, and therefore questions are necessary.

Close reading requires that a reader questions the text right from the beginning. Readers need to look for motives and meaning. Students need to question like a detective or an investigative reporter. Text-dependent questions can be answered only with evidence from the text.

Readers must question the theme, the word choice, the structure, the ideas, and the core understandings, as well as the author's purpose and background (Fisher, Frey, and Lapp, 2012).

The reader should ask: Who? What? When? Where? Why? How? This questioning pattern needs to be the backbone of all close reading and discussion of any text.

Then the questioning should endeavor to get the evidence and the information needed, including but not limited to the author's background and meaning. These are sample question starters but the possibilities are endless.

what's a possible explanation
what might be the future benefits
what evidence exists within the text
what conclusions can be drawn
what are the outcomes/results
what are the supporting details
what is the author's reasoning
what is the author's background with regard to the subject
what is the author's purpose for writing
what is the proof that supports your arguments
what does the author believe is the biggest problem
what does the author think just might be the solution
does the author explain things clearly
who are the people involved or affected
where did it take place
why did it happen
why is this important
how will this impact others
what's it really about

Guided Reading Question Cards—Nonfiction; Grades 3 & Up; by Edupress 2009 are an excellent source of question starters for nonfiction reading.

Common Core English Language Arts presents a new way to look at writing. With the emphasis on informational text and close reading, the writing becomes more purposeful. The three basic types of writing are: argument and opinion, informational, and narrative. Writing is closely associated with critical thinking. Writing requires a lot of practice. Teachers need to work together to plan an ever-spiraling writing curriculum to coordinate with the focus on text complexity and more informational titles. They need to make sure that writing skills are connected and fully developed each year.

When students write an opinion piece they must support their opinions with reasons or evidence from the text. It is crucial to understand the author's reasoning. Writing also must include domain or content-specific words and phrases. Students' writing must include accurately quoted statements from the text to support their explanations. Students are not required to agree with the texts they read, but if they disagree, they need to find other texts that support their reasoning.

Each reader brings his own background knowledge, understanding, and experience to the reading, so there may be a number of different interpretations of a text. Thoughtful academic conversation about texts helps students to think through their writing, which gives them ideas and material.

As a result of the focus on informational text and writing, a new set of writing assignments take center stage, which often are content related. Science might include a research paper, a lab report, a how-to paper, or a mini-book on a scientific topic. All writing must be backed up by evidence, which means that multiple sources on the topic need to be consulted, and the works should include an appropriate amount of academic vocabulary. As a result of a current scientific issue, a writing assignment might be a persuasive letter to an editor, a company, or a group. Again, specific academic vocabulary would be paramount as well as documented evidence from multiple sources. It is necessary to learn how to cite direct quotations of information properly.

For history studies, one might write historical fiction or historical research, again using appropriate vocabulary, a variety of examples of evidence, and properly written quotations from knowledgeable sources. This would also include the necessity of reading primary and secondary documents.

An argument or opinion essay can be assigned in any class. The key is gathering and organizing information in a logical way so that the reader can comprehend the issue. It is important to state all the evidence, so multiple sources must be consulted. The writer needs to persuade the reader so that he or she will agree with the stated point of view. To gather a variety of information to write a good paper, the students need to read the material carefully. The reader needs to find out exactly what the author is thinking and how those thoughts are organized and developed in the book. Once that has been accomplished then the writer can begin the task of creating an essay.

Narrative essay writing is also significant; students still need to create a beginning, middle, and ending. They need to set the scene and develop characters, a plot, and a resolution. The use of quality words and phrases to paint the picture clearly is still necessary. Ralph Fletcher (http://www.ralphfletcher.com) offers many suggestions for writers, especially boys. He knows that it is sometimes very difficult to come up with a creative idea for a narrative. He suggests: keeping a writing notebook for jotting down ideas and drawing pictures; recording bits of conversations and strange and unusual ideas; and creating a story line or a story web. Fletcher's ideas are well-suited for young writers.

# Chapter 4

# STRATEGIES FOR CHANGE

After reading the research it is apparent that it would be very helpful to boys if we made some changes in the ways we do things at school and at home. These strategies are organized by two areas: school (behaviors, reading, and writing) and home (Knowles and Smith, 2005).

## STRATEGIES FOR CHANGES AT SCHOOL

### Behaviors

- Provide all students with opportunities to move frequently, especially during lessons:

  *Classroom Fitness Breaks to Help Kids Focus: Fun-and-Easy Exercises for the Classroom That Boost Concentration and Get Kids Ready to Learn,* Sarah Longhi, Scholastic Teaching Resources, 2011

  *Energizing Brain Breaks,* David U. Sladkey, Corwin, 2013

  *Brain Gym: Simple Activities for Whole Brain Learning,* Paul E. and Gail E. Dennison, Edu Kinesthetics, 1992

- Provide boys with opportunities to show off through drama, sharing hobbies and interests, demonstrating something they have read about, and so on. (Knowles and Smith, 2005)
- Allow boys to move about the classroom as they work and think
- Give boys frequent breaks from work
- Give boys lots of opportunity for sensory activities and experiences
- Provide ample time to read

## Reading

- Make sure that classroom and school libraries have print materials that will interest boys: consult the school librarian to get ideas
- Provide boy friendly culminating activities after completing books; use art, film (Flip camera), and animation as a way to respond to literature
- Provide a Guinness Book of World Records in the classroom and several in the library
- Separate participants in literature circles and book discussion groups by gender and have a male teacher do a book club with middle school boys; establish a program where all the males in the school read aloud regularly to classes, and invite fathers and male community figures to be guest readers in the classroom
- Use readers' theater for developing fluency
- *Never* use round robin reading: Do *not* make students read out loud unless they have had time to prepare
- Read humorous poetry aloud and provide copies for boys to enjoy and share
- Demonstrate how to read and enjoy nonfiction, feature book talks on nonfiction books, and introduce nonfiction authors just as you would feature authors of fiction
- Be accepting of the reading needs of boys, give reluctant readers short passages to read
- On career day, ask guests to discuss what they have to read to succeed in their jobs
- Take advantage of free or inexpensive books offered through book clubs to build a classroom library of popular titles and offer books as prizes
- Read nonfiction books aloud
- Use retelling as a way to check comprehension
- Use graphic organizers to help boys understand their reading
- Model quality responses to literature
- Conduct frequent interest inventories to help boys find appropriate books and to put boys with similar interests together in book discussion groups; provide boys with a buddy reading program
- Provide boys with some review of prior knowledge before they begin to read a book
- Provide more titles similar in theme to the one a boy has selected or one read aloud and enjoyed
- Always allow choice in book selection
- Remember the appeal of comic books and graphic novels and capitalize on it
- Seek recommendations from boys for the classroom library and school library
- In the library frequently change displays that are geared toward the interests of boys

## Writing

- Accept the writing styles of boys—blood, guts, crashes, aliens, and so on; acceptance of such topics may help a boy become more comfortable with the writing process
- Refer to www.ralphfletcher.com for ideas

- Encourage boys if they prefer to read movie scripts and about movie and theater production, and then have them write plays
- Encourage boys to draw their thoughts first before they write
- Make writing a natural extension of reading through journaling and reflections where comments and questions can be written about what students have read

## Strategies for Changes for Parents

- Provide a wide variety of reading materials in the home
- Encourage fathers to become active in their sons' reading and encourage all adult males at home to share their reading preferences
- Set aside a daily time when everyone reads—turn off the TV, the video games, and the computer
- Read to/with kids long after the lower elementary grades
- Have reading parties for kids (Harry Potter, Percy Jackson)
- Purchase books or bookstore gift cards for gifts for kids' friends
- Rewards kids with trips to the book store/library
- Take advantage of any special kids' programs at the local public library
- Before or after seeing a movie, parents should read the book version with their kids and then compare and contrast the two versions
- Provide a wide variety of response activities to books, including the use of technology
- Support reading selections—never ridicule, always allow choice in book selection
- Promote graphic novels, comic books, and magazines

The following is a plan to change the school culture regarding to reading. The suggestions involve all members of the school community, some will require some fund raising, and all are favorable to providing a positive reading experience for boys especially.

## Whole School Reading Plan

- Read Aloud—at least once a week—with all members of the school community (especially the males) serving as readers and featuring nonfiction titles in each class-room or by grade-level group
- Drop Everything and Read (DEAR)—fifteen minutes a day, everyday, perhaps alternating classes, subject areas, or time periods, and all students should have a per-sonal selection reading time as part of homework
- Media Center Reading Environment—conducive to boys: chess and other games, a wide variety of magazines, displays of multiple nonfiction titles on interesting topics, the use of shelf-talkers, and graphic novels, students act as consultants and help select books and magazines for the media center, organize books by subjects like a book store
- Classroom Reading Environment—reading area with special seating, books avail-able, attention to a wide variety of titles and media incorporated within all content areas, time to read, time to talk about books, a Kindle or a Nook, and audiobooks

- Web Page—page for Media Center where students post reviews and the media specialist can introduce new titles, promotions, general information, lists of links of interest to boys
- Publishing Center—where writers can produce books for peers and younger students
- Book Clubs—for teachers to read and discuss current literature, for students to get together to all read one title or one author or on one subject and then share ideas and thoughts on their readings, for parents, students, by gender, grade levels—offer a father–son or mother–son book club in the library or after school/before school by classroom
- Curriculum Changes—include literature in all content areas, encourage all content area teachers to teach reading strategies, encourage all teachers to use nonfiction and picture books, teach students how to read nonfiction and feature nonfiction authors, and allow students time to read
- More Curriculum Changes— help traditional English literature teachers include fiction to compare and contrast with classics, emphasize students responding to literature on a personal level through literature circles and response journals, explore reading workshop where students select their own reading material and work at their own pace, and where skill teaching is done on an as-needed basis
- Visual Literacy—students should be taught to gather information and construct their own charts, graphs and diagrams; they need instruction in organizing large amounts of information – with special training in the use of a wide variety of graphic organizers; students also need to be taught skimming, scanning, note taking, and summarizing
- Special Events—connecting music and literature with plays, meaningful field trips, older students reading to and writing for younger students and vice-versa, author and illustrator visits or presentations on Skype, author-of-the-year focus for the entire school
- Booktalks and Trailers—librarians, teachers, and students all sharing a brief and tantalizing glimpse of excellent titles to promote recreational reading
- Lunch Time Read Alouds—have a male teacher read a book aloud to boys during lunch over a week, celebrate the end of the book with a special dessert
- Professional Development—sending teachers to reading conferences and workshops, opportunities to visit schools and libraries with good reading programs, memberships in professional reading organizations, professional libraries with lots of good books on reading, and professional journals for reading and discussion at faculty meetings
- State-Sponsored Reading Programs—Florida has Sunshine State Young Readers Award – where students read from a short list and vote on their favorite titles
- Bookshare—circulation of used books—kids bring in old books and buy back others for 50 cents each, teachers can have copies for classroom libraries and the leftovers can be donated to local charities

## STRATEGIES FOR CHANGE USING TECHNOLOGY

- Photography, photo sharing, and photo editing using simple tools and programs
- Screenwriting—have students turn their favorite book into a play

- Animation: http://www.abcya.com/animate.htm - online program (available as an app)
- Storyboarding—creating a comic strip to summarize a story already read or to create a new story
- News broadcasts—pattern school news after the nightly news, any kind of a video camera (on a cell phone, on a camera, or a Flip camera can be a good way to start)
- Virtual environments: http://www.zulaworld.com and http://www.animaljam.com are examples
- Google Earth: http://sitescontent.google.com/google-earth-for-educators/
- Skype: especially helpful for having information chats with authors, an interesting article on Edutopia: http://www.edutopia.org/blog/mock-elections-via-skype-suzie-boss
- Wordle: http://www.wordle.net - a toy for generating "word clouds" from text that you provide
- Webspiration: http://www.mywebspiration.com/ for students in grades 5–12, a great tool for developing thinking and writing skills and http://www.inspiration.com/Kidspiration for grades K–5, the visual way to explore and understand words, numbers, and concepts (available as an app)
- Virtual field trips: article from www.eschoolnews.com - http://www.eschoolnews.com/2013/04/07/ten-of-the-best-virtual-field-trips/
- Making videos using only still images
- Podcasts: Reading Rockets has a great information piece on creating podcasts in the classroom: http://www.readingrockets.org/article/25032/
- Social networking: Common Sense Media has information on safe social networking sites for kids: http://www.commonsensemedia.org/website-lists/social-networking-kids

## Collaborative writing, wikis, and blogs:

*Blogs, Wikis, Podcasts, and Other Powerful Web Tools for Classrooms*, Will Richardson, Corwin, 2010

*Teaching with Wikis, Blogs, Podcasts & More: Dozens of Easy Ideas for Using Technology to Get Kids Excited About Learning*, Kathleen Fitzgibbon, Scholastic Teaching Resources, 2010

## Uses for the Flip camera

- Create a digital twist on the book report
- Share a digital explanation of a math or science concept
- How-to's—in all subject areas
- Observations of events or phenomena
- Interviews
- Digital storytelling
- Student portfolios
- Music videos and song writing

- Advertisements/infomercials
- Movies and trailers about books
- Creating sequels for books or movies
- Arguments and discussions when comparing complex texts
- Weekly broadcast of current events

# Chapter 5

# ACTION AND ADVENTURE

Adventure stories have always been favorites of boys; the more thrilling and daring the plot, the better. Climbing mountains, battling snakes and alligators, rafting the white rapids, and swimming in shark-infested waters creates page-turning excitement for boys. These stories usually have strong main characters who are fearless, brave, and always heroic. They are aggressive and can survive the most incredible circumstances. When boys read these types of stories they imagine themselves in similar situations and can enjoy the action from afar.

## FEATURED AUTHORS

Name: Eoin (pronounced Owen) Colfer
Birth date: May 14, 1965
Place of Birth: Westford, Ireland
Most popular book(s): *Artemis Fowl* Series

*Have 1st 5 in series*

About: The *Artemis Fowl* series has sold over 20 million copies worldwide and is now concluding with the final book *The Last Guardian*. New series (2013) *WARP*
Web site: http://www.eoincolfer.com

Name: Sandra Markle
Birth date: November 10, 1946
Place of Birth: Fostoria, Ohio
Most popular book(s): *Snow School, The Case of the Vanishing Golden Frogs*

About: Markle is the author of more than 200 nonfiction books for children and has won numerous awards for this work, including the 2012 Prize for Excellence in Science Books by The American Association for the Advancement of Science.

Web site: http://sandra-markle.blogspot.com

## ANNOTATIONS

Horowitz, Anthony. *Eagle Strike*. Penguin, 2004. ISBN: 0-399-23979-0 YA.
    Teenage spy Alex Rider is visiting his girlfriend, Sabina, in the south of France when he spies the assassin Yassen Gregorovich on a large yacht. Yassen attempts to kill Sabina's father. Alex follows Yassen and learns that he is working for the famous, well-respected, pop singer Damian Cray. Why is Damian Cray hiring an assassin and what are his plans that require the use of a flash drive that cost $2 million? The adventures begin with Alex fighting in a bullfight, taking part in a high speed bicycle chase, and participating in a live video game with possible deadly consequences.

Lecreaux, Michele. *The Boy's Book of Adventure*. Barron's Educational Series, Inc., 2013. ISBN: 978-0-7641-6611-2.
    A handy outdoor activity book filled with facts, crafts, projects, and fun things for boys to make and do, from making a rain gauge and identifying poisonous snakes to using secret codes.

Logsted, Greg. *Alibi Junior High*. Aladdin, 2009. ISBN: 978-1-4169-4814-8.
    Cody, whose home has been in various parts of the world with his undercover agent father, attends a middle school for the first time. He gets a taste of what other students experience. Will he choose to go back to his former life?

Markle, Sandra. *Snow School*. Charlesbridge, 2013. ISBN: 978-1-5808-9410-4.
    It reads like fiction, but the author relates the early true-life lessons of two endangered snow cubs in Pakistan's Hindu Kush Mountains. After many adventures, the male cub makes his first kill signifying his independence as a solitary hunter.

Martel, Yann. *Life of Pi: A Novel*. Harcourt, Inc., 2002. ISBN: 0-15-100811-6.
    Sixteen-year-old Pi survives a ship sinking and spends seven months on a lifeboat with a Bengal tiger. By helping Richard Parker, the royal Bengal tiger, to survive, Pi also survives and reaches land in Mexico. Pi is questioned by officials who do not believe his real story, so he tells a more gruesome and horrible story. Because neither account can be proved, all agree that the story with the animals sounds better and it remains as part of the official report.

Nielsen, Jennifer A. *The False Prince*. Scholastic Inc., 2012. ISBN: 978-0-545-28414-1.
    Jaron, the prince and heir to the kingdom, is thought to be lost after an attack by pirates sink his ship. Connor, a regent of the court, selects four orphan boys in an action-filled plan to have one of them impersonate the lost heir. Who will be chosen to play the part of the prince, and what is the fate of the boys not selected?

Taylor, Theodore. *The Cay*. Random House, 1987. ISBN: 0-385-07906-0.
    After the Germans torpedo the freighter on which Phillip and his mother are traveling from wartime Curacao to the United States, Phillip finds himself dependent on

Timothy, an old, black West Indian sailor. Shipwrecked, there is just the two of them. This is the story of their struggle for survival and of Phillip's efforts to adjust to his new disability, blindness, and to understand the dignified, wise, and loving old man who is his companion. Classic.

## READ ALOUD

Fleming, Candace. *Amelia Lost: The Life and Disappearance of Amelia Earhart.* Schwartz & Wade, 2011. ISBN: 978-0-375-84198-9.

Lewin, Ted. *Tooth and Claw: Animal Adventures in the Wild.* HarperCollins, 2003. ISBN: 0-688-14105-6.

Osborne, Mary Pope. *American Tall Tales.* Knopf Books for Young Readers; First Edition, 1991. ISBN: 978-0-6798-0089-7. Classic.

Weaver, Janice. *Harry Houdini: The Legend of the World's Greatest Escape Artist.* Abrams Books, 2011. ISBN: 978-1-4197-014-9.

Webb, Sophie. *Far from Shore: Chronicles of an Open Ocean Voyage.* Houghton Mifflin, 2011. ISBN: 978-0-618-59729-1.

Williams, Marcia. *Greek Myths.* Candlewick, 2011. ISBN: 978-0-7636-5384-2.

## BIBLIOGRAPHY

Adam. Paul. *Attack at Dead Man's Bay.* Corgi Children's, 2012. ISBN: 978-0-5525-6034-4. Gr 4–6. Max Cassidy series.

Aguiar, Nadia. *Secrets of Tamarin.* Feiwel & Friends, 2011. ISBN: 978-0-312-38030-4. Gr 5–8.

Alexander, Lloyd. *The Golden Dream of Carlo Chuchio.* Holt, 2007. ISBN: 978-0-8050-8333-0. Gr 4–6.

Alexander, London C. *We Are Not Eaten by Yaks.* Puffin; Reprint edition, 2013. ISBN: 978-0-1424-2056-0. Gr 5 and up.

Almond, David. *The Boy Who Climbed into the Moon.* Candlewick, 2010. ISBN: 978-0-7636-4217-4. Gr 4–6.

Anderson, John David. *Sidekicked.* Walden Pond Press, 2013.ISBN: 978-0-0621-3314-4. Gr 3 and up.

Augarde, Steve. *X Isle.* David Fickling Books, 2010. ISBN: 978-0-3857-5193-3. YA.

Avi. *Poppy and Ereth.* HarperCollins, 2009. ISBN: 978-0-06-111969-9. Gr 4–6.

Balliett, Blue. *The Danger Box*. Scholastic, 2011. ISBN: 978-0-439-85209-8. Gr 5–7.

Bancks, Tristan. *Mac Slater vs. the City*. Simon & Schuster, 2011. ISBN: 978-1-4169 -8576-1. Gr 5–8.

Bell, Hilari. *Flame: Player's Ruse*. Harper Teen, 2010. ISBN: 978-0-0608-2509-X. Gr 4–6.

Bodeen, S. A. *The Raft*. Square Fish, 2013. ISBN: 978-1-2500-2739-9. Gr 7 and up.

Borgenicht, David. *Deadly Seas: You Decide How to Survive!* Chronicle, 2012. ISBN: 978-1-4521-0917-6. Gr 4–6. Worst-Case Scenario Ultimate Adventure series.

Bowler, Tim. *Out of the Shadows*. Philomel, 2010. ISBN: 0-3992-5187-1. Gr 8 and up. Blade series.

Bradford, Chris. *Bodyguard: Hostage (Book 1)*. Puffin Books, 2013. ISBN: 978-0-1413 -4005-0. YA.

Bradford, Chris. *The Ring of Sky*. Penguin Global, 2012. ISBN: 978-0-1413-3972-6. Gr 6 and up. Young Samurai series.

Bradley, F. T. *Double Vision*. HarperCollins, 2012. ISBN: 978-0-06-210437-3. Gr 4–6.

Bransford, Nathan. *Jacob Wonderbar for President*. Dial, 2012. ISBN: 978-0-80378-3538-5. Gr 4–6.

Broach, Elise. *Treasure on Superstition Mountain*. Henry Holt, 2013. ISBN: 978-0-8050 -7763-6. Gr 4–6.

Broach, Elise. *Missing on Superstition Mountain*. Square Fish; Reprint edition, 2012. ISBN: 978-1-2500-0477-2. Gr 4–6.

Brown, Jeff. *The Australian Boomerang Bonanza*. HarperCollins, 2011. ISBN: 978-0-0614 -3018-3. Gr 1–3. Worldwide Adventure series.

Brennan, Herbie. *The Secret Prophecy*. Balzer + Bray, 2012. ISBN: 978-0-0620-7180-4. Gr 4–6.

Buckley, Michael. *Attack of the Bullies*. Amulet Books, 2013. ISBN: 978-1-4197-0857-2. Gr 4–6. NERDS series.

Carman, Patrick. *3 Below: A Floors Novel*. Scholastic Press, 2012. ISBN: 978-0-545 -25520-2. Gr 4–6.

Castle, M. E. *Cloneward Bound*. Egmont, USA, 2013. ISBN: 978-1-6068-4233-1. Gr 4–6.

Chima, Cinda Williams. *The Crimson Crown (Seven Realms Series #4)*. Hyperion Books for Children, 2012. ISBN: 978-1-4231-4433-5 YA.

Clements, Andrew. *In Harm's Way*. Atheneum Books for Young Readers, 2013. ISBN: 978-1-4169-3889-7. Gr 2–5. Benjamin Pratt and the Keepers of the School series.

Colfer, Eoin. *Artemis Fowl: The Last Guardian*. Hyperion, 2012. ISBN: 978-1-4231-61615. Gr 4–6.

Colfer, Eoin. *WARP Book 1: The Reluctant Assassin*. Disney Hyperion, 2013. ISBN: 978-1-4231-6162-2. YA.

Collins, Suzanne. *Gregor and the Code of Claw*. Scholastic, 2008. ISBN: 978-0-4397-9144-1. Gr 4–6. Underland Chronicles series.

Conly, Jane Leslie. *Murder Afloat*. Hyperion, 2010. ISBN: 978-1-4231-0416-2. Gr 5–8.

Crocker, Carter. *Last of the Gullivers*. Philomel, 2012. ISBN: 978-0-3992-4231-1. Gr 5–7.

Cross, Gillian. *The Odyssey*. Candlewick, 2012. ISBN: 978-0-7636-4791-9. Gr 4–6.

Dashner, James. *The Kill Order (Maze Runner Prequel)*. Delacorte Books for Young Readers, 2012. ISBN: 978-0-3857-4288-7. Gr 7 and up.

De Guzman, Michael. *Finding Stinko*. Farrar, Straus and Giroux, 2007. ISBN: 978-0-3743-2305-9. Gr 4–6.

Doyle, Bill. *Everest*. Chronicle, 2011. ISBN: 978-0-8118-7123-5. Gr 4–8.

Dumas. *Count of Monte Cristo*. Random, 1996. ISBN: 0-679-60199-6. Gr 8–12. Classic.

Eames, Brian. *The Dagger Quick*. Simon & Schuster, 2011. ISBN: 978-1-4424-2311-4. Gr 4–7.

Fardell, John. *The 7 Professors of the Far North*. Puffin Books, 2006. ISBN: 978-0-1424-0735-6. Gr 5–8.

Flanagan, John. *The Hunters: Brotherband Chronicles, Book 3*. Philomel, 2012. ISBN: 978-0-3992-5621-9. Gr 4–6.

Garretson, Dee. *Wildfire Run*. HarperCollins, 2010. ISBN: 978-0-06-195347-7. Gr 4–7.

George, Jean Craighead. *My Side of the Mountain*. Puffin, 2004. ISBN: 978-0412-4011-18. Gr 4–6. Classic.

Gibbs, Stuart. *Spy School*. Simon & Schuster, 2012. ISBN: 978-1-4424-2182-0. Gr 4–7.

Gilman, David. *Blood Sun*. Delacorte Books for Young Readers, 2011. ISBN: 978-0-3857-3562-9. Gr 7–12. Danger Zone series.

Grant, Katy. *Hide and Seek*. Peachtree, 2010. ISBN: 978-1-5614-5542-3. Gr 5–8.

Gutman, Dan. *You Only Die Twice*. HarperCollins, 2013. ISBN: 978-0-0618-2770-9. Gr 4–6. The Genius Files series.

Gutman, Dan. *Ted & Me*. HarperCollins, 2012. ISBN: 978-0-0612-3487-3. Gr 4–6. Baseball Card Adventures series.

Haddix, Margaret Peterson. *Among the Free*. Simon & Schuster, 2007. ISBN: 978-0-6898-5799-7. Gr 4–6. Shadow Children series.

Hiaasen, Carl. *Scat*. Knopf, 2009. ISBN: 978-0-3759-3486-5. Gr 5–8.

Higgins, Jack. *Sharp Shot*. Putnam Juvenile, 2009. ISBN: 978-0-3992-5239-6. Gr 6–9 The Chance Twins series.

Higgins, Jack. *First Strike*. Putnam, 2010. ISBN: 978-0399-2524-2. Gr 5–8.

Higgins, Simon. *Moonshadow: Rise of the Ninja*. Little, Brown, 2010. ISBN: 978-0-316-05531-4. Gr 4–7.

Higson, Charlie. *The Sacrifice*. Hyperion, 2013. ISBN: 978-1-4231-6565-1. YA. An Enemy series.

Higson, Charlie. *Hurricane Gold*. Hyperion Book CH, 2010. ISBN: 978-1-4231-1415-4. Gr 5 and up The Young Bond series.

Hobbs, Will. *Never Say Die*. HarperCollins, 2013. ISBN: 978- 0-0617-0878-7. Gr 4–6.

Hobbs, Will. *Take Me to the River*. HarperCollins, 2012. ISBN: 978-0-0607-4146-4. Gr 4–6.

Holub, Joan. *Hades and the Helm of Darkness*. Aladdin, 2013. ISBN: 978-1-4424-5267-6. Gr 6–9. Hero in Training series.

Horowitz, Anthony. *Scorpia Rising*. Puffin, 2012. ISBN: 978-0-1424-1985-4. Gr 5 and up. Alex Rider series.

Jacobson, Jennifer Richard. *Small as an Elephant*. Candlewick, 2011. ISBN: 978-0-7636-4155-9. Gr 4–7.

Kipling, Rudyard. *Captains Courageous*. Simon & Brown, 2013. ISBN: 978-1-6138-2471-9. Classic.

Korman, Gordon. *The Summit*. Scholastic, Inc., 2012. ISBN: 978-0-5453-9234-1. Gr 4–6 Everest Book series.

Korman, Gordon. *S.O.S.* Scholastic Paperbacks, 2011. ISBN: 978-0-5451-2333-4. Gr 4–6. Titanic series.

Korman, Gordon. *The Medusa Plot*. Scholastic, 2011. ISBN: 978-0-545-29839-1. Gr 4–6. 39 Clues: Cahills vs. Vespers series.

Kuhlman, Evan. *Brother from a Box*. Atheneum, 2012. ISBN: 978-1-4424-2658-0. Gr 4–6.

Lacey, Josh. *Island of Thieves*. Houghton Mifflin Books for Children, 2012. ISBN: 978-0-5477-6327-9. Gr 4–6.

LaFevers, R. L. *The Unicorn's Tale*. Sandpiper, 2012. ISBN: 978-0-5478-5079-5. Gr 4–6. Nathaniel Fludd, Beastologist series.

Leach, Sara. *Count Me In*. Orca Paper, 2011. ISBN: 978-1-55469-404-4. Gr 4–6.

Lerangis, Peter. *The Colossus Rises*. HarperCollins, 2013. ISBN: 978-0-0620-7040-1. Gr 6–9. Seven Wonders series.

London, C. Alexander. *We Are Not Eaten by Yaks*. Philomel, 2011. ISBN: 978-0-399-25487-1. Gr 5–8.

Maddox, Jake. *Shipwreck!* Stone Arch, 2009. ISBN: 978-1-4342-0777-7. Gr 4–7.

Malaghan, Michael. *Greek Ransom*. Andersen Paper, 2010. ISBN: 978-1-84270-786-9. Gr 4–7.

McCaughrean, Geraldine. *Theseus*. Cricket Books, 2005. ISBN: 978-0-8126-2739-9. Gr 4–6. Heroes series.

McCaughrean, Geraldine. *The Death-Defying Pepper Roux*. HarperCollins, 2010. ISBN: 978-0-06-183666-4. Gr 5–8.

McCulloch, Amy. *The Oathbreaker's Shadow*. Doubleday Canada, 2013. ISBN: 978-0-3856-7824-7. YA.

Miller, Kirsten. *How to Lead a Life of Crime*. Razorbill, 2013. ISBN: 978-1-5951-4518-5. Gr 9 and up.

Mone, Gregory. *Fish*. Scholastic, 2010. ISBN: 978-0-545-11632-9. Gr 3–5.

Morpurgo, Michael. *Private Peaceful*. Scholastic Paperbacks, 2006. ISBN: 978-0-4396-3653-7. Gr 7–12.

Muchamore, Robert. *Guardian Angel*. Hodder & Stoughton, 2013. ISBN: 978-0-3409-9921-9. YA.

Muller, Rachel Dunstan. *Squeeze*. Orca Paper, 2010. ISBN: 978-1-55469-324-5. Gr 5–8.

Mulligan, Andy. *Trash*. Ember, Reprint, 2011. ISBN: 978-0-3857-5216-9. YA.

Nelson, N. A. *Bringing the Boy Home*. HarperCollins, 2008. ISBN: 0-0608-8698-6. Gr 4–6.

Osterweil, Adam. *The Comic Book Kid*. Namelos, 2011. ISBN: 978-1-6089-8092-5. Gr 4–6.

Paolini, Christopher. *Inheritance*. Random House Children's Books, 2012. ISBN: 978-0-3758-4631-1. YA.

Parkinson, Curtis. *Man Overboard*. Tundra Books, 2012. ISBN: 978-1-7704-9298-1. Gr 4 and up.

Paulsen, Gary. *Hatchet*. Simon, 2007. ISBN: 978-1-4169-2508-8. Gr 4–6.

Paulsen, Gary. *Road Trip*. Wendy Lamb Books, 2013. ISBN: 978-0-3857-4191-0. Gr 5 and up.

Pearson, Ridley. *Dark Passage*. Disney-Hyperion, 2013. ISBN: 978-1-4231-6489-0. Gr 5 and up. Kingdom Keepers series.

Pearson, Ridley. *Academy*. Hyperion Book CH, 2010. ISBN: 978-1-4231-1532-8. Steel Trap series. Gr 5–8.

Petersen, P. J. *Wild River*. Delacorte Books for Young Readers, 2009. ISBN: 978-0-3857-3724-1. Gr 4–6.

Pitchford, Dean. *Captain Nobody*. Puffin, 2010. ISBN: 978-0-3992-5034-7. Gr 4–6.

Philbrick, Rodman. *The Mostly True Adventures of Homer P. Figg*. Scholastic Paperbacks, 2011. ISBN: 978-0-4396-6821-7. Gr 5–8.

Potter, Ellen. *The Kneebone Boy*. Feiwel & Friends, 2010. ISBN: 978-0-312-37772-4. Gr 4–8.

Probst, Jeff. *Stranded*. Puffin, 2013. ISBN: 978-0-1424-2424-7. Gr 4–6.

Riordan, Rick. *Maze of Bones*. Scholastic, 2008. ISBN: 978-0-5450-6039-4. Gr 4–8.

Rodda, Emily. *The Golden Door*. Scholastic, 2012. ISBN: 978-0-545-42990-0. Gr 4–6.

Rodkey, Geoff. *Deadweather and Sunrise: The Chronicles of Egg, Book 1*. Putnam Juvenile, 2012. ISBN: 978-0-3992-5785-8. Gr 4–6.

Rollins, James. *Jake Ransom and the Howling Sphinx*. HarperCollins, 2011. ISBN: 978-0-06-147382-1. Gr 5–8.

Sachar, Louis. *Holes*. Dell Yearling, 2000. ISBN: 978-0-4404-1480-3. Gr 4–6. Classic.

Salisbury, Graham. *Night of the Howling Dogs.* Laurel Leaf, 2009. ISBN: 978-0-4402-3839-3. Gr 7 and up.

Salisbury, Graham. *Calvin Coconut: Hero of Hawaii.* Yearling, Reprint, 2012. ISBN: 978-0-3758-6505-3. Gr 2–5.

Sedgwick, Marcus. *Revolver.* Roaring Book, 2010. ISBN: 978-1-5964-3592-9. YA.

Selfors, Suzanne. *The Sasquatch Escape.* Little, Brown Books for Young Readers, 2013. ISBN: 978-0-3162-0934-2. Gr 3–5.

Selfors, Suzanne. *Smells Like Treasure.* Little, Brown, 2011. ISBN: 978-0-316-04399-1. Gr 4-7.

Smith, Roland. *Eruption.* Scholastic Paperbacks, Reprint, 2012. ISBN: 978-0-5450-8176-4. Gr 4–6. Storm Runners series.

Smith, Roland. *The Alamo.* Sleeping Bear Press, 2013. ISBN: 978-1-5853-6821-1. Gr 5–8. I Q series.

Soto, Gary. *Worlds Apart: Traveling with Fernie and Me.* Putnam, 2005. ISBN: 0-399-24218-X. Gr 4–6.

Soup, Cuthbert. *A Whole Nother Story.* Bloomsbury, 2010. ISBN: 978-1-5999-0435-1. Gr 3–6.

Strahan, Jonathan. *Life on Mars: Tales from the New Frontier.* Viking, 2011. ISBN: 978-0-670-0216-9. YA.

Strasser, Todd. *Boot Camp.* Simon Pulse, Reprint, 2008. ISBN: 978-1-4169-5942-7. Gr 8 and up.

Taylor, Theodore. *Ice Drift.* Sandpiper, Reprint, 2006. ISBN: 978-0-1520-5550-9. Gr 4–7.

Twain, Mark. *The Adventures of Huckleberry Finn.* Collector's Library: Reprint edition, 2010. ISBN: 978-1-9046-3346-4. Gr 9 and up. Classic.

Twain, Mark. *The Adventures of Tom Sawyer.* Penguin Barnes & Noble Classics; Later Printing edition, 2005. ISBN: 978-1-5930-8351-9. Gr 5 and up. Classic.

Van Tol. Alex. *Gravity Check.* Orca Paper, 2011. ISBN: 978-1-5546-9349-8. Gr 4–6.

Vinyoli, Joan and Albert. *Big Book of Pirates.* Sterling, 2011. ISBN: 978-1-4027-8056-1. Gr 4 and up.

Walden, Mark. *Dreadnought.* Simon & Schuster, 2011. ISBN: 978-1-4424-2186-8. Gr 5–8. H.I.V.E. series.

## INFORMATIONAL

Belanger, Jeff. *What It's Like to Climb Mount Everest, Blast Off into Space, Survive a Tornado, and Other Extraordinary Stories.* Sterling Paper, 2011. ISBN: 978-1-4027-6711-1. Gr 5–8.

Bledsoe, Lucy Jane. *How to Survive in Antarctica.* Holiday, 2006. ISBN: 0-8234-1890-1. Gr 4–6.

Blumberg, Rhoda. *The Remarkable Voyages of Captain Cook.* Atheneum, First Edition, 1991. ISBN: 978-0-0271-1682-3. Gr 6 and up.

*Boys' Book of Adventure.* Scholastic Nonfiction, 2010. ISBN: 978-0-5452-2326-3. Gr 4 and up.

Brown, Don. *Gold! Gold from the American River.* Roaring Brook, 2011. ISBN: 978-1-49643-223-9. Gr K–3.

Bredeson, Carmen. *After the Last Dog Died: The True-Life, Hair-Raising Adventure of Douglas Mawson and His 1912 Antarctic Expedition.* Holiday, 2006. ISBN: 0-8234-1890-1. Gr 4–6.

Cameron, Duncan. *Duncan Cameron's Shipwreck Detective.* DK Publishing, Inc., 2006. ISBN: 978-0-7566-2218-3. Gr 5 and up.

*Click: One Novel, Ten Authors.* Scholastic, 2007. ISBN: 978-0-439-41138-7. Gr 4–6.

Clifford, Barry. *Real Pirates: The Untold Story of the Whydah: From Slave Ship to Pirate Ship.* National Geographic Books, 2008. ISBN: 978-1-4263-0279-4. Gr K–3.

Clinton, Catherine. *Hold the Flag High.* HarperCollins, 2005. ISBN: 0-06-050428-5. Gr K–3.

Doeden, Matt. *Can You Survive the Jungle? An Interactive Survival Adventure.* Capstone, 2011. ISBN: 978-1-4296-6588-9. Gr 4–6.

Doubilet, David. *Face to Face with Sharks.* National Geographic Books, 2009. ISBN: 978-1-4263-0404-1. Gr 4–6.

Dunlap, Julie. *John Muir and Stickeen: An Icy Adventure with a No-Good Dog.* Northwood, 2004. ISBN: 1-55971-903-6. Gr K–3.

Earnest, Peter. *The Real Spy's Guide to Becoming a Spy.* Abrams, 2009. ISBN: 978-0-8109-8329-8. Gr 4–6.

Fritz, Jean. *Around the World in a Hundred Years: From Henry the Navigator to Magellan.* Puffin; Reprint edition, 1998. ISBN: 978-0-6981-1638-2. Gr 4–6.

Ganeri, Anita. *The Adventurers' Handbook: An Extreme, Extraordinary, and Exciting Journey Around the World.* Feiwel, 2010. ISBN: 978-0-312-58090-2. Gr 4–6.

Greenwood, Mark. *The Greatest Liar on Earth: A True Story*. Candlewick, 2012. ISBN: 978-0-7636-6155-7. Gr K–3.

Hagglund, Betty. *Epic Treks*. Kingfisher, 2011. ISBN: 978-0-7534-6668-1. Gr 5–9.

Hall, Daniel Weston, Jr. *Arctic Rovings: Or the Adventures of a New Bedford Boy on Sea and Land*. Nabu Press, 2011. ISBN: 978-1-1756-0583-2. Gr 7 and up.

Hanel, Rachael. *Can You Survive Antarctica? An Interactive Survival Adventure*. Capstone, 2011. ISBN: 978-1-4296-7345-7. Gr 4–6.

Hirschdelder, Arlene B. *Photo Odyssey: Solomon Carvalho's Remarkable Western Adventure, 1853–54*. Clarion, 2000. ISBN: 0-395-89123-X. Gr 5–9.

Junger, Sebastian. *The Perfect Storm: True Story of Men against the Sea*. Norton, 1997. Gr 9 and up. Classic.

Koehler-Pentacoff, Elizabeth. *John Muir and Stickeen: An Alaskan Adventure*. Lerner, 2003. ISBN: 0-7613-1997-2. Gr K–3.

Krakauer, Jon. *Into Thin Air*. Anchor; Later Printing edition, 1999. ISBN: 978-0-3854-9478-6. Gr 9 and up. Classic.

Lassieur, Allison. *Can You Survive the Titanic? An Interactive Survival Adventure*. Capstone, 2011. ISBN: 978-1-4296-6586-5. Gr 4–6.

Levinson, Nancy Smiler. *Magellan and the First Voyage Around the World*. Clarion, 2001. ISBN: 0-395-98773-3. Gr 4–6.

Lewin, Ted. *Top to Bottom Down Under*. HarperCollins, 2005. ISBN: 0-688-14114-5. Gr K–3.

Lewin, Ted. *Horse Hong: The Naadam of Mongolia*. Lee, 2008. ISBN: 978-1-58430-277-3. Gr K–3.

Lourie, Peter. *Yukon River: An Adventure to the Gold Fields of the Klondike*. Boyds Mills Press, 2000. ISBN: 978-1-8780-9390-5. Gr 5–8.

Macaulay, David. *Jet Plane: How It Works*. Square Fish, 2012. ISBN: 978-1-59643-764-7. Gr K–3.

Macaulay, David. *Castle: How It Works*. Square Fish, 2012. ISBN: 978-1-59643-744-9. Gr K–3.

Markle, Sandra. *Animals Marco Polo Saw: An Adventure on the Silk Road*. Chronicle, 2009. ISBN: 978-0-8118-5051-3. Gr 4–6.

Marrin, Albert. *Secrets from the Rocks: Dinosaur Hunting with Roy Chapman Andrews*. Dutton, 2002. ISBN: 0-525-46743-2. Gr 4–6.

Marrin, Albert. *The Great Adventure: Theodore Roosevelt and the Rise of Modern America*. Dutton, 2007. ISBN: 978-0-525-47659-7. YA.

Mundy, Carla. *Epic Voyages*. Kingfisher, 2011. ISBN: 978-0-7534-6574-5. Gr 5–9.

Nir, Yehuda. *The Lost Childhood: A World War II Memoir*. Scholastic, 2002. ISBN: 0-439-16389-7. YA.

Phelan, Matt. *Around the World*. Candlewick, 2011. ISBN: 978-0-7636-3619-7. Gr 4–7.

Rau, Dana Meachen. *Become an Explorer: Make and Use a Compass*. Norwood, 2010. ISBN: 978-1-59953-383-4. Gr 4–6.

Rose, Jamaica. *The Book of Pirates: A Guide to Plundering, Pillaging and Other Pursuits*. Gibbs Smith, 2010. ISBN: 978-1-4236-0670-3. Gr 5–10.

Ross, Stewart. *Into the Unknown: How Great Explorers Found Their Way by Land, Sea, and Air*. Candlewick, 2011. ISBN: 978-0-7636-4948-7. Gr 4–8.

Sandler, Martin W. *The Impossible Rescue: The True Story of an Amazing Arctic Adventure*. Candlewick, 2012. ISBN: 978-0-7636-5080-3. Gr 5 and up.

Sandler, Martin W. *The Impossible Rescue: An Amazing True Whaling Adventure*. Scholastic, 2006. ISBN: 0-439-74363-X. Gr 4–6.

Schanzer, Rosalyn. *John Smith Escapes Again*. National Geographic Books, 2006. ISBN: 0-7922-5930-0. Gr 4–6.

Sheinkin, Steve. *The Notorious Benedict Arnold: A True Story of Adventure, Heroism & Treachery*. Square Fish; Reprint edition, 2013. ISBN: 978-1-2500-2460-2. Gr 7 and up.

Stewart, Trenton Lee. *The Mysterious Benedict Society: Mr. Benedict's Book of Perplexing Puzzles, Elusive Enigmas, and Curious Conundrums*. Little, 2011. ISBN: 978-0-316-18193-8. Gr 4–6.

Thomson, Ruth. *Adventure Stories*. Sea to Sea, 2012. ISBN: 978-1-59771-406-8. Gr K–3.

Venables, Stephen. *To the Top: The Story of Everest*. Candlewick Press, 2003. ISBN: 0-7636-2115-3. Gr 4 and up.

Weaver, Janice. *Hudson*. Tundra, 2010. ISBN: 978-0-88776-814-9. Gr 3–6.

Zaunders, Bo. *Crocodiles, Camels and Dugout Canoes: Eight Adventurous Episodes*. Dutton, 1998. ISBN: 0-525-45858-1. Gr 4–6.

# PICTURE BOOKS

*Adventure Stories that Will Thrill You.* North-South, 2001. ISBN: 1-58717-101-5. Gr K–3.

Bania, Michael. *Kumak's River: A Tall Tale from the Far North.* Alaska, 2012. ISBN: 978-0-88240-886-6. Gr K–3.

Banks, Kate. *Max's Castle.* Farrar, 2011. ISBN: 978-0-374-39919-1. Gr K–3.

Blake, Robert J. *Swift.* Philomel, 2007. ISBN: 978-0-399-23383-8. Gr K–3.

Bliss, Harry. *Bailey at the Museum.* Scholastic, 2012. ISBN: 978-0-545-23345-3. Gr K–3.

Brown, Marc. *Arthur's First Sleepover.* Little Brown Books for Young Readers, 1996. ISBN: 978-0-316-11049-5. Gr K–3.

Buehner, Caralyn. *The Escape of Marvin the Ape.* Turtleback, 1999. ISBN: 978-0-6131-7791-7. Gr K–3.

Byrd, Robert. *The Hero and the Minotaur: The Fantastic Adventures of Theseus.* Dutton, 2005. ISBN: 0-525-47391-2. Gr K–3.

Crowley, Ned. *Nanook and Pryce: Gone Fishing.* HarperCollins, 2009. ISBN: 978-0-06-133641-6. Gr PK–2.

DiCamillo, Kate. *Louise, The Adventures of a Chicken.* HarperCollins, 2008. ISBN: 978-0-06-075554-6. Gr K–3.

Duddle, Jonny. *The Pirates Next Door.* Candlewick, 2012. ISBN: 978-0-7636-5842-7. K–2.

Fleming, Candace. *Clever Jack Takes the Cake.* Random House, 2010. ISBN: 978-0-375-84979-4. Gr PK–2.

Fritz, Jean. *The Great Adventure of Christopher Columbus: A Pop-up Book.* Putnam & Grosset, 1992. ISBN: 978-0-3992-2113-2. Gr 2–4.

Kajikawa, Kimiko. *Tsunami.* Philomel, 2009. ISBN: 978-0-3758-5583-2. Gr K–3.

Lane, Adam J. B. *Stop Thief.* Roaring Brook, 2012. ISBN: 978-1-5964-3693-0. Gr K–2.

Lewin, Ted. *Top to Bottom Down Under.* HarperCollins, 2005. ISBN: 0-688-14113-7. Gr K–3.

Livingstone, Star. *Harley.* North-South, 2001. ISBN: 1-58717-048-5. Gr K–3.

Quattlebaum, Mary. *Pirate vs. Pirate: The Terrific Tale of a Big, Blustery Maritime March.* Hyperion, 2011. ISBN: 978-1-4231-2201-2. Gr PK–2.

Shepard, Steven. *Fogbound*. Landmark, 1993. ISBN: 0-33849-43-5. Gr 1–3.

Van Dusen, Chris. *Randy Riley's Really Big Hit*. Candlewick, 2012. ISBN: 978-0-7636-4946-3. Gr 1–3.

## ANNOTATED PROFESSIONAL BOOK

Fletcher, Ralph. *Guy-Write: What Every Guy Writer Needs to Know*. Henry Holt and Co., 2012.

> Fletcher sympathizes with boys regarding their difficulties with writing for school—creativity boy-style is mostly unappreciated by teachers, clear handwriting is simply not possible, there is never a chance to free-write, and the teacher usually does not agree with the perception of their own work. Fletcher makes many suggestions to help boys with their genre writing. The book also offers suggestions to teachers for improving this situation for boys.

# Chapter 6

# ARTS AND MUSIC

The arts and music provide means of self-expression and acceptance for boys. They can read biographies about artists and musicians. The category also includes film, which has become an important and valued means of expression for boys. They can read about specific kinds of art as well as the creation of new and varied types of music. If they are interested in drawing, they can read books on how to draw. Books about artists demonstrate perseverance, dedication, and problem-solving skills. When boys participate in the arts and enjoy reading about the arts it encourages their creative endeavors and builds confidence. Boys can also learn about the commercial side of the arts and music through specific informational texts.

## FEATURED AUTHORS

Name: Kathleen Krull

Birth date: July 29, 1952

Place of Birth: Fort Leonard Wood, Missouri

Most popular book(s): *Lives of the Musicians, The Beatles Were Fab*

About: At fifteen, Krull was fired from her first job—in the library—for reading too much and not doing her work!

web site: http://www.kathleenkrull.com

Name: Bob Raczka

Birth date: 1963

Place of Birth: Chicago, Illinois

Most popular book(s): *Action Figures: Paintings of Fun, Daring, and Adventure*

About: As a child Raczka loved to draw, especially dinosaurs, cars, and airplanes. He also enjoyed making paper airplanes, plastic models, and model rockets. After 10 years in the ad business he began writing his first children's book. It took five years to sell the manuscript but it became the first in his Adventures in Art series.

Web site: http://www.bobraczka.com

## ANNOTATIONS

Applegate, Katherine. *The One and Only Ivan*. Harper, 2012. ISBN: 978-0-06-199225-4.
    Ivan, a silverback gorilla, has lived in his domain, a mall circus, 9,876 days. Before his elephant friend Stella died, Ivan promised her that he would save baby Ruby from Stella's fate. Ivan, an artist, has a plan with hopes for Ruby to be placed in a zoo with other elephants. It is not a perfect solution but better than being alone in a circus mall performing three times a day.

Krull, Kathleen. *Lives of the Musicians: Good Times, Bad Times (and What the Neighbors Thought)*. HMH Books for Young Readers, 2011. ISBN: 978-0152164362.
    This is a biography of many famous musicians such as Vivaldi, Mozart, and Beethoven from long ago to Guthrie and Joplin from more recent times. There are stylized caricatures of each one and descriptions of unusual personality quirks and unique possessions.

Raczka, Bob. *Action Figures: Paintings of Fun, Daring, and Adventure*. Millbrook Press, 2009. ISBN: 978-0-7613-4140-6.
    The title says it all, eighteen lively paintings in various styles dated from 1450 to 1962. Perfect for browsing along with fun facts to further stimulate your interest.

Van Hecke, Susan. *Raggin' Jazzin' Rockin': A History of American Musical Instrument Makers*. Boyds Mills Press, 2011. ISBN: 978-1-59078-574-4.
    The individuals and the amazing stories behind famous instruments include Fender and Martin guitars, the Steinway piano, and the Moog synthesizer for sculpting sound.

Wray, Anna. *This Belongs to Me: Cool Ways to Personalize Your Stuff*. RP Kids, 2013. ISBN: 978-0-7624-4929-3.
    Fourteen different projects to express your sense of style with cool designs. After the projects and techniques are introduced, free space is provided for practice.

## READ ALOUD

Bryant, Jen. *A Splash of Red: The Life and Art of Horace Pippin*. Knopf Books for Young Readers, 2013. ISBN: 978-0-3758-6712-5.

Burleigh, Robert. *George Bellows: Painter with a Punch*. Abrams, 2012. ISBN: 978-1-4197-0166-5.

Garriel, Barbara. *I Know a Shy Fellow Who Swallowed A Cello*. Boyds Mills Press, 2004. ISBN: 978-1-5907-8043-5.

Hill, Laban Carrick. *Dave the Potter: Artist, Poet, Slave.* Little, 2010. ISBN: 978-0-316-10731-0.

Schubert, Leda. *Monsieur Marceau: Actor Without Words.* Roaring Brook Press, 2012. ISBN: 978-1-5964-3529-1.

Stotts, Stuart. *We Shall Overcome: The Song That Changed the World.* Houghton Mifflin, 2010. ISBN: 978-0-547-18210-0.

Sweet, Melissa. *Balloons Over Broadway: The True Story of the Puppeteer of Macy's Parade.* Houghton, 2011. ISBN: 978-0-547-19945-0.

## BIBLIOGRAPHY

### Fiction

Auch, M. J. *Guitar Boy.* Henry Holt, 2010. ISBN: 978-0-8050-9112-0. Gr 5–8.

Balliett, Blue. *The Calder Game.* Scholastic, 2008. ISBN: 978-0-439-85207-4. Gr 4–6.

Balliett, Blue. *The Wright 3.* Scholastic, 2006. ISBN: 0-439-69367-5. Gr 4–6.

Balliett, Blue. *Chasing Vermeer.* Scholastic, 2004. ISBN: 0-439-37294-1. Gr 4–6.

Billout, Guy. *Something's Not Quite Right.* Godine, 2002. ISBN: 1-56792-230-9. Gr 4–6.

Bolognese, Don. *The Warhorse.* Simon, 2003. ISBN: 0-689-85458-7. Gr 4–6.

Booraem, Ellen. *The Unnameables.* Harcourt, 2008. ISBN: 978-0-15-206368-9. Gr 4–6.

Boyce, Frank Cottrell. *Framed.* HarperCollins, 2006. ISBN: 0-06-073402-7. Gr 4–6.

Broach, Elise. *Masterpiece.* Holt, 2008. ISBN: 978-0-8050-8270-8. Gr 4–6.

Creech, Sharon. *Replay.* HarperCollins Publishers, Reprint edition, 2007. ISBN: 978-0-0605-4021-0. Gr 4–6.

Duncan, Lois. *Movie for Dogs.* Scholastic, 2010. ISBN: 978-0-545-10854-6. Gr 4–6.

Federle, Tim. *Better Nate than Ever.* Simon & Schuster Books for Young Readers, 2013. ISBN: 976-1-4424-4689-2. Gr 5–8.

Flavin, Teresa. *The Blackhope Enigma.* Candlewick, 2011. ISBN: 978-0-7636-5695-2. Gr 4–6.

Fleischman, Paul. *Graven Images.* Candlewick, 2006. ISBN: 0-7636-2775-5. Gr 4–6.

Hale, Bruce. *Give My Regrets to Broadway.* The New York Review of Books, 2006. ISBN: 1-59017-212-4. Gr 4–6.

Henson, Heather. *Here's How I See It—Here's How It Is.* Simon & Schuster Children's Publishing, 2009. ISBN: 978-1-4169-4901-5. Gr 4–6.

Konigsburg, E. L. *From the Mixed-Up Files of Mrs. Basil E. Frankweiler.* Atheneum Books for Young Readers, Reprint edition, 2007. ISBN: 978-1-4169-4975-6. Gr 4–6. Classic.

Lerangis, Peter. *Summer Stars: Book Four.* Speak, 2008. ISBN: 978-0-1424-1116-2. YA. Drama Club series.

Marino, Nan. *Hiding Out at the Pancake Palace.* Roaring Brook Press, 2013. ISBN: 978-1-5964-3753-1. Gr 5–8.

Matti, Truus. *Mister Orange.* Enchanted Lion, 2013. ISBN: 978-1-59270-123-0. Gr 4–6.

Paulsen, Gary. *Paintings from the Cave: Three Novellas.* Random, 2011. ISBN: 978-0-385-74684-7. Gr 4–6.

Schmidt, Gary. *Okay for Now.* Sandpiper, Reprint, 2013. ISBN: 978-0-5440-2280-5. Gr 5 and up.

Tan, Shaun. *Lost & Found: Three by Shaun Tan.* Arthur A. Levine, 2011. ISBN: 978-0-5452-2924-1. Gr K–3.

Telgemeier, Raina. *Drama.* Graphix, 2012. ISBN: 978-0-5453-2698-8. Gr. 6–9.

## INFORMATIONAL

Adkins, Jan. *Up Close: Frank Lloyd Wright.* Viking, 2007. ISBN: 978-0-670-06138-9. YA.

Angleberger, Tom. *Art2-D2's Guide to Folding and Doodling: An Origami Yoda Activity Book.* Amulet Books, 2013. ISBN: 978-1-4197-0534-2. Gr 4 and up.

*Art Book for Children, The: Book Two.* Phaidon, 2007. ISBN: 978-0-7148-4706-1. Gr 4–6.

Bauer, Helen. *Beethoven for Kids: His Life and Music with 21 Activities.* Chicago Review Press, 2011. ISBN: 978-1-5697-6711-5. Gr 4 and up.

Bauer, Helen. *Verdi for Kids: His Life and Music with 21 Activities.* Chicago Review Press, 2013. ISBN: 978-1-6137-4500-7. Gr 5–8.

Bernier-Grand, Carmen T. *Diego: Bigger Than Life.* Marshall Cavendish, 2009. ISBN: 978-0-7614-5383-3. Gr 6–12.

Bingham, Jane. *Graffiti.* Raintree, 2009. ISBN: 978-1-4109-3401-7. Gr 5–7.

Bliss, John. *Art That Moves: Animation Around the World.* Raintree, 2011. ISBN: 978-1-4109-3922-7. Gr 5–8.

Brighton, Catherine. *Keep Your Eye on the Kid: The Early Years of Buster Keaton*. Roaring Brook, 2008. ISBN: 978-1-59643-158-4. Gr K–3.

Carlson-Berne, Emma. *Snoop Dogg*. Mason Crest Publishers, 2007. ISBN: 978-1-42220-2791. Gr 5–8. Hip-Hop series.

Carlson, Laurie. *Harry Houdini for Kids: His Life and Adventures*. Chicago Review Press, 2009. ISBN: 978-1-5565-2782-1. Gr 6–8.

Celenza, Anna Harwell. *Gershwin's Rhapsody in Blue*. Charlesbridge Publishing, 2006. ISBN: 978-1-5709-1556-7. Gr 4 and up.

*Children's Book of Art*. DK Children, 2009. ISBN: 978-0-7566-5511-2. Gr 3 and up.

*Children's Book of Music*. DK Publishing, 2010. ISBN: 978-0-7566-6734-4. Gr 3–6.

Christensen, Bonnie. *Django*. Square Fish, 2009. ISBN: 978-1-5964-3422-8. Gr 3–6.

Christensen, Bonnie. *Fabulous! A Portrait of Andy Warhol*. Henry Holt and Company, 2011. ISBN: 978-0-8050-8753-6. Gr 1–4.

Christensen, Bonnie. *Woody Guthrie: Poet of the People*. Dragonfly Books, 2009. ISBN: 978-0-5531-1203-0. Gr 3–7.

Close, Chuck. *Chuck Close: Face Book*. Abrams, 2012. ISBN: 978-1-4197-0163-4. Gr 4 and up.

Cohn, Jessica. *Animator*. Gareth Stevens, 2010. ISBN: 978-1-4339-1953-4. Gr 4–6.

Crossingham, John. *Learn to Speak Music: A Guide to Creating, Performing, and Promoting Your Songs*. Owlkids Books, 2009. ISBN: 978-1-8973-4965-6. Gr 5–8.

DeCarufel, Laura. *Learn to Speak Fashion: A Guide to Creating, Showcasing & Promoting Your Style*. Owlkids Books, 2012. ISBN: 978-1-9269-7337-1. Gr 6–10.

Dover. *Spot the Differences Book 1: Art Masterpieces*. Dover Publications, 2010. ISBN: 978-0-4864-7299-7. Gr 4 and up.

Finger, Brad. *13 Modern Artists Children Should Know*. Prestel, 2010. ISBN: 978-3-7913-7015-6. Gr 4 and up. Children Should Know series

Finger, Brad. *13 American Artists Children Should Know*. Prestel, 2010. ISBN: 978-3-7913-7036-1. Gr 2 and up.

Fleischman, Sid. *Sir Charlie Chaplin: The Funniest Man in the World*. Greenwillow Books, 2010. ISBN: 978-0-06-189640-8. Gr 6–12.

Fleming, Candace. *The Great and Only Barnum: The Tremendous, Stupendous Life of Showman P.T. Barnum.* Schwartz & Wade Books, 2009. ISBN: 978-0-3759-4597-7. Gr 3–7.

Gherman, Beverly. *Sparky: The Life and Art of Charles Schulz.* Chronicle Books, 2009. ISBN: 978-0-8118-6790-0. Gr 4–6.

Golio, Gary. *Spirit Seeker: John Coltrane's Musical Journey.* Clarion Books, 2012. ISBN: 978-0-5472-3994-1. Gr 5–8.

Golio, Gary. *Jimi Sounds Like a Rainbow: A Story of the Young Jimi Hendrix.* Clarion Books, 2010. ISBN: 978-0-6188-5279-6. Gr 6–9.

*Great Musicians.* DK Publishing, 2008. ISBN: 978-0-7566-3774-3. Gr 3 and up. DK Eyewitness Books series.

Heine, Florian. *13 Art Inventions Children Should Know.* Prestel, 2011. ISBN: 978-3-7913-7060-6. Gr 4 and up. Children Should Know series.

Helsby, Genevieve. *Those Amazing Musical Instruments with CD: Your Guide to the Orchestra Through Sounds and Stories.* Sourcebooks Jabberwocky, 2007. ISBN: 978-1-4022-0825-6. Gr 5–8.

Hosack, Karen. *Buildings.* Raintree, 2008. ISBN: 978-1-4109-3165-8. Gr 4–8.

Hosack, Karen. *Drawings and Cartoons.* Raintree, 2008. ISBN: 978-1-4109-3163-4. Gr 4–8.

Jocelyn, Marthe. *Sneaky Art: Crafty Surprises to Hide in Plain Sight.* Candlewick Press, 2013. ISBN: 978-0-7636-5648-5. Gr 2–5.

Krull, Kathleen. *The Beatles Were Fab (and They Were Funny).* Harcourt Children's Books, 2013. ISBN: 978-0-5475-0991-4. Gr 6–9.

Lach, William. *Can You Hear It?* Harry N. Abrams, 2006. ISBN: 978-0-8109-5721-3. Gr 2–6.

Laroche, Giles. *What's Inside? Fascinating Structures Around the World.* Houghton Mifflin, 2009. ISBN: 978-0-618-86247-4. Gr 4–8.

Mack, Jim. *Hip-Hop.* Heinemann-Raintree, 2010. ISBN: 978-1-4109-3393-5. Gr 3–6.

Markel, Michelle. *The Fantastic Jungles of Henri Rousseau.* Eerdmans, 2012. ISBN: 978-0-8028-5364-6. Gr K–3.

McCully, Emily Arnold. *The Secret Cave: Discovering Lascaux.* Heinemann-Raintree, 2010. ISBN: 978-0-374-36694-0. Gr 1–3.

McKendry, Joe. *One Times Square: A Century of Change at the Crossroads of the World.* David R. Godine, 2012. ISBN: 978-1-5679-2364-3. Gr 4–7.

Miles, Liz. *Making a Recording.* Raintree, 2009. ISBN: 978-1-4109-3392-8. Gr 3-6. Culture in Action series. Gr 3–6.

Miles, Liz. *The Orchestra.* Heinemann-Raintree, 2010. ISBN: 978-1-4109-3394-2. Gr 3–6.

Miles, Liz. *Movie Special Effects.* Heinemann-Raintree, 2010. ISBN: 978-1-4109-3399-7. Gr 3–6.

Miles, Liz. *Photography.* Heinemann-Raintree, 2010. ISBN: 978-1-4109-3400-0. Gr 3–6.

*My Art Book: Amazing Art Projects Inspired By Masterpieces.* DK, 2011. ISBN: 978-0-7566-7582-0. Gr 3–6.

*NatGeo Amazing! 100 People, Places and Things That Will Wow You.* National Geographic Society, 2010. ISBN: 978-1-4262-0649-8. YA.

O'Connor, Jim. *Who Is Bob Dylan?* Grosset & Dunlap, 2013. ISBN: 978-0-4484-6461-9. Gr 4 and up. Who Was series.

Ogier, Susan. *Objects and Meanings.* Cherrytree, 2010. ISBN: 978-1-84234-573-3. Gr 5–8.

Peot, Margaret. *Inkblot: Drip, Splat, and Squish Your Way to Creativity.* Boyds, 2011. ISBN: 978-1-59078-720-5. Gr 4–6.

Rappaport, Doreen. *John's Secret Dreams: The John Lennon Story.* Hyperion Book CH, 2004. ISBN: 978-0-7868-0817-5. Gr 4–8.

Roche, Art. *Create Your Own Comic Strips from Start to Finish.* Lark Books, 2007. ISBN: 978-1-5799-0788-4. Gr 4 and up.

Roeder, Annette. *13 Buildings Children Should Know.* Prestel, 2009. ISBN: 978-3-7913-4171-2. Children Should Know series. Gr 5 and up.

Rubalcaba, Jill. *I. M. Pei: Architect of Time, Space, and Purpose.* Marshall Cavendish, 2011. ISBN: 978-0-7614-5973-6. YA.

Rubin, Susan Goldman. *Music Was It: Young Leonard Bernstein.* Charlesbridge Pub Inc., 2011. ISBN: 978-1-5808-9344-2. Gr 5 and up.

Ryan, Pam Munoz. *When Marian Sang.* Scholastic Press, 2002. ISBN: 978-0-4392-6967-4. Gr 1–4.

Sabbeth, Carol. *Van Gogh and the Post-Impressionists for Kids: Their Lives and Ideas.* Chicago Review Press, 2011. ISBN: 978-1-5697-6275-2. Gr 5 and up.

Say, Allen. *Drawing From Memory*. Scholastic Press, 2011. ISBN: 978-0-5451-7686-6. Gr 5 and up.

Schubert, Leda. *Monsieur Marceau: Actor Without Words*. Roaring Brook Press, 2012. ISBN: 978-1-5964-3529-2. Gr PK–3.

Serres, Alain. *And Picasso Painted Guernica*. Allen & Unwin, 2011. ISBN: 978-1-74175-994-5. Gr 4–8.

Stoneham, Bill. *How to Create Fantasy Art for Video Games: Complete Guide to Creating Concepts, Characters, and Worlds*. Barron's, 2010. ISBN: 978-0-7641-4504-9. Adult.

Sturm, James. *Adventures in Cartooning: How to Turn Your Doodles into Comics*. Roaring Brook, 2009. ISBN: 978-1-5964-3369-4. Gr 6–8.

Tan, Shaun. *The Bird King: An Artist's Notebook*. Arthur A. Levine, 2013. ISBN: 978-0-5454-6513-7. Gr 3 and up.

Tate, Don. *It Jes' Happened: When Bill Traylor Started to Draw*. Lee & Low, 2012. ISBN: 978-1-6006-0260-3. Gr 2–4.

Temple, Kathryn. *Drawing: The Only Drawing Book You'll Ever Need to Be the Artist You've Always Wanted to Be*. Lark Books, 2005. ISBN: 978-1-5799-0587-3. Gr 4–7.

Tomecek, Stephen M. *Art and Architecture*. Chelsea House, 2010. ISBN: 978-1-60413-168-0. Gr 4–7.

Underwood, Deborah. *Staging a Play*. Raintree, 2009. ISBN: 978-1-4109-3396-6. Gr 3–6.

Wahl, Jan. *The Art Collector*. Charlesbridge, 2011. ISBN: 978-1-58089-270-4. PS–3.

Wenzel, Angela. *13 Artists Children Should Know*. Prestel, 2009. ISBN: 978-3-7913-4173-6. Children Should Know series. Gr 4 and up.

Wenzel, Angela. *13 Sculptures Children Should Know*. Prestel, 2010. ISBN: 978-3-7913-7010-1. Gr 4 and up.

Wenzel, Angela. *Thirteen Art Mysteries Children Should Know*. Prestel, 2011. ISBN: 978-3-7913-7044-6. Gr 5–7.

Williams, Freddie E. *The DC Comics Guide to Digitally Drawing Comics*. Watson-Guptill Publications, 2009. ISBN: 978-0-8230-9923-8. YA.

## PICTURE BOOKS

Bates, Katharine Lee. *America the Beautiful*. Orchard Books, 2013. ISBN: 978-0-5454-9207-2. Gr K–3.

Beaty, Andrea. *Iggy Peck, Architect*. Harry N. Abrams, 2007. ISBN: 978-0-8109-1106-2. Gr K–3.

Beaty, Andrea. *Artist Ted*. Simon & Schuster, 2012. ISBN: 978-1-4169-5374-6. Gr PK–2.

Davies, Jacqueline. *The Boy Who Drew Birds: A Story of John James Audubon*. Houghton Mifflin Books for Children, 2004. ISBN: 978-0-6182-4343-3. Gr K–3.

DePaola, Tomie. *The Art Lesson*. Puffin, 1997. ISBN: 978-0-7807-4073-0. Gr 1 and up. Classic.

Ernhardt, Karen. *This Jazz Man*. Harcourt Children's Books, 2006. ISBN: 978-0-1529-5307-9. Gr 1–5.

Falken, Linda. *Can You Find It? America*. Abrams Books for Young Readers, 2010. ISBN: 978-1-58839-334-0. Gr 2–5.

Gollub, Matthew. *The Jazz Fly (book with audio CD)*. Tortuga Pr, 2000. ISBN: 978-1-8899-1017-8. Gr 1 and up.

Greenberg, Jan. *Ballet for Martha: Making Appalachian Spring*. Flash Point, 2010. ISBN: 978-1-5964-3338-8. Gr 2–6.

Guarnaccia, Steven. *The Three Little Pigs: An Architectural Tale*. Abrams Books for Young Readers, 2010. ISBN: 978-0-8109-8941-2. Gr 1 and up.

Kalman, Esther. *Tchaikovsky Discovers America*. Orchard Books, 2005. ISBN: 978-0-5310-6894-6. Gr 3–5.

Lehman, Barbara. *Museum Trip*. Houghton Mifflin Books for Children, 2006. ISBN: 978-0-6185-8125-2. Gr 1–4.

Lewis, J. Patrick. *Tugg and Teeny*. Sleeping Bear, 2011. ISBN: 978-1-58536-514-2. Gr K–2.

Look, Lenore. *Brush of the Gods*. Schwartz and Wade, 2013. ISBN: 978-0-375-87001-9. Gr K–3.

Marsalis, Wynton. *Squeak! Rumble! Whomp! Whomp! Whomp! A Sonic Adventure*. Candlewick Press, 2012. ISBN: 978-0-7636-3991-4. Gr 1–4.

_____. *Jazz ABC: An A to Z Collection of Jazz Portraits with Art Print*. Candlewick, 2007. ISBN: 978-0-7636-3434-6. Gr 7 and up.

McCully, Emily Arnold. *The Secret Cave: Discovering Lascaux*. Farrar, 2010. ISBN: 978-0-374-36694-0. Gr 1–3.

Novesky, Amy. *Georgia in Hawaii: When Georgia O'Keefe Painted What She Pleased*. Harcourt Children's Books, 2012. ISBN: 978-0-15-205420-5. Gr 1–5.

Pinkney, Andrea. *Duke Ellington: The Piano Prince and His Orchestra*. Hyperion Book CH, 2006. ISBN: 978-0-7868-1420-6. Gr 1–5.

Polacco, Patricia. *The Art of Miss Chew*. Putnam Juvenile, 2012. ISBN: 978-0-3992-5703-2. Gr 1–4.

Reich, Susanna. *Jose! Born to Dance: The Story of Jose Limon*. Simon & Schuster, 2005. ISBN: 978-0-6898-6576-3. Gr 1 and up.

Reynolds, Peter H. *The Dot*. Candlewick, 2003. ISBN: 978-0-7636-1961-9. Gr PK–4.

Salvador, Ana. *Draw with Pablo Picasso*. Frances Lincoln Children's Books, 2008. ISBN: 978-1-8450-7819-5. Gr 1 and up.

Schwartz, Jeffrey. *The Rock & Roll Alphabet*. Mojo Hand LLC, 2011. ISBN: 978-0-6154-9521-7. Gr 1 and up.

Stanley, Diane. *Mozart: The Wonder Child: A Puppet Play in Three Acts*. HarperCollins, 2009. ISBN: 978-0-0607-2674-4. Gr K–3.

Stringer, Lauren. *When Stravinsky Met Nijinsky: Two Artists, Their Ballet, and One Extraordinary Riot*. Harcourt Children's Books, 2013. ISBN: 9789-0-5479-0725-3. Gr K–3.

Tullet, Herve. *Press Here*. Chronicle Books, 2011. ISBN: 978-0-8118-7954-5. Gr PK and up.

Warjin, Kathy-Jo. *M Is for Melody: A Music Alphabet*. Sleeping Bear Press, 2006. ISBN: 978-1-5853-6332-2. Gr 1 and up.

Weatherford, Carole Boston. *Before John Was a Jazz Giant: A Song of John Coltrane*. Henry Holt and Co., 2008. ISBN: 978-0-8050-7994-7. Gr K–4.

Wiesner, David. *Art & Max*. Clarion Books, 2010. ISBN: 978-0-6187-5663-6. Gr K–4.

Winter, Jonah. *Just Behave, Pablo Picasso!* Arthur A. Levine Books, 2012. ISBN: 978-0-545-13291-6. Gr 1–4.

Young, Ed. *The House Baba Built: An Artist Childhood in China*. Little, Brown Books for Young Readers, 2011. ISBN: 978-0-3160-7628-9. Gr 1 and up.

## ANNOTATED PROFESSIONAL BOOK

Allyn, Pam. *Best Books for Boys: How to Engage Boys in Reading in Ways That Will Change Their Lives*. Scholastic, 2011.
    Allyn details background information on the importance of identifying books specifically for boys, and she offers information on the READ model: ritual, environment, access,

and dialogue. Answers to 24 specific questions regarding boys and reading are included in the book. In addition, Allyn provides a thoughtfully annotated list of titles in a wide variety of genres such as: art and music, expeditions, how-to, learning to love reading, mechanics and technology, poetry, and biographies and memoirs. Finally, she includes a noteworthy list of magazines and other additional resources.

# Chapter 7

# COMICS AND GRAPHIC NOVELS

Graphic novels are full length original stories written in comic book format but presented in book form. They feature the sequential art that is highlighted in the comics. The format is totally visual, showing the unfolding story in panels of graphics and short text across the page. Graphic novels cover all genres. Teachers and librarians have taken a more serious look at these books and as a result are more accepting of graphic novels in the classroom and library. Graphic novels are a powerful incentive to many types of students: advanced, reluctant, struggling readers, special-needs students, and English-language learners. Graphic novels of today have sophisticated storylines and more advanced artwork than the comic books of days of old. But they also can have explicit language and intense violence; therefore, educators must scrutinize them carefully, and look at reviews in professional journals, before placing them in the hands of potential readers. Because of their unique format, graphic novels can motivate boys to investigate history, literature, science, and the arts.

## FEATURED AUTHORS

Name: Neil Gaiman

Birth date: November 10, 1960

Place of Birth: Portchester, England

Most popular book(s): *Coraline, The Graveyard Book*

About: When asked how he gets his ideas, Gaiman said, "You get ideas from daydreaming. You get ideas from being bored. You get ideas all the time. The only difference between writers and other people is we notice when we're doing it."

Web site: http://www.neilgaiman.com

Name: Jim Ottaviani

Most popular book(s): *Primates: The Fearless Science of Jane Goodall, Dian Fossey, and Biruté Galdikas*

About: Ottaviani has worked as a nuclear engineer and is currently employed as a reference librarian in Ann Arbor, Michigan. He writes comic books.

Web site: http://www.gt-labs.com

## ANNOTATIONS

Garcia, Tracey J. *Thomas Edison*. Rosen Publishing Group, Inc., 2013. ISBN: 978-0-531-20949-3.
This is a short graphic biography of America's famous inventor and businessman, Thomas Edison. He had over 1,093 patents in his lifetime, including the phonograph and improved light bulb.

McKissack, Patricia. *Best Shot in the West: The Adventures of Nat Love*. Chronicle Books, 2012. ISBN: 978-0-8118-5749-9.
Nat Love, who was also known as Deadwood Dick, was born into slavery in 1854. He was freed after the Civil War, and went west, to become a legendry cowpuncher and crack shot. Twenty years later, the railroad modernized the West, cowboys were no longer required, and Nat Love bid farewell to "the exciting adventures, good horses, good and bad men, long rides, and last but foremost, the friends I have made." Wonderfully illustrated by Randy DuBurke.

Ottaviani, Jim. *Primates: The Fearless Science of Jane Goodall, Dian Fossey, and Birute Galdikas*. First Second Books, 2013. ISBN: 978-1-5964-3865-1.
A graphic novel of three famous women who spent their years making a difference researching chimpanzees, mountain gorillas, and orangutans. Some of what is written is fiction, but the significant details can be trusted and the story is often humorous.

*Star Wars: Clone Wars, Volume 3, Last Stand on Jabiim*. Dark Horse Books, 2004. ISBN: 978-1-5930-7006-9.
The Jedi forces are a day's trek from the shelter base, and they fear the Confederacy will attack once they find their weak spot. After thirty-seven days of rain, the Force pushes on to the cobalt station where they plan to be evacuated. Whereas the Separatists have just received reinforcements and their orders are to make the Jedi suffer. The Force is between the planned evacuation and the Separatists. Anakin Skywalker has been ordered to leave and oversee the evacuation, but he does not want to abandon his friends in the upcoming battle.

Spiegelman, Art. *Maus: A Survivor's Tale: My Father Bleeds History*. Pantheon Books, 1986. ISBN: 0-394-74723-2. Adult classic.
Author and cartoonist Art Speigelman interviews his father, Vladek, for a book he is writing about his father's survival in Poland from 1936 through the war years. In the graphic novel the mice are the Jews, the cats are the Nazis, and the Poles are the pigs. The story moves from his father's unhappy present circumstances to the gradual deterioration of his comfortable life in Poland. Vladek marries into a wealthy family, serves in the Polish army, and is captured and becomes a war prisoner. He is released as a war prisoner and volunteers for labor assignment to a big German company. Thus begins

Vladek's struggle to survive through his cleverness, wealth, and family connections. All the time he struggles to live because to die is easy. At the end of *Maus*, his father and mother have just arrived at Camp Auschwitz. Most of their family is already dead, including their young son. *Maus II: And Here My Troubles Began* begins with life in the barracks of the concentration camp.

## READ ALOUD

Coudray, Philippe. *Benjamin Bear in Bright Ideas*. Candlewick, 2013. ISBN: 978-1-93617-622-5.

Nobleman, Marc Tyler. *Boys of Steel: the Creators of Superman*. Knopf Books for Young Readers, 2008. ISBN: 978-0-3758-3802-6.

O'Malley, Kevin. *Captain Raptor and the Space Pirates*. Walker Children's, 2005. ISBN: 978-0-8027-8935-8.

Williams, Marcia. *Ancient Egypt: Tales of Gods and Pharaohs*. Candlewick, 2011. ISBN: 978-0-7636-5308-8.

## BIBLIOGRAPHY

Aguirre, Jorge. *Giants Beware*. First Second Books, 2012. ISBN: 978-1-5964-3582-7. Gr 2–5.

Almond, David. *Slog's Dad*. Candlewick Press, 2011. ISBN: 978-0-7636-4940-1. Gr 6 and up.

Amir. *Zahra's Paradise*. First Second Books, 2012. ISBN: 978-1-59643-642-8. Adult.

Arcudi, John. *The Creep*. Dark Horse Comics, 2013. ISBN: 978-1-6165-5061-5. YA.

Baltazar, Art. *Billy Batson and the Magic of Shazam: Mr. Mind Over Matter*. DC Comics Paper, 2011. ISBN: 978-1-4012-2993-1. Gr 3–5.

Beard, George and Harold Hutchins. *Super Diaper Baby 2: The Invasion of the Potty Snatchers*. The Blue Sky Press, 2011. ISBN: 978-9-545-17532-6. Gr 2 and up.

Bedard, Tony. *Revenge of the Black Hand*. DC Comics, 2013. ISBN: 978-1-4012-3766-0. Green Lantern series.

Black, Holly. *The Good Neighbors: Kin*. Graphix, 2008. ISBN: 978-0-439-85562-4. YA.

Brown, Jeffrey. *Star Wars: Darth Vader and Son*. Chronicle Books, 2012. ISBN: 978-1-4521-0655-7. Gr 3–7.

Brown, Jeffrey. *Star Wars: Jedi Academy*. Scholastic Inc., 2013. ISBN: 978-0-5455-0517-8. Gr 3–7.

Cammuso, Frank. *Otto's Orange Day.* Toon Books, 2013. ISBN: 978-1-9351-7927-6. Gr 1–4.

Cammuso, Frank. *The Battling Bands.* Graphix, 2011. ISBN: 978-0-4399-0318-9. Knights of the Lunch Table series. Gr 4 and up.

Chad, Jon. *Leo Geo and His Miraculous Journey Through the Center of the Earth.* Roaring Brook, 2012. ISBN: 978-15964-3661-9. Gr 3–6.

Colfer, Eoin and Andrew Donkin. *The Arctic Incident: The Graphic Novel.* Hyperion Books, 2009. ISBN: 978-1-4231-1402-4. Gr 5 and up.

Conway, Gerry. *Crawling with Zombies.* Papercutz, 2010. ISBN: 978-1-5970-7220-5. Gr 3–6.

Cosentino, Ralph. *Superman: The Story of the Man of Steel.* Viking, 2010. ISBN: 978-0-670-06285-0. Gr 1–3.

Craddock, Eric. *Robot Frenzy.* Random House Books for Young Readers, 2013. ISBN: 978-0-3758-6913-6. Gr 3-6. Stone Rabbit series.

Dahl, Michael. *The Last Super Hero.* Stone Arch Books, 2011. ISBN: 978-1-4342-3082-9. Gr 4 and up. Green Lantern series.

Dahl, Michael. *Dawn of the Dragons.* Stone Arch Books, 2011. ISBN: 978-1-4342-3455-1. Gr 1–3. Dragon Blood series.

Davis, Jim. *The Curse of the Cat People.* Papercutz, 2011. ISBN: 978-1-59707-267-0-. Gr 2–5.

de Saint-Exupery, Antoine. *The Little Prince.* Houghton Mifflin, 2010. ISBN: 978-0-5473-3802-6. Gr 5–9.

Dini, Paul. *Batman: Heart of Hush.* DC Comics, 2010. ISBN: 978-1-4012-2124-9. Gr. 6–12.

Dixon, Chuck. *Batman: Knightquest.* DC Comics, 2012. ISBN: 978-1-4012-3536-9. YA. Batman: Knightfall series.

Emerson, Sharon. *Zebrafish.* Simon & Schuster, 2010. ISBN: 978-1-4169-9525-8. Gr 5–8.

Everheart, Chris. *Shadow Cell Scam.* Recon Academy, 2009. ISBN: 978-1-4342-1166-8. Gr 4–8.

Farshtey, Greg and Randy Elliott. *Biontcle: #3 City of Legends.* Papercutz, 2008. ISBN: 978-1-59707-121-8. Gr 4–6.

Fearing, Mark. *Earthling!* Chronicle, 2012. ISBN: 978-1-8118-7106-8. Gr 4–6.

Friesen, Ray. *Piranha Pancakes.* Don't Eat Any Bugs Paper, 2010. ISBN: 978-0-9802-3143-4. Gr 3–5.

Gaiman, Neil. *Coraline: The Graphic Novel*. HarperCollins, 2009. ISBN: 978-0-0608-2545-4. Gr 4–6.

Giarrusso, Chris. *G-Man: Learning to Fly*. Image Paper, 2010. ISBN: 978-1-6070-6270-7. Gr 3–5.

Gulledge, Laura Lee, *Will & Whit*. Amulet Books, 2013. ISBN: 978-1-4197-0546-5. Gr 7 and up.

Herge, *The Adventures of Tintin: Red Rackham's Treasure*. Little, Brown and Company, 2011. ISBN: 978-0-316-13384-5. Gr 4–6.

Hinds, Gareth. *The Odyssey*. Candlewick, 2010. ISBN: 978-0-7636-4268-6. YA.

Holm, Jennifer L. *Babymouse Burns Rubber*. Random House, 2010. ISBN: 978-0-3759-5713-0. Gr 4–6.

Holm, Jennifer L. *Babymouse for President*. Random, 2012. ISBN: 978-0-375-96780-1. Gr 3–5.

Horowitz, Anthony. *Skeleton Key: The Graphic Novel*. Philomel, 2009. ISBN: 978-0-3992-5418-5. Alex Rider series. Gr 5 and up.

Hunter, Erin. *Warriors: Escape from the Forest*. HarperCollins Publishers, 2009. ISBN: 978-0-06-154793-5. Tigerstar & Sasha series. Gr. 4 and up.

Jacques, Brian. *Redwall: The Graphic Novel*. Philomel, 2007. ISBN: 978-0-3992-4481-0. Gr 4 and up.

Kibuishi, Kazu. *Prince of the Elves*. Graphix, 2012. ISBN: 978-0-5452-0889-5. Amulet series. Gr 4 and up.

Kibuishi, Kazu. *Explorer: The Mystery Boxes*. Amulet Books, 2012. ISBN: 978-1-4187-0009-5. Gr 5 and up.

Kinney, Jeff. *The Third Wheel*. Amulet Books, 2012. ISBN: 978-1-4197-0584-7. Diary of a Wimpy Kid series. Gr 4 and up.

Krosoczka, Jarrett. *Lunch Lady and the Mutant Mathletes*. Random House, Inc., 2012. ISBN: 978-0-375-87028-6. Gr 2–5. Lunch Lady series.

*Lego Ninjago Masters of Spinjitzu #2: Mask of the Sensei*. Papercutz, 2012. ISBN: 978-1-59707-310-3. Gr 1–4.

L'Engle, Madeleine. *A Wrinkle in Time: The Graphic Novel*. Farrar, Straus and Giroux, 2012. ISBN: 978-0-3743-8615-3. Gr 5 and up.

Lobdell, Scott. *Chaos at 30,000 Feet (The Hardy Boys #19)*. Papercutz, 2010. ISBN: 978-1-59707-169-7. Gr 4 and up.

London, Jack. *The Call of the Wild: The Graphic Novel*. Campfire; Reprint edition, 2010. ISBN: 978-9-3800-2833-0. Gr 4 and up. Campfire Graphic Novels series.

Loux, Matthew. *The Truth About Dr. True*. Oni paper, 2009. ISBN: 978-1-9349-6404-0. Gr 3–6.

Lutes, Jason. *Houdini: The Handcuff King*. Hyperion, 2007. ISBN: 978-0-7868-3902-5. Gr 4–6.

Marunas, Nathaniel. *Manga Claus: The Blade of Kringle*. Penguin, 2006. ISBN: 1-59514-134-0. Gr 4–6.

McCranie, Stephen. *Mal and Chad: The Biggest, Bestest Time Ever*. Philomel Paper, 2011. ISBN: 978-0-3992-5221-1. Gr 2–5.

McGuiness, Dan. *Pilor and Huxley: The First Adventure*. Scholastic Paper, 2010. ISBN: 978-0-5452-6504-1. Gr 2–4.

Mucci, Tim. *The Odyssey*. Sterling, 2010. ISBN: 978-1-4027-3155-6. Gr 6 and up.

O'Malley, Bryan Lee. *Scott Pilgrim's Finest Hour*. Oni Press, 2010. ISBN: 978-1-9349-6438-7. Scott Pilgrim series. Gr 10–12.

Ottaviani, Jim. *T-Minus: The Race to the Moon*. Aladdin, 2009. ISBN: 978-1-4169-4960-2. Gr 4 and up.

Ottaviani, Jim. *Two-Fisted Science*. G. T. Labs, 2009. ISBN: 978-0-9788-0374-2. Gr 4 and up.

Parker, Jake. *Rescue on Tankium 3*. Graphix, 2011. ISBN: 978-0-5451-1717-3. Gr 4 and up. Missle Mouse series.

Pastis, Stephen. *Timmy Failure: Mistakes Were Made*. Candlewick, 2013. ISBN: 978-0-7636-6050-5. Gr 4 and up.

Phelan, Matt. *The Storm in the Barn*. Candlewick Press, 2009. ISBN: 978-0-7637-3618-0. Gr 5 and up.

Pierce, Lincoln. *Big Nate Out Loud*. Andrews McMeel Publishing, 2011. ISBN: 978-1-4494-0718-6. Gr 4–6.

Pilkey, Dav. *The Adventures of Ook and Gluk, Kung-fu Cavemen from the Future*. Scholastic, 2010. ISBN: 978-0-545-17530-2. Gr 4–6.

Pilkey, Dav. *Super Diaper Baby 2: The Invasion of the Potty Snatchers*. Scholastic, 2011. ISBN: 978-0-5451-7532-6. Gr 1–3.

Renier, Aaron. *The Unsinkable Walker Bean*. First Second Paper, 2010. ISBN: 978-1-5964-3453-0. Gr 5–8.

Reynolds, Aaron. *Big Hairy Drama*. Henry Holt and Co., 2010. ISBN: 978-0-8050-9110-6. Gr 3–6. Joey Fly, Private Eye series.

Riordan, Rick. *The Lightning Thief: The Graphic Novel*. Hyperion Book CH, 2010. ISBN: 978-1-4231-1710-0. Gr 5 and up.

Rodriguez, Pedro. *Chilling Tales of Horror: Dark Graphic Short Stories*. Enslow, 2012. ISBN: 978-0-7660-4085-4. Gr 4–6.

Roman, Dave. *Astronaut Academy: Zero Gravity*. First Second Paper, 2011. ISBN: 978-1-5964-3620-6. Gr 5–8.

Rosa, Don. *The Life and Times of Scrooge McDuck*. Boom!, 2010. ISBN: 978-1-60886-538-3. Gr 5–8.

Sakai, Stan. *A Town Called Hell*. Dark Horse, 2013. ISBN: 9781-5958-2970-2. Usagi Yojimbo series. Gr 7 and up.

Santat, Dan. *Sidekicks*. Scholastic, 2011. ISBN: 978-0-439-29811-7. Gr 4–6.

Sfar, Joann. *Little Vampire*. First Second Books, 2008. ISBN: 978-1-5964-3233-8. Gr 5 and up.

Shaw, Murray. *Sherlock Holmes and a Scandal in Bohemia*. Lerner, 2010. ISBN: 978-0-7613-6185-5. Gr 4–6.

Shiga, Jason. *Meanwhile*. Abrams, 2010. ISBN: 978-0-8109-8423-3. Gr 4–9.

Slott, Dan. *Dying Wish*. Marvel, 2013. ISBN: 978-0-7851-6523-1. Spider-Man series.

Smith, Jeff. *BONE Prequel: Rose*. Graphix, 2009. ISBN: 978-0-5451-3542-6. Gr 5 and up. Bone series.

Sonneborn, Scott. *Shell Shocker*. DC Super Heroes, 2011. ISBN: 978-1-4342-2615-0. Gr 2–4.

Spector, Baron. *The Second Adventure: Chasing Whales Aboard the Charles W, Morgan*. Magic Wagon, 2011. ISBN: 978-1-60270-771-9. Gr 4–6.

Spires, Ashley. *Binky under Pressure*. Kids Can, 2011. ISBN: 978-1-5545-3767-9. Gr 2–4.

Stahlberg, Lance. *Moby Dick: The Graphic Novel*. Campfire, 2010. ISBN: 978-9-3800-2822-4. Gr 7–10. Campfire Graphic Novels series.

*Strange Allies*. Dark Horse Books, 2011. ISBN: 978-1-59582-766-1. *Star Wars, the Clone War* series.

Telgemeier, Raina. *Drama*. Graphix, 2012. ISBN: 978-0-5453-2698-8. Gr 6–9.

TenNapel, Doug. *Cardboard*. Graphix, 2012. ISBN: 978-0-5454-1872-0. Gr 4–6.

TenNapel, Doug. *Bad Island*. Scholastic, Inc., 2011. ISBN: 978-0-5453-1480-0. Gr 4–6.

Tolkien, J. R. R. *The Hobbit: An Illustrated Edition of the Fantasy Classic (Abridged)*. Ballantine Books, 2001. ISBN: 0-613-53684-3. Gr 5–8. Classic.

Twain, Mark. *The Adventures of Tom Sawyer*. Papercutz, 2009. ISBN: 978-1-5970-7152-9. Gr 5–8.

Urasawra, Naoiki. *Pluto*. Viz, 2009. ISBN: 978-1-4215-9180. YA.

Vaughn, Brian K. *Pride of Baghdad*. Vertigo, 2008. ISBN: 978-1-4012-0315-9. YA.

Vernon, Ursula. *Dragonbreath: Revenge of the Horned Bunnies*. Dial, 2012. ISBN: 978-0-8037-3677-1. Gr 4–6.

Waid, Mark. *Agent of S.H.I.E.L.D*. Marvel, 2013. ISBN: 978-0-7851-6831-7. Indestructible Hulk series.

Weigel, Jeff. *Thunder from the Sea: Adventure on Board the HMS Defender*. Putnam, 2010. ISBN: 978-0-399-25089-7. Gr 3–5.

Wooding, Chris. *Pandemonium*. Scholastic, 2012. ISBN: 978-0-545-25221-8. YA.

Wooding, Chris. *Malice*. Scholastic Paperbacks, 2010. ISBN: 978-0-5451-6044-5. YA.

## INFORMATIONAL

Abel, Jessica. *Drawing Words & Writing Pictures: Making Comics; Manga, Graphic Novels and Beyond*. First Second Books, 2008. ISBN: 978-1-5964-3131-7. YA.

Amara, Philip. *So You Want to Be a Comic Book Artist?* Simon & Schuster Children's Publishing, 2012. ISBN: 978-1-58270-358-9. Gr 4–6.

Bacchin, Matteo. *T. Rex and the Great Extinction*. Abbeville, 2010. ISBN: 978-0-7892-1014-2. Gr 4–6.

Barnard, Bryn. *The Genius of Islam: How Muslims Made the Modern World*. Alfred A. Knopf, 2011. ISBN: 978-0-3758-4072-2. Gr 6–12.

Beauregard, Lynda. *In Search of the Fog Zombie: A Mystery About Matter*. Lerner, 2012. ISBN: 978-0-7613-5689-9. Gr 3–5.

Biskup, Agnieszka. *The Surprising World of Bacteria with Max Axiom, Super Scientist.* Capstone, 2009. ISBN: 978-1-4296-3975-0. Gr 1–3.

Butzer, C. M. *Gettysburg: The Graphic Novel.* HarperCollins, 2009. ISBN: 978-0-06-156176-4. Gr 6–9.

Debon, Nicolas. *The Strongest Man in the World: Louis Cyr.* Groundwood, 2007. ISBN: 978-0-88899-731-9. Gr 4–6.

Doeden, Matt. *The Battle of the Alamo.* Capstone, 2005. ISBN: 0-7368-3832-5. Gr 4–6.

Doxiadis, Apostolos. *Logicomix: An Epic Search for Truth.* Bloomsbury, 2009. ISBN: 978-1-5969-1452-0. YA.

Ebine, Kazuki. *Gandhi: A Manga Biography.* Penguin, 2011. ISBN: 978-01431-2024-7. Gr 6–9.

Gherman, Beverly. *Sparky: The Life and Art of Charles Schulz.* Chronicle Books, 2009. ISBN: 978-0-8118-6790-0. Gr 4–6.

Gladstone, Brooke. *The Influencing Machine.* W. W. Norton, 2012. ISBN: 978-0-393-07779-7. Adult.

Glidden, Sarah. *How to Understand Israel in 60 Days or Less.* Vertigo, 2012. ISBN: 978-0-4012-2233-8. Gr 10 and up.

Hama, Larry. *The Battle of Iwo Jima: Guerrilla Warfare in the Pacific.* Rosen Central, 2007. ISBN: 978-1-4042-0781-3. Gr 5 and up.

Hinds, Gareth. *King Lear.* Candlewick, 2009. ISBN: 978-0-7636-4343-0. YA.

Hinds, Gareth. *The Merchant of Venice.* Candlewick, 2008. ISBN: 978-0-7636-3024-9. YA.

Kallen, Stuart. *Manga.* Lucent, 2011. ISBN: 978-1-4205-0535-1. YA.

Lambert, Joseph. *Annie Sullivan and the Trials of Helen Keller.* Hyperion, 2012. ISBN: 978-1-4231-1336-2. YA.

McCloud, Scott. *Making Comics: Storytelling Secrets of Comics, Manga, and Graphic Novels.* HarperPerennial, 2006. ISBN: 978-0-06-078094-4. Gr 6 and up.

Neufeld, Josh. *A.D.: New Orleans After the Deluge.* Pantheon Books, 2009. ISBN: 978-0-3073-7814-9. Gr 6–12.

Noyes, Deborah. *Sideshow: Ten Original Tales of Freaks, Illusionists and Other Matters Odd and Magical.* Candlewick, 2009. ISBN: 978-0-7636-3752-1. Gr 7–10.

O'Brien, Patrick. *The Mutiny on the Bounty.* Walker, 2007. ISBN: 978-0-8027-9587-8. Gr 4–6.

O'Connor, George. *Zeus: King of the Gods*. First Second Paper, 2010. ISBN: 978-1-59643-431-8. Gr 5–9.

Ottaviani, Jim. *Feynman*. First Second, 2011. ISBN: 978-1-5964-3259-8. YA.

Peters, Jeffrey Edward. *Write a Graphic Novel in 5 Simple Steps*. Enslow, 2012. ISBN: 978-0-7660-3888-2. Gr 4–6.

Phelan, Matt. *Around the World*. Candlewick, 2011. ISBN: 978-0-7636-3619-7. Gr 4–7.

Robbins, Trina. *Lily Renee, Escape Artist: From Holocaust Survivor to Comic Book Pioneer*. Lerner, 2011. ISBN: 978-0-7613-6010-0. Gr 4–6.

Roche, Art. *Art for Kids: Comic Strips: Create Your Own Comic Strips from Start to Finish*. Sterling, 2011. ISBN: 978-1-57990-788-4. Gr 4–6.

Rodriguez, Pedro. *Chilling Tales of Horror: Dark Graphic Short Stories*. Enslow, 2012. ISBN: 978-0-7660-4084-4. Gr 4–6.

Rosinsky, Natalie M. *Write Your Own Graphic Novel*. Compass Point, 2008. ISBN: 978-0-7565-3856-9. Gr 4–8.

Santiago, Wilfred. *21: The Story of Roberto Clemente*. Fantagraphics, 2012. ISBN: 978-1-56097-892-3. YA.

Say, Allen. *Drawing from Memory*. Scholastic, Inc., 2100. ISBN: 978-0-5451-7686-6. Gr 6 and up.

Stanley, Mark Alan. *Alia's Mission: Saving the Books of Iraq*. Knopf, 2004. ISBN: 0-375-83217-3. Gr K–3.

Sturm, James. *Adventures in Cartooning Activity Book*. Roaring Brook, 2010. ISBN: 978-1-5964-3598-8. Gr 2–5.

Sturm, James. *Satchel Paige: Striking Out Jim Crow*. Hyperion, 2007. ISBN: 978-0-7868-3900-1. Gr 6–12.

Townsend, Michael. *Where Do Presidents Come From? And Other Presidential Stuff of Super-Great Importance*. Dial Books, 2012. ISBN: 978-0-8037-3748-8. Gr 4–9.

Williams, Freddie. E. *The DC Comics Guide to Digitally Drawing Comics*. Watson-Guptill, 2009. ISBN: 978-0-8230-9923-8. Gr 9–12.

Williams, Marcia. *Chaucer's Canterbury Tales*. Candlewick, 2007. ISBN: 978-0-7636-3197-0. Gr 4–6.

# PICTURE BOOKS

Bar-el, Dan. *That Spooky Night*. Kids Can, 2012. ISBN: 978-1-55453-751-8. Gr 1–3.

Bliss, Harry. *Luke on the Loose*. Toon Books, 2009. ISBN: 978-1-9351-7900-9. Gr PK–2.

Burks, James. *Beep and Bah*. Carolrhoda, 2012. ISBN: 978-0-7613-6567-9. Gr 1–2.

Burks, James. *Bird & Squirrel: On the Run*. Graphix, 2012. ISBN: 978-0-5453-1283-7. Gr K–3.

Coudray, Philippe. *Benjamin Bear in Fuzzy Thinking*. Toon, 2011. ISBN: 978-1-9351-7912-2. Gr K–2.

Eaton, Maxwell III. *The Flying Beaver Brothers and the Fish Business*. Knopf, 2012. ISBN: 978-0-375-96448-0. Gr 1–5.

Hayes, Geoffrey. *Benny and Penny in the Toy Breaker*. Toon, 2010. ISBN: 978-1-935179-07-8. Gr PK–2.

Hayes, Geoffrey. *Patrick in a Teddy Bear's Picnic and Other Stories*. Toon, 2011. ISBN: 978-1-9351-7909-2. Gr K–2.

Johnson, Kikuo. *The Shark King*. Toon Books, 2012. ISBN: 978-1-9351-7916-0. Gr 2–4.

Kochalka, James. *Johnny Boo and the Happy Apples*. Top Shelf, 2009. ISBN: 978-1-6030-9041-4. Gr K–3.

Lechner, John. *Stickt Burr: Adventures in Burrwood Forest*. Candlewick Press, 2008. ISBN: 978-0-7636-3567-1. Gr K–3.

Long, Ethan. *Rick and Rack and the Great Outdoors*. Blue Apple, 2010. ISBN: 978-1-6090-5034-4. Gr 1–3.

Luciani, *Brigitte. The Meeting*. Lerner, 2010. ISBN: 978-0-7613-5625-7. Gr K–3.

*Nursery Rhyme Comics: 50 Timeless Rhymes from 50 Celebrated Cartoonists*. First Second, 2011. ISBN: 978-1-5964-3600-8. Gr PK–3.

Ponti, Claude. *Chick and Chickie Play All Day*. Toon, 2012. ISBN: 978-1-9351-7929-0. Gr PK–K.

O'Connor, George. *Kapow*. Aladdin, 2004. ISBN: 978-1-4169-6847-4. Gr PK–1.

Smith, Jeff. *Little Mouse Gets Ready*. Toon, 2009. ISBN: 978-1-9351-7901-6. Gr PK–K.

Spiegelman, Nadja. *Zig and Wikki in Something Ate My Homework*. Toon, 2010. ISBN: 978-1-9351-7902-3. Gr K–2.

Viva, Frank. *A Trip to the Bottom of the World With Mouse*. Toon, 2012. ISBN: 978-1-9351-7919-1. Gr PK–1.

## ANNOTATED PROFESSIONAL BOOK

Zbaracki, Matthew D. *Best Books for Boys: A Resource for Educators*. Libraries Unlimited, 2008.

> Zbaracki discusses boys and books, including such factors as interest, choice, social factors, involvement, and text types to consider when choosing books for boys. The chapters cover a variety of genres, including humor, realistic fiction, fantasy, historical fiction, poetry, graphic novels, nonfiction, and modern classics. Each chapter is set up with an introduction, annotated titles arranged by author, and is divided into picture books, novels, and short stories.

# Chapter 8

# EXCEPTIONALITIES

Children and young adults with both physical and mental exceptionalities still have difficulty in our society. In 1975, the Education for All Handicapped Children Act required a free and appropriate education with related services for each child in the least restrictive environment. This created inclusion, the practice of educating all or most children with physical, mental, and developmental disabilities in regular classrooms. Often, a special assistant to the classroom teacher was required. Therefore, students with exceptionalities were mixed in with regular kids, and students were exposed to greater diversity than ever before (The Education for All Handicapped Children Act, 1975. Public Law (PL) 94-142). Exceptionalities cover a wide range of topics including mental and physical disabilities as well as social conditions. An exceptional student could have a hearing impairment, autism, dyslexia, ADHD, or even be gifted. Very often, an exceptional student has social issues in the school setting, and may look to books for dealing with issues such as shyness, behavior issues, bullying, and self-consciousness. By reading these types of books, boys may also develop greater understanding, empathy, and accommodation for exceptional students.

## FEATURED AUTHORS

Name: Jack Gantos

Birth date: July 2, 1951

Most popular book(s): *Joey Pigza* Series

About: The seeds for Jack's writing career were planted in sixth grade, when he read his sister's diary and decided he could write better than she could. He begged his mother for a diary and began to collect anecdotes he overheard at school, mostly from standing outside the teachers' lounge and listening to their lunchtime conversations.

Web site: http://www.jackgantos.com

Name: Patricia Polacco

Birth date: July 11, 1944

Place of Birth: Lansing, Michigan

Most popular book(s): *Bully, Just in Time, Abraham Lincoln, The Art of Miss Chew, January's Sparrow*

About: When Polacco was in elementary school she wasn't a very good student and had a terrible time with reading and math. She did not learn how to read until she was almost 14 years old when it was learned that she had dyslexia. Her book *Thank You, Mr. Falker* is Polacco's retelling of the teacher who helped her learn to read.

Web site: http://www.patriciapolacco.com

## ANNOTATIONS

Hoopman, Kathy. *All Cats Have Asperger Syndrome*. Jessica Kingsley Publishers, 2006. ISBN: 978-1-84310-481-0.
> This book provides an explanation of Asperger Syndrome, with charming pictures of kittens and cats to match the descriptors.

Lynch, Chris. *Kill Switch*. Simon and Schuster, 2012. ISBN: 978-1-4169-2702-0.
> Daniel is not sure what is the truth and what is his grandfather's dementia, when Da lets a few comments slip about his past life of assassinations and coups. Daniel tries to protect his grandfather by leaving home and avoiding the perceived threats. Da believes everybody has a kill switch and once it is flipped, you can do everything you thought you couldn't or wouldn't want to do. What will happen to Daniel when he flips his kill switch?

Palacio, R. J. *Wonder*. Knopf Books for Young Readers, 2012. ISBN: 978-0-3758-6902-0.
> Wonder is told from the point of view of Auggie, who has had numerous operations to correct a genetic chromosome deficiency. Auggie was never expected to live let alone attend fifth grade in a private school. Much of the story is told through the eyes of his sister, Via, and newly acquired friends. Auggie goes from being a victim of the "plague" to winning the "Henry Ward Beecher medal to (for) the student whose quiet strength has carried up the most hearts."

Park, Barbara. *The Graduation of Jake Moon*. Simon & Schuster, 2002. ISBN: 0-689-839855.
> Jake and two eighth-grade friends are on the way home from school when they begin to make fun of an old man in a dumpster. Jake lets it happen and doesn't let on that the old man is his grandfather, Skelly. Jake was always very close with his grandfather but he doesn't know how to handle Skelly's Alzheimer's disease. As Jake reminisces about Skelly his guilt lessens and he reconciles with Skelly. Jake is forced to publicly acknowledge and rescue his grandfather during his eighth-grade graduation.

Vawter, Vince. *Paperboy*. Delacorte Press, 2013. ISBN: 978-0-385-74244-3.

The substitute paperboy for one month in Memphis, 1959, is an eleven-year-old boy who stutters. This is a challenge because he has to communicate and words are hard for him. At the end of this remarkable summer in the segregated South, he realizes that what he says is more important than how he says it. The paperboy is typing his story, and the words on the paper will last forever as opposed to just speaking the same words.

## READ ALOUD

Snicket, Lemony. *The Dark*. Little, Brown Books for Young Readers, 2013. ISBN: 978-0-3161-8748-0.

Stefanski, Daniel. *How to Talk to an Autistic Kid*. Free Spirit Publishing. 2011. ISBN: 978-1-57542-365-4.

Stout, Glenn. *Able to Play: Overcoming Physical Challenges*. Turtleback; Reprint edition, 2012. ISBN: 978-0-6062-4613-2.

## BIBLIOGRAPHY

### Fiction

Abbott, Tony. *Firegirl*. Little, Brown Books for Young Readers, 2007. ISBN: 978-0-3160-1170-9. Gr 4–6.

Alexie, Sherman. *The Absolutely True Diary of a Part-Time Indian*. Little, 2007. ISBN: 978-0-316-01368-0. YA.

Aronson, Sarah. *Head Case*. Roaring Brook, 2007. ISBN: 978-1-59643-214-7. YA.

Auch, M. J. *One-Handed Catch*. Henry Holt and Co., 2009. ISBN: 978-0-8050-7900-5. Gr 4–6.

Baskin, Nora Raleigh. *Anything But Typical*. Simon & Schuster Books for Young Readers, 2009. ISBN: 978-1-4169-6378-3. Gr 4–6.

Berk, Josh. *The Dark Days of Hamburger Halpin*. Knopf, 2010. ISBN: 978-0-375-85699-0. YA.

Canfield, Jack. *Chicken Soup for the Soul: Children with Special Needs: Stories of Love and Understanding for Those Who Care for Children with Disabilities*. Kindle Edition.

Chambers, Aidan. *Dying to Know You*. Abrams, 2012. ISBN: 978-1-4197-0165-8. YA.

Choldenko, Gennifer. *Al Capone Shines My Shoes*. Dial, 2009. ISBN: 978-0-8037-3460-9. Gr 4–6.

Choldenko, Gennifer. *Al Capone Does My Homework*. Dial, 2013. ISBN: 978-0-8037-3472-2. Gr 6–8.

Crutcher, Chris. *Anger Management*. Greenwillow Books; Reprint edition, 2011. ISBN: 0-0605-0248-7. YA.

Deans, Sis. *Riding Out the Storm*. Holt, 2012. ISBN: 978-0-8050-9355-1. YA.

Dowd, Siobhan. *The London Eye Mystery*. Random, 2008. ISBN: 978-0-375-94976-0. Gr 4–6.

Draper, Sharon M. *Out of My Mind*. Atheneum Books for Young Readers, 2012. ISBN: 978-1-4169-7171-9. Gr 4–6.

Erskine, Kathryn. *Mockingbird*. Philomel, 2010. ISBN: 978-0-399-25264-8. Gr 4–7.

Flake, Sharon. *Pinned*. Scholastic Press, 2012. ISBN: 978-0-5450-5718-9. Gr 4–6.

Gantos, Jack. *Joey Pigza Swallowed the Key*. Square Fish, Reprint edition, 2011. ISBN: 978-0-3126-2355-5. Gr 5 and up. Joey Pigza series.

Gifaldi, David. *Listening for Crickets*. Holt, 2008. ISBN: 978-0-8050-7385-0. Gr 4–6.

Ginsberg, Blaze. *Episodes: My Life As I See it*. Roaring Brook, 2009. ISBN: 978-1-59643-461-5. YA.

Graff, Lisa. *The Thing About Georgie*. HarperCollins, 2007. ISBN: 978-0-06-087589-3. Gr 4–6.

Green, John. *The Fault in Our Stars*. Dutton Juvenile, 2012. ISBN: 978-0-5254-7881-2. YA.

Gutman, Dan. *The Million Dollar Putt*. Dial, 2009. ISBN: 978-0-8037-3346-6. Gr 4–6.

Hinwood, Christinen. *The Returning*. Dial, 2011. ISBN: 978-0-8037-3528-6. YA.

Hostetter, Joyce Moyer. *Comfort*. Boyds Mills Press, 2009. ISBN: 978-1-59078-606-2. Gr 4–6.

Houtman, Jacqueline Jaeger. *The Reinvention of Edison Thomas*. Front Street, 2010. ISBN: 978-1-59078-708-3. Gr 5–8.

Jinks, Catherine. *Genius Squad*. Harcourt, 2008. ISBN: 978-0-15-205985-9. YA.

Keller, Julia. *Back Home*. Egmont, 2009. ISBN: 978-1-60684-005-4. Gr 4–6.

Klimo, Kate. *Dog Diaries #2: Buddy*. Random House Books for Young Readers, 2013. ISBN: 978-0-3079-7904-9. Gr 2–5.

Koertge, Ron. *Stoner and Spaz*. Candlewick, 2002. ISBN: 0-7636-1608-7. YA.

Koertge, Ron. *Now Playing: Stoner & Spaz II*. Candlewick, 2011. ISBN: 978-0-7636-5081-0. YA.

Korman, Gordon. *Ungifted*. Balzer + Bray, 2012. ISBN: 978-0-0617-4266-8. Gr. 4–6.

Lawrence, Caroline. *The Case of the Deadly Desperados: Western Mysteries, Book One.* Putnam Juvenile, 2012. ISBN: 978-0-3992-5633-2. Gr 4–6.

Lord, Cynthia. *Rules*. Scholastic Paperbacks, 2008. ISBN: 978-0-4394-4383-8. Gr 4–6.

Mazer, Harry. *Somebody, Please Tell Me Who I Am*. Simon & Schuster Children's Publishing, 2012. ISBN: 978-1-4169-3895-8. YA.

Mikaelsen, Ben. *Petey*. Hyperion Book CH; Reprint edition, 2010. ISBN: 978-1-4231-3174-8. YA.

Miller, Ashley Edward and Zack Stentz. *Colin Fischer*. Razorbill, 2012. ISBN: 978-1-5951-4578-9. YA.

Miller-Lachmann, Lyn. *Gringolandia*. Curbstone, 2009. ISBN: 978-1-931896-490-8. YA.

Monninger, Joseph. *Wish*. Delacorte, 2010. ISBN: 978-0-385-73941-2. YA.

Patterson, James. *I Funny: A Middle School Story*. Little, Brown and Company, 2012. ISBN: 978-0-3162-0693-8. Gr 4–6.

Philbrick, Rodman. *Freak the Mighty*. Scholastic Paperbacks, 2001. ISBN: 978-0-4392-9606-0. Gr 3–7. Classic.

Roy, Jennifer. *Mindblind*. Cavendish, 2010. ISBN: 978-0-7614-5716-9. YA.

Schmatz, Pat. *Bluefish*. Candlewick, 2011. ISBN: 978-0-7636-5334-7. YA.

Selznick, Brian. *Wonderstruck*. Scholastic, 2011. ISBN: 978-0-545-02789-2. Gr 4–8.

*Shining On: 11 Star Authors' Illuminating Stories*. Delacorte, 2007. ISBN: 978-0-385-90470-4. YA.

Slepian, Jan. *The Alfred Summer*. Philomel, 2001. ISBN: 0-399-23747-X. Gr 4–6.

Stork, Francisco X. *Marcelo in the Real World*. Scholastic, 2009. ISBN: 978-0-545-05474-4. YA.

Sullivan, Tara. *Golden Boy. Putnam Juvenile, 2013*. ISBN: 978-0-3992-6112-4. YA.

Tashjian, Janet. *My Life As a Book*. Henry Holt and Co., 2013. ISBN: 978-0-8050-9609-5. Gr 4–6.

Trueman, Terry. *Cruise Control*. Harper Tempest, 2004. ISBN: 0-06-623960-5. YA.

Trueman, Terry. *Life Happens Next*. Harper Teen, 2012. ISBN: 978-0-06-202803-7. YA.

Vaught, Susan. *Trigger*. Bloomsbury, 2006. ISBN: 1-58234-920-7. YA.

Wait, Lea. *Finest Kind*. McElderry, 2006. ISBN: 1-4169-09524. Gr 4–6.

White, Andrea. *Window Boy*. Bright Sky, 2008. ISBN: 978-1-9339-7914-4. Gr 5–8.

## INFORMATIONAL

Abbott, Jim. *Imperfect: An Improbable Life*. Ballantine Books; Reprint edition, 2013. ISBN: 978-0-3455-2326-6. Adult.

Alexander, Sally Hobart. *Do You Remember the Color Blue?: And Other Questions Kids Ask about Blindness*. Viking, 2000. ISBN: 0-670-88043-4. Gr 4–6.

Andrews, Beth. *Why Are You so Scared? A Child's Book about Parents with PTSD*. Magination, 2011. ISBN: 978-1-4338-1045-9. Gr 1–4.

Bessinger, Buzz. *Father's Day: A Journey into the Mind and Heart of My Extraordinary Son*. Eamon Dolan/Mariner Books, Reprint edition, 2013. ISBN: 978-0-5440-0228-9. Adult.

Chilman-Blair, Kim. *What's Up with Max? Medikids Explain Asthma*. Rosen, 2010. ISBN: 978-1-4358-3534-4. Gr 4–7. Superheroes on a Medical Mission series.

Cook, Julia. *Wilma Jean the Worry Machine*. National Center for Youth Issues, 2012. ISBN: 978-1-9378-7001-0. Gr 2–5.

Corman, Catherine A. *Positively ADD: Real Success Stories to Inspire Your Dreams*. Walker, 2006. ISBN: 0-8027-8988-9. Gr 4–6.

DeLand, M. Maitland. *The Great Katie Kate Discusses Diabetes*. Greenleaf Book Group Press, 2010. ISBN: 978-1-60832-039-4. Gr K–3.

Fonseca, Christine. *101 Success Secrets for Gifted Kids*. Prufrock Press, 2011. ISBN: 978-1-5936-3544-2. Gr 4–6.

Ginsberg, Blaze. *Episodes: My Life As I See It*. Roaring Brook, 2009. ISBN: 978-1-59643-461-5. YA.

Heller, Lora. *Sign Language for Kids: A Fun and Easy Guide to American Sign Language*. Sterling, 2004. ISBN: 978-1-4027-0672-1. Gr 4–6.

Kent, Deborah. *What Is It Like to be Blind?* Enslow Publishers, Inc., 2012. ISBN: 978-1-46440153-4. Gr K–3.

Lauren, Jill. *That's Like Me*. Star Bright Books, 2009. ISBN: 978-1-5957-2207-2. Gr 4–6.

Markle, Sandra. *Leukemia: True Survival Stories*. Lerner, 2010. ISBN: 978-0-8225-8700-2 Gr 5–8 Powerful Medicine series.

McElwain, Jason. *The Game of My Life: A True Story of Challenge, Triumph, and Growing Up*. New American Library, 2008. ISBN: 978-0-4512-2301-2. Gr 9–12.

Meyer, Don. *The Sibling Slam Book: What it's Really Like to Have a Brother or Sister with Special Needs*. Woodbine House, 2005. ISBN: 978-1-8906-2752-2. Gr 6 and up.

Montgomery, Sy. *Temple Grandin: How the Girl Who Loved Cows Embraced Autism and Changed the World*. Houghton, 2012. ISBN: 978-1-547-44315-7. Gr 4–6.

Naik, Anita. *Read the Signals: The Body Language Handbook*. Crabtree, 2009. ISBN: 978-0-7787-4388-0. Gr 4–8. Really Useful Handbooks series.

Rotner, Shelley. *I'm Adopted*. Holiday House, 2011. ISBN: 978-0-8234-2294-4. Gr PK–K.

Schwartz, John. *Short: Walking Tall When You're Not Tall at All*. Flash Point, 2010. ISBN: 978-1-59643-323-6. Gr 4–8.

Schuette, Sarah L. *Adoptive Families*. Capstone, 2009. ISBN: 978-1-4296-3977-4. Gr PK–2. My Family series.

Skrypuchm, Marsha Forchuk. *Last Airlift: A Vietnamese Orphan's Rescue from War*. Pajama Press, 2012. ISBN: 978-0-9869495-4-8. Gr 4–6.

Small, David. *Stitches: A Memoir*. W. W. Norton & Company, 2009. ISBN: 978-0-3930-6857-3. YA.

Stout, Glenn. *Able to Play: Overcoming Physical Challenges*. Sandpiper, 2012. ISBN: 978-0-5474-1733-2. Gr 4 and up. Good Sports series.

Sullivan, George. *Tom Thumb: The Remarkable True Story of a Man in Miniature*. Clarion, 2011. ISBN: 978-0-547-18203-2. Gr 4–6.

Taylor, John F. *The Survival Guide for Kids with ADD or ADHD*. Free Spirit Publishing, 2006. ISBN: 978-1-5754-2195-7. Gr 4–6.

Verdick, Elizabeth. *The Survival Guide for Kids with Autism Spectrum Disorders (and Their Parents)*. Free Spirit Publishing, 2012. ISBN: 978-1-5754-2385-2. Gr 4–6.

Zucker, Bonnie. *Take Control of OCD: The Ultimate Guide for Kids with OCD*. Prufrock Press, 2010. ISBN: 978-1-5936-3429-2. Gr 5 and up.

## PICTURE BOOKS

Cottin, Menena. *The Black Book of Colors*. Groundwood Books, 2008. ISBN: 978-0-8889-9873-6. Gr K–8.

Esham, Barbara. *Last to Finish: A Story About the Smartest Boy in Math Class*. Mainstream Connections Publishing, 2008. ISBN: 978-1-6033-6456-0. Gr 1 and up. The Adventures of Everyday Geniuses series.

Gaynor, Kate. *Tom's Special Talent—Dyslexia*. Special Stories Publishing, 2009. ISBN: 978-0-9561-7510-6. Gr K–3. Special Stories series.

Girnis, Meg. *ABC for You and Me*. Whitman, 2000. ISBN: 0-8075-0101-8. Gr PK.

Hopkinson, Deborah. *Annie and Helen*. Schwartz & Wade, 2012. ISBN: 978-0-375-85706-5. Gr K–3.

Keats, Ezra Jack. *Apt. 3*. Viking, 1999. ISBN: 0-670-88342-5. Gr K–3. Classic.

Lears, Laurie. *Ian's Walk: A Story about Autism*. Whitman, 1998. ISBN: 0-8075-3480-3. Gr K–3.

Lyons, George Ella. *The Pirate of Kindergarten*. Simon & Schuster, 2010. ISBN: 978-1-4169-5024-0. Gr PK–2.

Mackntosh, David. *Marshall Armstrong Is New to Our School*. Abrams Books for Young Readers, 2011. ISBN: 978-1-4197-0036-1. Gr K–3.

Peete, Holly Robinson. *My Brother Charlie*. Scholastic, 2010. ISBN: 978-0-545-09466-5. Gr K–3.

Polacco, Patricia. *Thank You, Mr. Falker*. Philomel; Gift edition, 2012. ISBN: 978-0-3992-5782-9. Gr K–3.

Polacco, Patricia. *Junkyard Wonders*. Philomel, 2010. ISBN: 978-0-3992-5078-1. Gr 2–5.

Robb, Diane Burton. *The Alphabet War: A Story About Dyslexia*. Albert Whitman, 2004. ISBN: 978-0-8075-0302-7. Gr K–4.

Techel, Barbara Gail. *Frankie, the Walk 'N Roll Dog*. Joyful Paw Prints, 2008. ISBN: 978-0-9800-0520-2. Gr 1–4.

Tourville, Amanda Doering. *My Friend Has Autism*. Picture Window Books, 2010. ISBN: 978-11-40486109-1. Gr K–3.

Wise, Bill. *Silent Star: The Story of Deaf Major Leaguer William Hoy*. Lee, 2012. ISBN: 978-1-60060-411-9. Gr K–3.

## ANNOTATED PROFESSIONAL BOOK

Cleveland, Kathleen. *Teaching Boys Who Struggle in School: Strategies that Turn Underachievers into Successful Learners.* ASCD, 2011.

Cleveland offers some very practical tools for helping boys who struggle in school. She begins by replacing four factors that interfere with boys' academic success with four new directions: replace, reconnect, rebuild, and reduce. She addresses the Boy Code (a term coined by Dr. William S. Pollack in a list of myths that describe life challenges for boys) and how it shapes and influences boys. Cleveland then shares a long-term, integrated, multifaceted approach to helping boys succeed. Part two discusses six pathways to reengagement.

# Chapter 9

# EXPLORATIONS AND JOURNEYS

The sky's the limit for titles in this category. There may be a book about an experienced traveler or a first-time adventurer. The story could have a historical setting or it could be about an exploration occurring now. Reading about humankind's desire to explore and conquer the unknown, along with their sometimes ill-fated journeys, can be riveting. These books can teach us about new places and cultures. They also provide boys with ideas and dreams about where they would like to go and what they might like to do in the future.

## FEATURED AUTHORS

Name: Will Hobbs

Birth date: August 22, 1947

Place of Birth: Pittsburgh, Pennsylvania

Most popular book(s): *Take Me to the River*, *Jason's Gold*, *Go Big or Go Home*, *Crossing the Wire*

About: Hobbs's dad was in the Air Force so he lived in many different states. During the years he lived in Alaska he fell in love with mountains, rivers, fishing, and books.

Web site: http://www.willhobbsauthor.com

Name: Russell Freedman

Birth date: October 11, 1929

Place of Birth: San Francisco, California

Most popular book(s): *Lincoln: A Photobiography*, *Children of the Wild West*

About: Freedman is an American biographer and the author of nearly fifty books for young people. He may be best known for winning the 1988 Newbery Medal with his work, *Lincoln: A Photobiography*.

Web site: http://www.scholastic.com/teachers/contributor/russell-freedman

## ANNOTATIONS

Cadnum, Michael. *Blood Gold*. Viking, 2004. ISBN: 0-670-05884-X.

One cannot help but like Ezra although he leaves Elizabeth behind with child while he seeks gold in the American West. William, who is a good friend of Elizabeth, departs for San Francisco by way of the Isthmus of Panama with the idea of informing Ezra about Elizabeth's condition. Along the way William encounters many adventures and it seems that William is not the only one looking for Ezra. Red-haired Murray, with two companions, is just ahead of William and he is not the kind of person one wants as an enemy. The closer William gets to the gold fields the more distracted he becomes with all the possible wealth and the attention of a certain young lady. William knows immediately that something is wrong when he arrives at Spanish Bar, the location of Ezra's camp. Murray has already been there and now William is following the man who murdered Ezra and is leaving a trail of blood.

Demi. *Columbus*. Amazon Children's Publishing, 2013. ISBN: 978-0-7614-6167-8.

Christopher was fascinated by the sea at a young age and at 14 he left home and became a sailor. He believed it was possible to reach the East and its riches by sailing west around the Earth. When they reached what is now San Salvador, Columbus thought they had reached Eastern Asia. After crossing the Atlantic Ocean eight times, he claimed many distant lands for Isabella and Ferdinand but never produced the gold and spices that he promised. Columbus died at the age of fifty-four, a failure who "destroyed the Taino culture and enslaved the islanders."

Hobbs, Will. *Never Say Die*. Harper, 2013. ISBN: 978-0-06-170879-4.

Nick, an Inuit hunter, and his half-brother Ryan, a wildlife photographer, embark on a journey to photograph the rarely seen gathering of the migrating caribou. Evidence of global warming, severe storms, and several encounters with a huge grolar bear (part grizzly and part polar bear) test Nick and Ryan's survival instincts as Nick uses the way his ancestors hunted polar bears in the past to save both of their lives.

Morley, Jacqueline. *You Wouldn't Want to Be Cursed by King Tut*. Franklin Watts, 2012. ISBN: 978-0-531-20949-3.

King Tut's tomb was robbed twice shortly after his death and it wasn't until 1922 that Lord Carnarvon and Howard Carter rediscovered his tomb. Less than two months later, Lord Carnarvon dies and thus begins reports of a curse to those closely involved with the discovery.

Ross, Stewart. *Into the Unknown: How Great Explorers Found Their Way by Land, Sea, and Air*. Candlewick Press, 2011. ISBN: 978-0-7636-4948-7.

This story of exploration begins with Pytheas the Greek around 340 BC and ends with Neil Armstrong standing on the moon in 1969. Each featured section includes several detailed drawings by Stephen Biesty to further illustrate each explorer's amazing journey.

## READ ALOUD

Bailey, Linda. *Stanley's Wild Ride.* Kids Can Press, 2006. ISBN: 978-1-5545-3254-X.

Becker, Aaron. *Journey.* Candlewick, 2013. ISBN: 978-0-7636-6053-6.

Freedman, Russell. *Who Was First? Discovering the Americas.* Clarion. 2007. ISBN 978-0-618-66391-0.

Yaccarino, Dan. *Go, Go America.* Scholastic Press, 2008. ISBN: 978-0-439-70338-3.

## BIBLIOGRAPHY

Abdel-Fattah, Randa. *Where the Streets Had a Name.* Scholastic, 2010. ISBN: 978-0-545-17292-9. Gr 4–6.

Avi. *Crispin: At the Edge of the World.* Hyperion, 2006. ISBN: 0-7868-5152-X. Gr 4–6.

Avi. *Crispin: The End of Time.* HarperCollins, 2010. ISBN: 978-0-06-174082-4. Gr 4–6.

Banks, Kate. *The Magician's Apprentice.* Farrar, 2012. ISBN: 978-0-374-34716-1. Gr 4–6.

Barnes, John. *Losers in Space.* Viking, 2012. ISBN: 978-0-670-06156-3. YA.

Blackwood, Gary. *Around in the World in 100 Days.* Dutton Juvenile, 2010. ISBN: 978-0-5254-2295-1. Gr 4–6.

Bodeen, S. A. *The Raft.* Feiwel, 2012. ISBN: 978-0-312-65010-0. YA.

Bossee, Malcolm. *The Examination.* Square Fish; Reprint edition, 1996. ISBN: 978-0-3744-2223-3. Gr 6–10.

Bray, Libba. *Going Bovine.* Delacorte, 2009. ISBN: 978-0-385-73397-7. YA.

Cadnum, Michael. *Blood Gold.* Viking, 2004. ISBN: 0-670-05884-X. YA.

Card, Orson Scott. *Ruins.* Simon Pulse, 2012. ISBN: 978-1-4169-9177-9. YA.

Collins, Suzanne. *Gregor the Overlander.* Scholastic, 2003. ISBN: 0-439-43536-6. Gr 4–6.

Conly, Jane. *Murder Afloat.* Hyperion, 2010. ISBN: 978-1-4231-0416-2. Gr 4–6.

Cooper, Patrick. *I Is Someone Else.* Delacorte, 2006. ISBN: 0-385-73269-4. YA.

Crockett, S. D. *After the Snow.* Feiwel, 2012. ISBN: 978-0-312-64169-6. YA.

Dahl, Roald. *James and the Giant Peach: A Children's Story.* Knopf, 1996. ISBN: 978-0-8403-7682-4. Gr 4–6. Classic.

Divakaruni, Chitra Banerjee. *The Conch Bearer*. Roaring Brook, 2003. ISBN: 0-7613-1935-2. Gr 4–6.

Engle, Margarita. *Hurricane Dancers: The First Caribbean Pirate Shipwreck*. Holt, 2011. ISBN: 978-0-8050-9240-0. YA.

Erdrich, Louise. *Chickadee*. HarperCollins, 2012. ISBN: 978-0-06-057790-2. Gr 4–6.

Flores-Galbis, Enrique. *90 Miles to Havana*. Roaring Book Press, 2010. ISBN: 978-1-5964-3168-3. Gr 4–7.

Gaiman, Neil. *Odd and the Frost Giants*. HarperCollins, 2009. ISBN: 978-0-06-167173-9. Gr 4–6.

Gavin, Jamilla. *The Blood Stone*. Farrar, 2005. ISBN: 0-374-30846-2. YA.

Haddix, Margaret Peterson. *Torn*. Simon, 2011. ISBN: 978-1-4169-8980-6. Gr 4–6.

Heneghan, James. *Wish Me Luck*. Farrar, 1998. ISBN: 978-0-4402-2764-9. Gr 4–6.

Hobbs, Will. *Take Me to the River*. HarperCollins, 2011. ISBN: 978-0-06-074144-0. Gr 4–6.

Ibbotson, Eva. *One Dog and His Boy*. Scholastic, 2012. ISBN: 978-0-545-35196-6. Gr 4–6.

Jacques, Brian. *The Angel Command*. Philomel, 2003. ISBN: 0-399-23999-5. Gr 4–6.

Kang, Hildi. *Chengli and the Silk Road Caravan*. Tanglewood, 2011. ISBN: 978-1-933718-54-5. Gr 4–6.

LaFevers, R. L. *The Basilisk's Lair*. Houghton Mifflin, 2010. ISBN: 978-0-547-23867-8. Gr 2–5. Nathaniel Fludd, Beastologist series.

Kokie, E. M. *Personal Effects*. Candlewick, *2012*. ISBN: 978-0-7636-5527-3. YA.

Marchetta, Melina. *Finnikin of the Rock*. Candlewick, 2010. ISBN: 978-0-7636-4361-4. YA.

Matson, Morgan. *Amy & Roger's Epic Detour*. Simon & Schuster, 2010. ISBN: 978-1-4169-9065-9. YA.

Mulligan, Andy. *Trash*. Random, 2010. ISBN: 978-0-385-75214-5. YA.

Murphy, Jim. *The Journal of Brian Doyle: A Greenhorn on an Alaskan Whaling Ship*. Scholastic, 2004. ISBN: 0-439-07814-8. Gr 4–6. My Name is America series.

Olson, Tod. *How to Get Rich in the California Gold Rush: An Adventurer's Guide to the Fabulous Riches Discovered in 1848 by Yours Truly, Thomas Hartley*. National Geographic, 2008. ISBN: 978-1-4263-0315-9. Gr 4–6.

Osborne, Mary Pope. *Land of the Dead*. Hyperion, 2002. ISBN: 0-7868-0771-7. Gr 4–6.

Park, Linda Sue. *A Long Walk to Water: Based on a True Story*. Clarion, 2010. ISBN: 978-0-547-25127-1. Gr 4–6.

Preus, Margi. *Heart of a Samurai*. Abrams, 2010. ISBN: 978-0-8109-8981-8. Gr 4–6.

Rapp, Adam. *Punkzilla*. Candlewick, 2009. ISBN: 978-0-7636-3031-7. YA.

Stewart, Trenton Lee. *The Mysterious Benedict Society and the Perilous Journey*. Little, 2008. ISBN: 978-0-316-05780-6. Gr 4–6.

Vanderpool, Clare. *Navigating Early*. Delacorte, 2013. ISBN: 978-0-385-74209-2. Gr 4–6.

Wells, Rosemary. *On the Blue Comet*. Candlewick, 2010. ISBN: 978-0-7636-3722-4. Gr 4–6.

Zelnick, Brian. *Wonderstruck*. Scholastic Press, 2011. ISBN: 978-0-5450-2789-2. Gr 4 and up.

## INFORMATIONAL

Aretha, David. *Magellan: First to Circle the Globe*. Enslow, 2009. ISBN: 978-1-59845-097-2. YA. Great Explorers of the World series.

Aronson, Marc. *The World Made New: Why the Age of Exploration Happened and How It Changed the World*. National Geographic Children's Books, 2007. ISBN: 978-0-7922-6454-5. Gr 4 and up.

Athans, Sandra K. *Tales from the Top of the World: Climbing Mount Everest with Pete Athans*. Millbrook Press, 2012. ISBN: 978-0-7613-6506-8. Gr 4–8.

Brown, Don. *Gold! Gold from the American River!* Roaring Brook, 2011. ISBN: 978-1-5964-3223-9. Gr 2-4.

Clements, Gillian. *The Picture History of Great Explorers*. Frances Lincoln Children's Books, 2009. ISBN: 978-1-8450-7464-7. Gr 2–4.

Demi. *Marco Polo*. Marshall Cavendish Children, 2008. ISBN: 978-0-7614-5433-5. Gr 4–6.

Dunlap, Julie. *John Muir and Stickeen: An Icy Adventure with a No-Good Dog*. NorthWord, 2004. ISBN: 1-55971-903-6. Gr K–3.

Freedman, Russell. *Adventures of Marco Polo*. Arthur A. Levine Books, 2006. ISBN: 978-0-4395-2394-3. Gr 4–6.

Hagglund, Betty. *Epic Treks*. Kingfisher, 2011. ISBN: 978-0-7534-6668-1. Gr 5–9.

Iggulden, Conn. *The Dangerous Book for Boys*. HarperCollins, 2007. ISBN: 978-0-06-124385-5. Gr 4–8.

Jenkins, Steve. *The Top of the World: Climbing Mount Everest*. Houghton Mifflin, 1999. ISBN: 978-0-395-94218-5. Gr 3–5.

Koestler-Grack, Rachel A. *Vasco da Gama and the Sea Route to India*. Chelsea, 2005. ISBN: 0-7910-8611-9. Gr 4–6. Explorers of New Lands series.

Kramer, Sydelle. *Who Was Ferdinand Magellan?* Grosset, 2004. ISBN: 0-448-43356-7. Gr 4–6. Who was . . .? series.

Leacock, Elspeth. *Journeys in Time: A New Atlas of American History*. Houghton, 2001. ISBN: 0-395-97956-0. Gr 4–6.

Lavender, David. *Snowbound: The Tragic Story of the Donner Party*. Holiday, 1996. ISBN: 978-0-8234-1231-0. Gr 5–7.

Mooney, Carla. *Explorers of the New World: Discover the Golden Age of Exploration*. Nomad Paper, 2011. ISBN: 978-1-936313-44-0. Gr 4 and up.

Mundy, Robyn. *Epic Voyages*. Kingfisher, 2011. ISBN: 978-0-7534-6574-5. Gr 5–9.

Murphy, Jim. *Across America on an Emigrant Train*. Perfection, 2003. ISBN: 978-0-7569-9144-9. Gr 5–8.

Phelan, Matt. *Around the World*. Candlewick, 2011. ISBN: 978-0-7636-3619-7. Gr 4–7.

Philbrick, Nathaniel. *The Mayflower and the Pilgrims' New World*. Putnam, 2008. ISBN: 978-0-399-24795-8. YA.

Revkin, Andrew. *The North Pole Was Here: Puzzles and Perils at the Top of the World*. Kingfisher, 2006. ISBN: 978-0-7534-5993-5. Gr 6–9.

Ross, Stewart. *Into the Unknown: How Great Explorers Found Their Way By Land, Sea, and Air*. Candlewick, 2011. ISBN: 978-0-7636-4948-7. Gr 4–8.

Rumford, James. *Traveling Man: The Journey of Ibn Battuta, 1325–1354*. Houghton, 2001. ISBN: 0-618-08366-9. Gr 4–6.

Sandler, Martin W. *The Impossible Rescue: The True Story of an Amazing Arctic Adventure*. Candlewick, 2012. ISBN: 978-0-7636-5080-3. YA.

Sandler, Martin W. *Trapped in Ice! An Amazing True Whaling Adventure*. Scholastic Nonfiction, 2006. ISBN: 978-0-4397-4363-1. Gr 4–6.

Schwartz, Heather E. *Foul, Filthy American Frontier: The Disgusting Details About the Journey Out West*. Capstone, 2010. ISBN: 978-1-4296-3957-6. Gr 4–8. Fact Finders: Disgusting History series.

Shulevitz, Uri. *The Travels of Benjamin of Tudela: Through Three Continents in the Twelfth Century*. Farrar, 2005. ISBN: 0-374-37754-5. Gr 4–6.

Sutcliff, Rosemary. *The Wanderings of Odysseus: The Story of The Odyssey*. Frances Lincoln Children's Books, 2005. ISBN: 978-1-8450-7360-2. Gr 5–8.

Timmesh, Catherine. *Team Moon: How 400,000 People Landed Apollo 11 on the Moon*. Houghton Mifflin Company, 2006. ISBN: 978-0-6185-0757-3. Gr 5 and up.

Weaver, Janice. *Hudson*. Tundra, 2010. ISBN: 978-0-88776-814-9. Gr 3–6.

Webb, Sophie. *Far from Shore: Chronicles of an Open Ocean Voyage*. Houghton, 2011. ISBN: 978-0-618-59729-1. Gr 4–6.


## PICTURE BOOKS

Brown, Don. *Alice Ramsey's Grand Adventure*. HMH Books for Young Readers; Reprint edition, 2000. ISBN: 978-0-61-807316-0. Gr K–3.

Carnesi, Monica. *Little Dog Lost: The True Story of a Brave Dog Named Baltic*. Penguin, 2012. ISBN: 978-0-399-25666-0. Gr K–3.

Crowley, Ned. *Nanook & Pryce: Gone Fishing*. HarperCollins, 2009. ISBN: 978-0-06-133641-6. Gr K–3.

Egan, Tim. *Dodsworth in Tokyo*. Houghton, 2013. ISBN: 978-0-547-87745-7. Gr 1–3.

Jeffers, Oliver. *Lost and Found*. Philomel, 2006. ISBN: 0-399-24503-0. Gr K–3.

Kerby, Mona. *Owney, the Mail-Pouch Pooch*. Farrar, 2008. ISBN: 978-0-374-35685-9. Gr K–3.

Lewin, Ted. *Lost City: The Discovery of Machu Picchu*. Philomel, 2003. ISBN: 978-0-3992-3302-9. Gr K–3.

Lewis, J. Patrick. *A World of Wonders: Geographic Travels in Verse and Rhyme*. Dial, 2002. ISBN: 0-8037-2579-5. Gr K–3.

Mayer, Bill. *All Aboard: A Traveling Alphabet*. McElderry, 2008. ISBN: 978-0-689-85249-7. Gr K–3.

McClintock, Barbara. *Adele & Simon in America*. Farrar, 2008. ISBN: 978-0-374-39924-5. Gr K–3.

McCully, Emily Arnold. *Manjiro: The Boy Who Risked His Life for Two Countries*. Farrar, 2008. ISBN: 978-0-374-34792-5. Gr K–3.

Potter, Alicia. *Mrs. Harkness and the Panda*. Knopf, 2012. ISBN: 978-0-375-84448-5. Gr K–3.

Provensen, Alice. *Klondike Gold*. Simon & Schuster Children's Publishing, 2005. ISBN: 978-0-6898-4885-8. Gr K–3.

Say, Allen. *Grandfather's Journey*. HMH Books for Young Readers; Reprint edition, 2008. ISBN: 978-0-5470-7680-5. Gr K–3.

Sis, Peter, *Follow the Dream*. Knopf, 2003. ISBN: 978-0-6798-0628-8. Gr 2–4.

St. George, Judith. *So You Want to Be an Explorer?* Philomel, 2005. ISBN: 978-0-3992-3868-0. Gr K–3.

Teague, Mark. *LaRue Across America: Postcards from the Vacation*. Scholastic, 2011. ISBN: 978-0-439-91502-1. Gr K–4.

Van Allsburg, Chris. *The Wretched Stone*. Houghton Mifflin, 1991. ISBN: 978-0-3955-3307-9. Gr 2–4.

Viva, Frank. *A Trip to the Bottom of the World with Mouse*. Toon, 2012. ISBN: 978-1-935179-1. Gr K–3.

Wallner, Alexandra. *The First Air Voyage in the United States: The Story of Jean-Pierre Blanchard*. Holiday, 1996. ISBN: 978-0-8234-1224-2. Gr K–3.

Williams, Mo. *Knuffle Bunny Free: An Unexpected Diversion*. HarperCollins, 2010. ISBN: 978-0-06-192958-8. Gr PK.

Weatherford, Carole Boston. *I, Matthew Henson: Polar Explorer*. Walker Children's, 2007. ISBN: 978-0-8027-9688-2. Gr 1–4.

## ANNOTATED PROFESSIONAL BOOK

Campbell, Kimberly Hill and Kristi Latimer. *Beyond the Five Paragraph Essay*. Stenhouse, 2012.

Even though the five-paragraph essay is the most frequently taught form of writing in classrooms, it is rarely seen outside the school walls. Research shows that the five-paragraph formula restricts creativity, emphasizes structure rather than content, does not improve standardized test scores, and does not prepare students for college and career writing. The authors share thoughts on reading as a writer, writing to support thinking, writing to explore, writing as an authority, and writing with mentors.

# Chapter 10

# FANTASY AND SCIENCE FICTION

Space travel, aliens, and life on other planets have special meaning for most boys. They can imagine themselves time warping into other galaxies and brandishing laser weapons to triumph over horrible-looking aliens. They can picture life on Mars and exploring barren landscapes in zero gravity. Boys certainly have been exposed to enough imagery of what all this might be like through movies and video games. Having all this come to life in their imaginations through the pages of a great science fiction novel allows a boy's courageous spirit to reach new levels. Boys enjoy reading stories about animals that talk and lead creative lives and whole civilizations of people who live under the subway system in big cities. Sometimes fantasy stories are about time travel and going back or ahead in time and trying to adjust to different ways of life. Boys enjoy reading about strong male main characters who deal with problems relevant to them.

## FEATURED AUTHORS

Name: Rick Riordan

Birth date: June 5, 1964

Place of Birth: San Antonio, Texas

Most popular book(s): Percy Jackson and the Olympians series

About: For fifteen years Riordan taught English and history in public and private middle schools in the San Francisco Bay area and Texas. He wrote *The Lightning Thief* for his son as a bedtime story. Web site: http://www.rickriordan.com

Name: Orson Scott Card

Birth date: August, 24, 1951

Place of Birth: Richland, Washington

Most popular book(s): Pathfinder Series and the fantasy series Mithermages

About: It was as a theater student that Card first began to school himself to be a writer. "It's the best training in the world for a writer, to have a live audience." At one time, he founded a repertory theater company and was the first to produce plays at The Castle, an outdoor amphitheater that was located directly behind the state mental hospital in Provo, Utah, and was built as a government project during the Depression.

Web site: http://www.hatrack.com

## ANNOTATIONS

Bradbury, Ray. *Fahrenheit 451: The Temperature at Which Book Paper Catches Fire, and Burns*. Ballantine Books, 1987. ISBN: 0-345-34296-8.

> When all houses are finally fireproofed there is no need for firemen as they originally functioned. Now their job is to ensure that everyone is happy all the time, and the way to do this is to burn all books and the houses where they are hidden. Montag likes his job until he meets a young girl named Clarisse, who is not merely satisfied to know how things are done but wants to know why. He is also affected by a woman who, when surrounded by her kerosene-soaked books, refuses to leave her house and strikes a kitchen match against the porch railing, committing suicide. Montag, too, has been hoarding books and develops a plan to hide them in firemen's houses, turn in the alarm, and then see the firemen's houses burn. However, Montag is forced to make life-altering decisions when he answers one last special assignment when the firemen and their book-burning equipment stop in front of his own house. Classic.

Drake, Ernest. *Dragonology. The Complete Book of Dragons*. Candlewick Press, 2003. ISBN: 0-7636-2329-6.

> A scientific fantasy treatment of dragons that includes locations of dragons in the world, different species of dragons, natural history of dragons, working with dragons, and appendices that include a dragonological laboratory, useful spells and charms, dragonologists and dragons layers of history, and the work of a dragonologist.

Haddix, Margaret Peterson. *Among the Brave*. Simon & Schuster, 2004. ISBN: 0-689-85794-2.

> It is declared illegal to have more than two children because of the food shortage. The Population Police have taken control of the society, and their ranks are increasing in order to seek out and destroy all third children. Trey is a third child, and it is up to him to rescue his friends who have been captured by the Population Police. Bravely he joins the dreaded Population Police, flees from a rioting crowd, and drives to the Nazerree Prison. He narrowly escapes with his friends and the leader of the Liber, or Free the Third Children movement. The adults are terrified of the future so it is up to the third children to discover the weakness of the Population Police and try to bring them down from within. Will any of Trey's friends join him in this new adventure?

Riordan, Rick. *The House of Hades (The Heroes of Olympus, Book Four)*. Disney, 2013. ISBN: 978-1-4231-4672-8.

> In the Heroes of Olympus series, seven modern Roman demigod heroes try to prevent the waking of Gaia. Gaia gave birth to Earth, and she wants to control Earth and

overthrow Olympus. The series includes the following titles: *The Lost Hero, The Son of Neptune, The Mark of Athena, The House of Hades,* and *Book 5* (Winter 2014).

Shusterman, Neal. *Bruiser.* Harper Teen, 2010. ISBN: 978-0-06-113408-1.
Bruiser is voted most likely to get the death penalty by his entire school. Most people do not know that Bruiser's real name is Brewster. Brewster is fifteen, lonely, and misunderstood. He has an unusual paranormal gift that is also a curse: he is able to take away the physical and mental pain of those he loves. The story is told from four points of view as though this could happen in a dark fairy tale where there is no happily ever after.

## READ ALOUD

Pullman, Philip. *The Scarecrow and His Servant.* Yearling, Reprint edition, 2007. ISBN: 978-0-4404-2130-6.

Riordan, Rick. *The Demigod Files (A Percy Jackson & the Olympian Guide).* Hyperion Book CH, 2009. ISBN: 978-1-4231-2166-4.

Yolen, Jane. *Grumbles from the Forest.* Boyds Mills, 2013. ISBN: 978-1-5907-8867-7.

## BIBLIOGRAPHY

### Fantasy

Alexander, Lloyd. *The Rope Trick.* Dutton, 2002. ISBN: 0-525-47020-4. Gr 4–7.

Allen, Will. *Swords for Hire: Two of the Most Unlikely Heroes You'll Ever Meet.* CenterPunch Paper, 2003. ISBN: 0-9724882-0-0. Gr 5–8.

Armstrong, K. L. *Loki's Wolves.* Little, Brown for Young Readers, 2013. ISBN: 978-0-3162-0496-5. Gr 4 and up. The Blackwell Pages series.

Appelt, Kathi. *The True Blue Scouts of Sugarman Swamp.* Atheneum Books for Young Readers, 2013. Gr 3 and up.

Atwater-Rhodes, Amelia. *Hawksong.* Delacorte, 2003. ISBN: 0-385-73071-3. Gr. 7–10.

Banks, Kate. *The Magician's Apprentice.* Farrar, Straus and Giroux, 2012. ISBN 978-0-3743-4716-1. Gr 6 and up.

Banks, Lynn Reid. *Indian in the Cupboard.* Yearling, 2010. ISBN: 978-0-3758-4753-0. Gr 4 and up. Classic.

Baker, Clive. *Thief of Always.* Harper Perennial; Reprint edition, 2008. ISBN: 978-0-0616-8426-5. YA.

Bell, Hilari. *Flame.* Simon & Schuster, 2003. ISBN: 0-689-85413-7. Gr 6–10.

Bell, Hilari. *The Goblin Wood.* HarperCollins, 2003. ISBN: 0-06-051371-3. Gr 6–10.

Blackwood, Sage. *Jinx*. HarperCollins, 2013. ISBN: 978-0-0621-2990-1. Gr 4–8.

Bowman, Erin. *Taken*. Harper Teen, 2013. ISBN: 978-0-0621-1726-7. Gr 8 and up.

Clement-Davies, David. *The Sight*. Dutton, 2003. ISBN: 0-525-46723-8. Gr 7–12.

Collins, Suzanne. *Gregor the Overlander*. Scholastic, 2003. ISBN: 0-439-43536-6. Gr 4–6.

Dahl, Roald. *Charlie and the Chocolate Factory*. Perfection Learning, 2007. ISBN: 978-0-7569-82113-3. Gr 4 and up. Classic.

Dahl, Roald. *James and the Giant Peach*. Perfection Learning, 2007. ISBN: 978-0-7560-8213-3. Gr 4 and up. Classic.

Delaney, Joseph. *Slither*. Greenwillow Books, 2013. ISBN: 978-0-0621-9234-9. YA. The Last Apprentice series.

Dickinson, Peter. *The Tears of the Salamander*. Random, 2003. ISBN: 0-385-73098-5 Gr 6–9.

Duane, Diane. *Wizard's Holiday*. Harcourt, 2003. ISBN: 0-15-204771-9 Gr. 6–9.

Farrey, Brian. *The Vengekeep Prophecies*. Harper, 2012. ISBN: 978-0-0620-4928-5. Gr 4–8.

Flanagan, John. *The Royal Ranger*. Philomel, 2013. ISBN: 978-0-3991-6360-9. Gr 6 and up. Ranger's Apprentice series.

Forward, Toby. *Dragonborn*. Bloomsbury, 2013. ISBN: 978-1-5999-0983-7. Gr 4 and up.

Funke, Cornelia. *Fearless: A Mirrorworld Novel*. Little, Brown, 2013. ISBN: 978-0-3160-5610-6. Gr 7–10.

Gordon, Roderick. *Tunnels*. Chicken House, 2008. ISBN: 978-0-4398-7177-8. Gr 4 and up.

Grant, Michael. *Light*. Katherine Tegan Books, 2013. ISBN: 978-0-0614-4918-5. YA. Gone series.

Healy, Christopher. *The Hero's Guide to Saving Your Kingdom*. Walden Pond Press, 2012. ISBN: 978-0-0621-1743-4. Gr 4 and up.

Hulme, John. *The Glitch in Sleep*. Bloomsbury Children's Books, 2007. ISBN: 978-1-5999-0129-9. Gr 5 and up.

Hunter, Erin. *Fire and Ice*. HarperCollins, 2003. ISBN: 0-06-000003-1. Gr 6–9.

Jacques, Brian. *The Angel's Command: A Tale from the Castaways of the Flying Dutchman*. Putnam, 2003. ISBN: 0-399-23999-5. Gr 5–9.

Jacques, Brian. *Loamhedge*. Philomel, 2003. ISBN: 0-399-23724-0. Gr 5–8.

Jennings, Patrick. *The Wolving Time*. Scholastic, 2003. ISBN: 0-439-39555-0. Gr 6–10.

Jobling, Curtis. *Storm of Sharks*. Viking Juvenile, 2013. ISBN: 978-0-6707-8558-2. Gr 5 and up. Wereworld series.

Jones, Diana Wynne. *The Merlin Conspiracy*. HarperCollins, 2003. ISBN: 0-06-052318-2. Gr 6–10.

Kay, Elizabeth. *The Divide*. Scholastic, 2003. ISBN: 0-439-45696-7. Gr 5–9.

La Fevers, R. L. *The Falconmaster*. Dutton, 2003. ISBN: 0-525-46993-1. Gr 6–8.

Landry, Derek. *The Faceless Ones*. Harper, 2009. ISBN: 978-0-0612-4091-1. Gr 4 and up.

Lasky, Kathryn. *Guardians of Ga'Hoole: Book One: The Capture*. Scholastic, 2003. ISBN: 0-439-40557-2. Gr 4–8.

Lewis, C. S. *The Lion, the Witch and the Wardrobe*. HarperFestival, 2005. ISBN: 978-0-0607-6548-4. Gr 3–6. Classic.

Lowry, Lois. *The Giver*. Houghton, 1993. ISBN: 0-395-64566-2. Gr 6–9. Classic.

Lowry, Lois. *Son*. Houghton Mifflin Books for Children, 2012. ISBN: 978-0-5478-8720-3. Gr 6 and up.

Lu, Marie. *Prodigy: A Legend Novel*. Putnam Juvenile, 2013. ISBN: 978-0-3992-5676-9. YA.

MacHale, D. J. *The Lost City of Fear*. Simon & Schuster, 2003. ISBN: 0-7434-3732-2. Gr 5–8.

Mahy, Margaret. *Alchemy*. Simon & Schuster, 2003. ISBN: 0-689-85053-0. Gr 7–10.

Meloy, Maile. *The Apprentices*. G. P. Putnam's Sons, 2013. ISBN: 978-0-3991-6245-9. Gr 5–9.

Nielsen, Jennifer A. *The Runaway King*. Scholastic Press, 2013. ISBN: 978-0-5452-8415-8. Gr 6 and up.

Nimmo, Jenny. *Charlie Bone and the Invisible Boy*. Scholastic, 2004. ISBN: 0-439-54526-9. Gr 4–6.

Nimmo, Jenny. *Charlie Bone and the Time Twister*. Scholastic, 2003. ISBN: 0-439-49687-X. Gr 5–7.

Nimmo, Jenny. *Midnight for Charlie Bone*. Scholastic, 2003. ISBN: 0-439-47429-9. Gr 4–6.

Nix, Garth. *Mister Monday*. Scholastic paper, 2003. ISBN: 0-439-55123-4. Gr 5–8.

November, Sharyn (editor). *Firebirds: An Anthology of Original Fantasy and Science Fiction.* Firebird; Reprint edition, 2007. ISBN: 978-0-1424-0936-7. Gr 7–10.

Oppel, Kenneth. *Sunwing.* Simon & Schuster, 2008. ISBN: 978-1-4169-4997-8. Gr 4–8.

Paolini, Christopher. *Eragon.* Knopf, 2003. ISBN: 0-375-82668-8. Gr 7–12.

Pierce, Tamora. *Battle Magic.* Scholastic Press, 2013. ISBN: 978-0-4398-4297-6. YA.

Pratchett, Terry. *Dodger.* HarperCollins, 2012. ISBN: 978-0-0620-0949-4. Gr 7 and up.

Pullman, Philip. *The Amber Spyglass.* Knopf, 2000. ISBN: 0-679-87926-9. Gr 7–12.

Pullman, Philip. *The Golden Compass.* Knopf, 1996. ISBN: 0-679-87924-2. Gr 7–12.

Pyle, Howard. *The Story of King Arthur.* ABDO Publishing, 2002. ISBN: 978-1-5776-5691-3. Classic.

Reeve, Philip. *No Such Thing as Dragons.* Scholastic Press, 2010. ISBN: 978-0-5452-2224-2. Gr 4–6.

Riordan, Rick. *The Serpent's Shadow (Kane Chronicles, Book 3).* Hyperion Books, 2012. ISBN: 978-1-4231-4057-5. Gr 5 and up.

Rodda, Emily. *The Silver Door.* Scholastic Press, 2013. ISBN: 978-0-5454-2992-4. Golden Door series. Gr 3 and up.

Rodda, Emily. *Return to Del.* Scholastic Inc., Reprint, 2012. ISBN: 978-0-5454-6028-6. Deltora Quest series. Gr 3 and up.

Rowling, J. K. *Harry Potter and the Sorcerer's Stone.* Scholastic, 2003. ISBN: 0-439-55493-4. Gr 5 and up. Harry Potter series.

San Souci, Robert D. *Robin Hood and the Golden Arrow.* Orchard, 2010. ISBN: 978-0-4396-2538-8. Gr K–3.

Sanderson, Brandon. *The Rithmatist.* Tor Teen, 2013. ISBN: 978-0-7653-2032-2. YA.

Schmidt, Gary D. *What Came From the Stars.* Clarion Books, 2012. ISBN: 978-0-5476-1213-3. Gr 6–8.

Sleator, William. *Marco's Millions.* Dutton, 2001. ISBN: 0-525-46441-7. Gr 5–9.

Spinelli, Jerry. *Hokey Pokey.* Knopf Books for Young Readers, 2013. ISBN: 978-0-3758-3198-0. Gr 5–8.

Stewart, Paul. *Beyond the Deepwoods.* David Fickling Books, 2004. ISBN: 978-0-3857-5069-1. Gr 4 and up.

Stiefvater, Maggie. *The Scorpio Races*. Scholastic Press, 2011. ISBN: 978-0-5452-2490-1. YA.

Stroud, Jonathan. *The Amulet of Samarkand*. Hyperion, 2003. ISBN: 0-7868-1859-X. Gr 6–12.

Taylor, S. S. *The Expeditioners and the Treasure of Drowned Man's Canyon*. McSweeney's McMullens, 2012. ISBN: 978-1-9380-7306-9. Gr 6 and up.

Toft, Di. *Wolven*. Scholastic, 2010. ISBN: 978-0-5451-7109-0. Gr 4 and up.

Tolkien, J. R. R. *The Fellowship of the Ring: Being the First Part of the Lord of the Rings*. Houghton Mifflin, 1988. ISBN: 0-395-48931-8 Gr. 7 and up. Lord of the Rings series.

Vaughan, M. M. *The Ability*. Margaret K. McElderry Books, 2013. ISBN: 978-1-4424-5200-8. Gr 3 and up.

Vizzini, Ned. *The Other Normals*. Balzer + Bray, 2012. ISBN: 978-0-0620-7990-9. Gr 7–10.

Wilson, N. D. *The Dragon's Tooth*. Random House, 2011. ISBN: 978-0-3758-6439-1. YA.

Yancy, Rick. *The 5th Wave*. Putnam Juvenile, 2013. ISBN: 978-0-3991-6241-1. Gr 9 and up.

## Science Fiction

Armstrong, Jennifer. *The Keepers of the Flame*. HarperCollins, 2002. ISBN: 0-06-029411-6. Gr 7–10.

Bacigalupi, Paolo. *Ship Breaker*. Little, Brown and Company, 2010. ISBN: 978-0-3160-5621-2. Gr 9 and up.

Bell, Hilari. *The Goblin War*. Harper Teen, 2011. ISBN: 978-0-0616-5105-2. Gr 5–8.

Blakemore, Megan Frazer. *The Water Castle*. Walker Children's, 2013. ISBN: 978-0-8027-2839-5. Gr 6 and up.

Bracken, Alexandra. *The Darkest Minds*. Hyperion, 2012. ISBN: 978-1-4231-5737-3. Gr 9 and up.

Brezenoff, Steven. *Time Voyage*. Stone Arch Books, 2012. ISBN: 978-1-4342-3299-1. Gr 2 and up.

Calhoun, Dia. *Firegold*. Winslow, 1999. ISBN: 1-890817-10-4. Gr 7–12.

Card, Orson Scott. *Shadow of the Giant*. Tom Doherty, 2006. ISBN: 978-0-8125-7139-4. YA. Last of the Ender Shadow series.

Cart, Michael (editor). *Tomorrowland: Ten Stories about the Future*. Scholastic, 1999. ISBN: 0-590-37678-0. Gr 6–12.

Castro, Adam-Troy. *Spider-Man: Secret of the Sinister Six*. Berkley Paper, 2002. ISBN: 0-7434-4464-7. Gr 7–12.

Clancy, Tom, and Steve Pieczenik. *Virtual Vandals*. Berkley Paper, 1999. ISBN: 0-425-16173-0 Gr. 7-12 YA.

Colfer, Eoin. *The Reluctant Assassin*. Hyperion, 2013. ISBN: 978-1-4231-6162-2. Gr 8 and up.

Cooper, Susan. *Green Boy*. Simon & Schuster, 2002. ISBN: 0-689-84751-3. Gr 4–8.

Coville, Bruce (compiler and editor). *Bruce Coville's UFOs*. HarperCollins, 2000. ISBN: 0-380-80257-0. Gr 4–8.

Coville, Bruce. *Half-Human*. Scholastic, 2001. ISBN: 0-590-95944-1. Gr 7–10.

Coville, Bruce. *Odder Than Ever*. Harcourt, 1999. ISBN: 0-15-201747-X. Gr 5–9.

Crossley-Holland, Kevin. *At the Crossing Places*. Scholastic, 2002. ISBN: 0-439-26598-3. Gr 5–8.

Crossley-Holland, Kevin. *The Seeing Stone*. Scholastic, 2001. ISBN: 0-439-26326-3. Gr 4–8.

DiTerlizzi, Tony. *A Hero for Wondla*. Simon & Schuster for Young Readers, 2012. ISBN: 978-1-4169-8312-5. Gr 6 and up.

DuPrau, Jeanne. *The City of Ember*. Random, 2003. ISBN: 0-375-82273-9. Gr 5–7.

Farmer, Nancy. *The House of the Scorpion*. Atheneum, 2002. ISBN: 0-689-85222-3. Gr 7–10.

Fisher, Catherine. *Obsidian Mirror*. Dial, 2013. ISBN: 978-0-8037-3969-7. Gr 8 and up.

Gutman, Dan. *The Edison Mystery*. Simon & Schuster, 2001. ISBN: 0-689-84124-8. Gr 4–8.

Haddix, Margaret Peterson. *Turnabout*. Simon & Schuster, 2000. ISBN: 0-689-82187-5. Gr 7–10.

Hesse, Karen. *Phoenix Rising*. Holt, 1994. ISBN: 0-8050-3108-1. Gr 6–8.

Howard, Chris. *Rootless*. Scholastic Press, 2012. ISBN: 978-0-5453-8789-7. Gr 7–10.

Hughes, Monica. *The Keeper of the Isis Light*. Simon & Schuster, 1981. ISBN: 0-689-83390-3. Gr 6–9.

Junks, Catherine. *Living Hell*. Harcourt, 2010. ISBN: 978-0-15-206193-7. YA.

Kenyon, Sherrilyn. *Inferno: Chronicles of Nick*. St. Martin's Griffin, 2013. ISBN: 978-1-2500-0283-9. Gr 8 and up.

Klaus, Annette Curtis. *Alien Secrets*. Random, 1993. ISBN: 0-440-22851. Gr 5–8.

L'Engle, Madeleine. *A Wrinkle in Time*. Farrar, Straus & Giroux, 1962. ISBN: 978-0-3743-8613-9. Gr 6 and up. Classic.

Lore, Pittacus. *I am Number Four*. HarperCollins, 2010. ISBN: 978-0-0619-6955-3. Gr 9 and up.

Lubar, David. *Flip*. Tor, 2003. ISBN: 0-765-30149-0. Gr 5–8.

Mackel, Kathy. *Can of Worms*. HarperCollins, 2000. ISBN: 0-380-97681-1. Gr 4–7.

Mackel, Kathy. *From the Horse's Mouth*. HarperCollins, 2002. ISBN: 0-06-029415-9. Gr 5–7.

Martin, George R. *A Dance with Dragons: A Song of Ice and Fire: Book 5*. Bantam, 2013. ISBN: 978-0-5533-8595-3. YA.

Mass, Wendy. *Pi in the Sky*. Little, Brown and Company. 2013. ISBN: 978-0-3160-8916-6. Gr 5–8.

McMann, Lisa. *The Trap Door*. Scholastic, 2013. ISBN: 978-0-5454-8456-5. Gr 4 and up.

Mieville, China. *Railsea*. Del Rey, 2012. ISBN: 978-0-3455-2452-2. Gr 9–12.

Paulsen, Gary. *The Transall Saga*. Delacorte, 1998. ISBN: 0-385-32196-1. Gr 7–12.

Pierce, Tamora. *Street Magic*. Scholastic Paper, 2001. ISBN: 0-590-39628-5. Gr 5–9.

Pratchett, Terry. *The Bromeliad Trilogy: Truckers, Diggers, and Wings*. HarperCollins, 2003. ISBN: 0-06-009493-1. Gr 4–6.

Reeve, Philip. *Fever Crumb*. Scholastic Press, 2010. ISBN: 978-0-5452-0719-5. Gr 5–7.

Shulman, Polly. *The Wells Bequest*. Nancy Paulsen Books, 2013. ISBN: 978-0-3992-5646-2. Gr 5 and up.

Skurzynski, Gloria. *The Clones: The Virtual War Chronologs*. Simon & Schuster, 2002. ISBN: 0-689-84463-5. Gr 6–9.

Sleator, William. *Parasite Pig*. Dutton, 2002. ISBN: 0-525-46918-4. Gr 7–10. Classic.

*Star Wars, The Clone Wars: Incredible Vehicles*. DK Publishing, 2011. ISBN: 978-0-7566-8691-8. Gr 3 and up.

Vizzini, Ned. *The Other Normals*. Balzer + Bray, 2012. ISBN: 978-0-0620-7990-9. Gr 7–10.

White, Ruth. *You'll Like It Here*. Yearling, Reprint, 2012. ISBN: 978-0-3758-6596-1. Gr 4 and up.

Wilson, Daniel H. *A Boy and His Bot*. Bloomsbury Books, 2011. ISBN: 978-1-5999-0280-7. Gr 4 and up.

## PICTURE BOOKS

Agee, Jon. *The Other Side of Town*. Michael di Capua Books, 2012. ISBN: 978-0-5451-6204-3. Gr K–4.

Bunting, Eve. *Night of the Gargoyles*. Clarion Books, 1994. ISBN: 0-395-66553-1. Gr K–3.

Donaldson, Julia. *A Gold Star for Zog*. Arthur A. Levine, 2012. ISBN: 978-0-5454-1724-2. Gr K–4.

Joyce, William. *A Day with Wilbur Robinson*. HarperCollins, 1993. ISBN: 0-06-443339-0. Gr PS and up. Classic.

Joyce, William. *The Fantastic Flying Books of Mr. Morris Lessmore*. Atheneum Books for Young Readers, 2012. ISBN: 978-1-4442-5702-7. Gr PK and up.

Pinfold, Levi. *Black Dog*. Templar 2012. ISBN: 978-0-7636-6097-0. Gr K–5.

Say, Allen. *The Boy in the Garden*. Houghton Mifflin, 2010. ISBN: 978-0-5472-1410-8. Gr K–4.

Snicket, Lemony. *The Dark*. Little, Brown, 2013. ISBN: 978-0-3161-8748-0. Gr PK–1.

Spires, Ashley. *Binky Takes Charge*. Kids Can 2012. ISBN: 978-1-55453-703-7. Gr 3–6.

Spires, Ashley. *Binky to the Rescue*. Kids Can, 2012. ISBN: 978-1-55453-502-6. Gr 3–6.

Tan, Shaun. *Lost & Found: Three by Shaun Tan*. Arthur A. Levine, 2011. ISBN: 978-0-5452-2924-3. Gr K–4.

Van Allsburg, Chris. *The Wreck of the Zephyr*. Houghton Mifflin, 1983. ISBN: 0-395-33075-0. Gr K–4.

Wiesner, David. *Free Fall*. HarperCollins, 1991. ISBN: 0-688-10990-X. Gr K–4.

## ANNOTATED PROFESSIONAL BOOK

Baxter, Kathleen & Marcia Agness Kochel. *Get Those Guys Reading!: Fiction and Series Books that Boys Will Love*. Libraries Unlimited, 2012.

This book is organized by genres, including: action, adventure, spy, animal stories, graphic novels, historical fiction, humor, mystery, suspense, horror, realistic fiction, science fiction, fantasy, and sports. Each chapter is organized by younger guys and older guys and includes an author spotlight. The books are arranged by author, include a general short summary, and a list of other titles by the same author.

# Chapter 11

# HISTORY AND HISTORICAL FICTION

History and historical fiction can be appealing subjects to boys. These types of books offer high-action stories with strong male characters; compelling adventures about knights and castles; rip-snorting tales from the Old West; and war-time heroics. There are also fascinating books about dinosaurs, woolly mammoths, and even ancient Egypt with its mummies and hieroglyphs. Books that bring history to life help boys make a connection to things that they have heard about or seen on television or in the movies.

## FEATURED AUTHORS

Name: Avi

Birth date: 1937

Place of Birth: New York City, New York

Most popular book(s): *Sophia's War, Nothing But the Truth, City of Orphans*

About: Avi's name was given to him as a child by his twin sister. In elementary school he did well in science, but he was a poor writer. When he got to high school he failed all his courses. Then his folks put him in a small school that emphasized reading and writing. Even beyond that he needed special tutoring. He began as a playwright but when he had children of his own he started writing for kids.

Web site: http://www.Avi-writer.com

Name: Jim Murphy

Birth date: September 25, 1947

Place of Birth: Newark, New Jersey

Most popular book(s): *The Great Fire, Blizzard*

About: Murphy's nonfiction books often feature kids—because kids—even very young kids—weren't typically part of the events that shaped our nation's history. In his books, kids often participate in an active, heroic way and then eloquently tell about their experiences. Unfortunately, many historians focus exclusively on the important adults involved—a president, general, scientist or other powerful individual—and never let us see who else was there.

Web site: http://www.jimmurphybooks.com

## ANNOTATIONS

Avi. *Nothing But the Truth.* Turtleback, 2010. ISBN: 978-0-6061-2300-6.
Philip is looking for a way to get transferred out of Mrs. Narwin's homeroom and English class. Philip does not fulfill the requirements of his English class, so he receives a D, which means he cannot be on the track team. After the morning announcements, students are asked to rise and stand in respectful silent attention during the playing of the national anthem. In spite of Mrs. Narwin's request for silence, Philip insists that he is not disrespectful when he continues "singing" the national anthem. Furthermore, he still wants to be transferred out of her homeroom and English class. How far is Philip willing to press this issue?

Kerley, Barbara. *Those Rebels, John & Tom.* Scholastic, Inc., 2012. ISBN: 978-0-5452-2268-6.
John Adams and Thomas Jefferson were very different in their temperaments and upbringing. John loved to speak and voice his opinions, whereas Tom worked quietly thinking and writing. Together, they helped to launch a new nation on July 4, 1776 with *The Unanimous Declaration of the Thirteen United States of America.*

McCormick, Patricia. *Never Fall Down.* Balzer + Bray, 2012. ISBN: 978-0-06-173093-1.
Before the Khmer Rouge, Arn was just an eleven-year-old boy selling ice cream with his younger brother. One day, with bullhorns blaring and a warning of an invasion by Americans, soldiers marched everyone out of his town into the countryside. All of Cambodia was on the road, and all of their possessions were taken away, now that they were all considered equal. They were issued black pajamas and Arn remembered his aunt's solution, "Do whatever they say, be like the grass, bend low, bend low, then bend lower. The wind blows one way, you blow that way. It blows the other way you do to. That is the way to survive. Cry only in your mind." This powerful novel is based on Arn's many close brushes with death, his survival, and journey to America. Arn chooses to live and dedicates his life to helping many young people in need around the world.

Murphy, Jim. *The Crossing: How George Washington Saved the American Revolution.* Scholastic Press, 2010. ISBN: 978-0-439-69186-4.
George Washington was considered an amateur compared to the British officers. He had never commanded more than 5,000 troops at one time. He avoided direct contact with the British and adopted a hit-and-run style of combat. Over time, he "created and organized, a disciplined army willing to follow him into the most dangerous situations."

O'Reilly, Bill and Dwight Jon Zimmerman. *Lincoln's Last Days: The Shocking Assassination That Changed America Forever.* Henry Holt and Company, 2012. ISBN: 978-0-8050-9675-0.

*Lincoln's Last Days* is an adapted version for younger readers of Bill O'Reilly's best seller *Killing Lincoln.* Robert E. Lee has been defeated and essentially the Civil War is over. Within days Lincoln would be assassinated by John Wilkes Booth fulfilling Lincoln's belief that he would die in office. Short chapters with many illustrations, pictures and maps enhance the telling of this memorable event.

Osborne, Mary Pope. *Abraham Lincoln.* Random House, 2011. ISBN: 978-0-375-97024-5

This nonfiction companion to the Magic Tree House Book # 47, *Abe Lincoln at Last!* includes Abe's early years, growing up, practicing law, presidency, and assassination. Additional information may be found in the list of books, museums, landmarks, Internet sites, and DVDs.

Pinkney, Andrea Davis. *Hand in Hand: Ten Black Men Who Changed History.* Jump at the Sun Books, 2012. ISBN: 978-1 4231-4257-7.

This book moves from Colonial America (Benjamin Banneker) to the Civil War (Booker T. Washington) to the turn of the century (W.E.B. DuBois) to World War I (A. Philip Randolph) to the Great Depression (Thurgood Marshall) to the Civil Rights Movement (Martin Luther King), and finally to the modern day (Barack H. Obama II). Each of the ten men shares common themes both strong and significant for the youth of today.

Tarshis, Lauren. *The Battle of Gettysburg, 1863.* Scholastic, 2013. ISBN: 978-0-545-49936-5.

In this action-packed, historical novel, runaway slaves, Thomas and his little sister Birdie, escape Mr. Knox's farm and head north. Thomas saves the life of Henry, a Union soldier. Henry takes Birdie and Thomas with him as the Union Army travels to Gettysburg. How will Thomas and Birdie survive Gettysburg, the biggest and bloodiest battle of the Civil War?

Yolen, Jane, and Heidi Elisabeth Yolen Stemple. *Roanoke the Lost Colony: An Unsolved Mystery from History.* Simon & Schuster, 2003. ISBN: 0-689-82321-5.

In 1587, 92 colonists, 60 men, 20 women, and 12 children, left England for the New World. The previous colonists at Roanoke were not prepared and had problems with the Native Americans, so they returned to England. Soldiers remained at the fort in anticipation of the new group of colonists. When the new group arrived, led by John White, no soldiers were around, and only a single skeleton was found. The colonists had not planned on staying in Roanoke but there was not another option. White was pressured to go back to England to get supplies and soldiers. When he returned three years later the colony was empty and the colonists gone. The authors propose five common theories of what might have happened and leave it up to the reader to draw their own conclusions or propose a new theory.

## READ ALOUD

Burleigh, Robert. *Fly, CherAmi, Fly! The Pigeon Who Saved the Lost Battalion.* Abrams, 2008. ISBN: 978-0810970977.

Ellis, Deborah. *Kids of Kabul: Living Bravely Through a Never-Ending War.* Groundwood Books, 2012. ISBN: 978-1-55498-181-6.

Hodge, Deborah. *Rescuing the Children: The Story of the Kindertransport.* Tundra Books, 2012. ISBN: 978-1-77049-256-1.

Tunnell, Michael O. *Candy Bomber: The Story of the Berlin Airlift's "Chocolate Pilot."* Charlesbridge, 2010. ISBN: 978-1-58089-336-7.

Woodson, Jacqueline. *This Is the Rope: A Story from the Great Migration.* Nancy Paulsen Books, 2013. ISBN: 978-0-3992-3986-1.

## BIBLIOGRAPHY

Abbott, Tony. *Lunch-Box Dream.* Farrar, 2011. ISBN: 978-0-374-34673-7. Gr 5–8.

Anderson, Laurie Halse. *Forge.* Simon & Schuster, 2010. ISBN: 978-1-4169-6144-4. Gr 5–8.

Avi. *City of Orphans.* Atheneum, 2011. ISBN: 978-1-4169-7102-3. Gr 5 and up.

Avi. *Iron Thunder: The Battle Between the Monitor & the Merrimac: A Civil War Novel.* Hyperion, 2009. ISBN: 978-1-4231-0446-3. Gr 3 and up.

Avi. *Crispin: The End of Time.* HarperCollins, 2010. ISBN: 978-0-06-174082-0. Gr 5–8.

Bartoletti, Susan Campbell. *The Boy Who Dared.* Scholastic Press, 2008. ISBN: 978-0-4396-8013-4. Gr 6–9.

Bradley, Kimberly. *Jefferson's Sons: A Founding Father's Secret.* Dial, 2011. ISBN: 978-0-1424-2184-0. Gr 3 and up.

Bruchac, Joseph. *Hidden Roots.* Lulu.com, 2011. ISBN: 978-0-5577-1168-0. Gr 5–9.

Calkhoven, Laurie. *Michael at the Invasion of France, 1943.* Dial, 2012. ISBN: 978-0-8037-3724-2. Gr 3 and up. Boys of Wartime series.

Carbone, Elisa. *Blood on the River: James Town 1607.* Perfection Learning, 2010. ISBN: 978-1-6068-6385-5. Gr 4 and up.

Carbone, Elisa. *Night Running: How James Escaped with the Help of His Faithful Dog.* Knopf Books for Young Readers, 2008. ISBN: 978-0-3758-2247-6. Gr K–3.

Cooper, Afua. *My Name Is Henry Bibb: A Story of Slavery and Freedom.* Kids Can, 2009. ISBN: 978-1-55337-813-6. Gr 5–8.

Cooper, Susan. *Ghost Hawk.* Margaret K. McElderry Books, 2013. ISBN: 978-1-4424-8141-1. Gr 5 and up.

Couloumbis, Audrey. *War Games*. Yearling; Reprint edition, 2011. ISBN: 978-0-3758-5629-7. Gr 5–8.

Crowe, Chris. *Mississippi Trial*. Penguin Putnam, 2002. ISBN: 0-8037-2745-3. Gr 7–12. Classic.

Curtis, Christopher Paul. *Bud, Not Buddy*. Delacorte, 1999. ISBN: 0-385-32306-9. Gr 4–7.

Curtis, Christopher Paul. *The Watsons Go to Birmingham*. Delacorte Books for Young Readers, 1995. ISBN: 978-0-3853-2175-4. Gr 3 and up. Classic.

D'Adamo, Francesco. *Iqbal*. Aladdin; Reprint edition, 2005. ISBN: 978-1-4169-0329-1. Gr. 4–6.

Davis, Tony. *Roland Wright: At the Joust*. Yearling, 2011. ISBN: 978-0-3758-7328-7. Gr 2–4.

Davis, Tony. *Future Knight*. Delacorte, 2009. ISBN: 978-0-3859-0706-4. Gr 2–4.

Dowd, Siobhan. *Bog Child*. David Fickling Books, 2008. ISBN: 978-0-3758-4135-4. Gr 7 and up.

Engle, Margarita. *Hurricane Dancers: The First Caribbean Pirate Shipwreck*. Henry Holt and Co., 2011. ISBN: 978-0-8050-9240-0. Gr 7 and up.

Erdrich, Louise. *Chickadee*. HarperCollins, 2012. ISBN: 978-0-0605-7790-2. Gr 3 and up.

Flores-Galbis, Enrique. *90 Miles to Havana*. Roaring Book Press, 2010. ISBN: 978-1-5964-3168-3. Gr 6–9.

Ford, Michael. *Legacy of Blood*. Walker Children's, 2009. ISBN: 978-0-8027-9844-2. Gr 3 and up. Spartan Quest series.

Fussell, Sandy. *Shaolin Tiger*. Candlewick, 2011. ISBN: 978-0-7636-5702-4. Gr 4 and up Samurai Kids series.

Gantos, Jack. *Dead End in Norvelt*. Farrar, Straus and Giroux, 2011. ISBN: 978-0-3743-7993-3. Gr 5 and up.

Haddix, Margaret Peterson. *Caught*. Simon & Schuster Books for Young Readers, 2013. ISBN: 978-1-4169-8983-7. Gr 3–7. Missing series.

Hanel, Rachael. *Life as a Knight: An Interactive History Adventure*. Capstone Press, 2010. ISBN: 978-1-4296-4866-0. Gr 3 and up.

Harrar, George. *The Trouble with Jeremy Chance*. Milkweed, 2007. ISBN: 1-5713-1669-8. Gr 4–7.

Hartnett, Sonya. *The Midnight Zoo*. Candlewick, 2011. ISBN: 978-0-7636-5339-2. Gr 5 and up.

Hughes, Shirley. *Hero on a Bicycle*. Candlewick Press, 2013. ISBN: 978-0-7636-6037-6. Gr 5 and up.

Jinks, Catherine. *Pagan's Scribe: Book Four of the Pagan Chronicles*. Candlewick, 2006. ISBN: 0-7636-2973-1. YA.

Kang, Hildi. *Chengli and the Silk Road Caravan*. Tanglewood, 2011. ISBN: 978-1-9337-1854-5. Gr 4–6.

Korman, Gordon. *Unsinkable*. Scholastic Paper, 2011. ISBN: 978-0-545-12331-0. Gr 5–8. Titanic series.

Korman, Gordon. *Titanic #3: S. O. S.* Scholastic Paperbacks, 2011. ISBN: 978-0-5451-2333-4. Gr 3 and up.

Lester, Julius. *Day of Tears*. Hyperion Book CH, 2007. ISBN: 978-1-4231-0409-4. Gr 6–9.

Lloyd, Alison. *Year of the Tiger*. Holiday House, 2010. ISBN: 978-0-8234-2277-7. Gr 5–8.

Magoon, Kekla. *The Rock and the River*. Aladdin, 2010. ISBN: 978-1-4169-7803-9. Gr 7 and up.

Mazer, Harry. *Somebody, Please Tell Me Who I Am*. Simon & Schuster Books for Young Readers, 2013. ISBN: 978-1-4169-3896-5. Gr 7 and up.

Meyer, Susan Lynn. *Black Radishes*. Yearling, 2011. ISBN: 978-0-3758-5822-2. Gr 4–7.

Mitchell, Jack. *The Ancient Ocean Blues*. Tundra Paper, 2008. ISBN: 978-0-8877-6832-3. Gr 5–8.

Moran, Katy. *Bloodline Rising*. Candlewick Press, 2011. ISBN: 978-0-7636-4508-3. Gr 5 and up. Bloodline series.

Morgpugo, Michael. *War Horse*. Scholastic Press, 2011. ISBN: 978-0-5454-0335-1. Gr 3–7.

Morris, Gerald. *The Adventures of Sir Gawain the True*. Sandpiper, 2013. ISBN: 978-0-5440-2264-5. Gr 3–5. The Knights Tales series.

Murphy, Jim. *On Enemy Soil: Journal of James Edmond Pease, a Civil War Union Soldier*. Scholastic Inc., Reprint edition, 2012. ISBN: 978-0-5453-9887-8. Gr 3 and up.

Myers, Anna. *Spy!* Walker's Children, 2008. ISBN: 978-0-8027-9742-1. Gr 5 and up.

Myers, Laurie. *Escape by Night: A Civil War Adventure*. Henry Holt, 2011. ISBN: 978-0-8050-8825-0. Gr 3–5.

Myers, Walter Dean. *Fallen Angels.* Scholastic Paperbacks, 2008. ISBN: 978-0-5450-5576-5. Gr 7 and up.

Myers, Walter Dean. *Sunrise Over Fallujah.* Scholastic Press; Reprint edition, 2009. ISBN: 978-0-4399-1625-7. Gr 7 and up.

Nelson, Kadir. *Heart and Soul: The Story of America and African Americans.* Balzer + Bray, 2011. ISBN: 978-0-0617-3074-0. Gr 1–5.

Olson, Tod. *How to Get Rich in the California Golf Rush: An Adventurer's Guide to the Fabulous Riches Discovered in 1848.* National Geographic, 2008. ISBN: 978-1-4263-0315-9. Gr 4–8.

Oppel, Kenneth. *This Dark Endeavor.* Simon & Schuster, 2011. ISBN: 978-1-4424-0315-4. YA.

Osterweil, Adam. *Cooper and the Enchanted Metal Detector.* Namelos, 2013. ISBN: 978-1-6089-8149-6. Gr 4–7.

Park, Linda Sue. *A Long Walk to Water.* Clarion Books, 2010. ISBN: 978-0-5472-5127-1. Gr 6–9.

Paulsen, Gary. *Woods Runner.* Wendy Lamb Books, 2011. ISBN: 978-0-3758-5908-3. Gr 7 and up.

Pearsall, Shelley. *Jump into the Sky.* Knopf, 2012. ISBN: 978-0-3758-3699-2. Gr. 5–8.

Perkins, Mitali. *Bamboo People.* Charlesbridge, 2010. ISBN: 978-1-58089-328-2. Gr 5–8.

Preus, Margi. *Shadow on the Mountain.* Amulet Books, 2012. ISBN: 978-1-4197-1159-6. Gr 5 and up.

Pratchett, Terry. *Dodger.* Harper, 2012. ISBN: 978-0-0620-0949-4. Gr 8 and up.

Salisbury, Graham. *Eyes of the Emperor.* Laurel Leaf, 2007. ISBN: 978-0-4402-2956-8. Gr 7–10.

Schmidt, Gary D. *Okay for Now.* Sandpiper; Reprint edition, 2013. ISBN: 978-0-5440-2280-5. Gr 5 and up.

Sheth, Kashmira. *Boys Without Names.* HarperCollins, 2010. ISBN: 978-0-06-185760-7. Gr 4–7

Spinelli, Jerry. *Milkweed.* Knopf, 2003. ISBN: 0-375-81374-8. Gr 7 and up.

Spradlin, Michael P. *Keeper of the Grail.* Putnam, 2008. ISBN: 978-0-399-24763-7. Gr 5–8. The Youngest Templar series.

Strickland, Brad and Thomas E. Fuller. *Heart of Steele*. Simon & Schuster, 2003. ISBN: 0-689-85298-3. Gr 5–8.

Swain, Gwenyth. *Hope and Tears: Ellis Island Voices*. Boyds Mills, 2012. ISBN: 978-1-5907-8765-6. Gr 5–8.

Tarshis, Lauren. *I Survived the Shark Attacks of 1916*. Scholastic, 2010. ISBN: 978-0-545-20688-4. Gr 3–7. I Survived series.

Timberlake, Amy. *One Came Home*. Knopf Books for Young Readers, 2013. ISBN: 978-0-3758-6925-9. Gr 4 and up.

Thomason, Mark. *Moonrunner*. Kane, 2009. ISBN: 978-1-9352-7903-7. Gr 4–8.

Thompson, Kate. *Most Wanted*. HarperCollins, 2010. ISBN: 978-0-06-17037-5. Gr 3–5.

Tooke, Wes. *King of the Mound: My Summer with Satchel Paige*. Simon & Schuster, 2012. ISBN: 978-1-4424-3346-5. Gr 5–7.

Vanderpool, Clare. *Navigating Early*. Delacorte Books for Young Readers, 2013. ISBN: 978-0-3857-4209-2. Gr 5 and up.

Wallace, Rich. *War and Watermelon*. Viking, 2011. ISBN: 978-0-670-01152-0. Gr 5–8.

Whelan, Gloria. *After the Train*. HarperCollins, 2009. ISBN: 978-0-0602-9596-1. Gr 5–8.

Whelan, Gloria. *Voices for Freedom*. Sleeping Bear Press, 2013. ISBN: 978-1-5853-6886-0. Gr 3–6.

Woelfle, Gretchen. *All the World's a Stage: A Novel in Five Acts*. Holiday House, 2011. ISBN: 978-0-385-75199-8. Gr 4–7.

Wolf, Allan. *The Watch That Ends the Night*. Candlewick, 2011. ISBN: 978-0-7636-3703-3. YA.

Woodruff, Elvira. *George Washington's Spy*. Scholastic Paperbacks; Reprint edition, 2012. ISBN: 978-0-5451-0488-3. Gr 3 and up. Time Travel Adventures series.

Yelchin, Eugene. *Breaking Stalin's Nose*. Henry Holt and Co., 2011. ISBN: 978-0-8050-9216-5. Gr 4 and up.

Yep, Laurence. *The Star Maker*. HarperCollins, 2011. ISBN: 978-0-06-025315-8. Gr 3–5.

Yolen, Jane. *Sword of the Rightful King*. Harcourt, 2003. ISBN: 0-15-202527-8. Gr. 6–9.

## INFORMATIONAL

Abramson, Andra Serlin. *Inside Dinosaurs*. Sterling, 2010. ISBN: 978-1-4027-7074-6. Gr 4–6.

Adamson, Heather. *Ancient Egypt: An Interactive History Adventure.* Capstone, 2009. ISBN: 978-1-4296-3415-1. Gr 3–5.

Albee, Sarah. *Poop Happened: A History of the World from the Bottom Up.* Walker's Children, 2010. ISBN: 978-0-8027-2077-1. Gr 4–8.

Allen, Kathy. *The Horrible, Miserable Middle Ages: The Disgusting Details About Life During Medieval Times.* Capstone, 2010. ISBN: 978-1-4296-3958-3. Gr 4–8.

Aronson, Marc. *If Stones Could Speak: Unlocking the Secrets of Stonehenge.* National Geographic Books, 2010. ISBN: 978-1-4263-0599-3. Gr 4–6.

Aronson, Marc. *Sugar Changed the World: A Story of Magic, Spice, Slavery, Freedom, and Science.* Clarion. 2010. ISBN 978-0-61857-492-6. Gr 8 and up.

Bardoe, Cheryl. *Mammoths and Mastodons: Titans of the Ice Age.* Abrams, 2010. ISBN: 978-0-8109-8413-4. Gr 4–7.

Barrow, Randi. *Saving Zasha.* Scholastic, 2011. ISBN: 978-0-545-20632-7. Gr 4–7.

Bartoletti, Susan Campbell. *They Called Themselves the K.K.K.: The Birth of an American Terrorist Group.* Houghton Mifflin Books for Children, 2010. ISBN: 978-0-6184-4033-7. Gr 7–10.

Bausum, Ann. *Marching to the Mountaintop: How Poverty, Labor Fights, and Civil Rights Set the Stage for Martin Luther King, Jr's Final Hours.* National Geographic, 2012. ISBN: 978-1-4263-0939-7. Gr 5–8.

Beccia, Carlyn. *The Raucous Royals: Test Your Royal Wits: Crack Codes, Solve Mysteries, and Deduce Which Royal Rumors Are True.* Houghton Mifflin, 2008. ISBN: 978-0-6188-9130-6. Gr 4–7.

Blair, Margaret Whitman. *Liberty or Death: The Surprising Story of Runaway Slaves Who Sided with the British During the American Revolution.* National Geographic, 2010. ISBN: 978-1-4263-0590-0. Gr 5–8.

Blumenthal, Karen. *Bootleg: Murder, Moonshine, and the Lawless Years of Prohibition.* Flash Point, 2011. ISBN: 978-1-5964-3449-3. Gr 7 and up.

Bolden, Tonya. *Emancipation Proclamation: Lincoln and the Dawn of Liberty.* Abrams Books for Young Readers, 2013. ISBN: 978-1-4197-0390-4. Gr 5–9.

Bragg, Georgia. *How They Croaked: The Awful Ends of the Awfully Famous.* Walker's Children; Reprint edition, 2012. Gr 5 and up.

Brimner, Larry Dane. *Birmingham Sunday.* Boyds Mills Press, 2010. ISBN: 978-1-5907-8613-0. Gr 6 and up.

Brimner, Larry Dane. *Black and White: The Confrontation Between Reverend Fred L. Shuttleworth and Eugene "Bull" Connor.* Boyds Mills Press, 2011. ISBN: 978-1-5907-8766-3. Gr 7 and up.

Brown, Don. *All Stations! Distress! April 15, 1912, the Day the Titanic Sank*. Roaring Brook Press, 2008. ISBN: 978-1-5964-3222-2. Gr 1–5.

Brown, Don. *America Is Under Attack: September 11, 2001: The Day the Towers Fell*. Roaring Brook, 2011. ISBN: 978-1-59643-694-7. Gr 1–5.

Burgan, Michael. *Breaker Boys: How a Photograph Helped End Child Labor*. Compass Point. 2012. ISBN 978-0-7565-4510-9. Gr 6–9.

Calkhoven, Laurie. *I Grew Up to Be President*. Scholastic, 2011. ISBN: 978-0-545-33152-4. Gr 3–5.

Clifford, Barry. *Real Pirates: The Untold Story of the Whydah from Slave Ship to Pirate Ship*. National Geographic, 2008. ISBN: 978-1-4263-0279-4. Gr 4–7.

Corrigan, Jim. *The 1900s Decade in Photos: A Decade of Discovery*. Enslow, 2010. ISBN: 978-0-7660-3129-6. Gr 4–9. Amazing Decades in Photos series.

Crowe, Chris. *Getting Away with Murder: The True Story of the Emmett Till Case*. Fogelman Books, 2003. 0-8037-2804-21. Gr 8–12.

Cullen, Dave. *Columbine*. Twelve, 2009. ISBN: 978-0-4465-4693-5. YA.

Cushman, Karen. *Will Sparrows Road*. Clarion Books, 2012. ISBN: 978-0-5477-3962-5. Gr 5 and up.

Deem, James M. *Bodies from the Ash*. Houghton Mifflin, 2005. ISBN: 978-0-6184-7308-3. Gr 4–6.

Dennis, Yvonne Wakim and Maha Addasi. *A Kid's Guide to Arab American History*. Chicago Review Press, 2013. ISBN: 978-1-6137-4017-0. Gr 2–4.

Ellis, Deborah. *Children of War: Voices of Iraqi Refugees*. Groundwood Books, 2009. ISBN: 978-0-8889-9907-8. Gr 6–12.

England, Victoria. *Top 10 Worst Things About Ancient Egypt You Wouldn't Want to Know*. Gareth Stevens, 2012. ISBN: 978-1-4339-6688-0. Gr 4–7.

Evans, Shane W. *Underground: Finding the Light to Freedom*. Roaring, 2011. ISBN: 978-1-59643-538-4. Gr 1–3.

Fleming, Candace. *The Lincolns: A Scrapbook Look at Abraham and Mary*. Schwartz & Wade, 2008. ISBN: 978-0-3758-3618-3. Gr 7 and up.

Freedman, Russell. *The Boston Tea Party*. Holiday House, 2012. ISBN: 978-0-8234-2266-1. Gr 2–5.

Freedman, Russell. *Abraham Lincoln & Frederick Douglass: The Story Behind an American Friendship*. Clarion, 2012. ISBN: 978-0-5473-8562-4. Gr 5–9.

Giblin, James Cross. *Good Brother, Bad Brother: The Story of Edwin Booth and John Wilkes Booth.* Clarion Books, 2006. ISBN: 978-0-6180-9642-8. Gr 5–8.

Giblin, James Cross. *The Boy Who Saved Cleveland.* Henry Holt and Co., 2006. ISBN: 978-0-8050-7355-3. Gr 3–6.

Gonzales, Doreen. *The Secret of the Manhattan Project.* Enslow, 2012. ISBN: 978-0-7660-3954-4. Gr 5–8. Stories in American History series.

Graham, Ian. *You Wouldn't Want to Be a World War II Pilot! Air Battles You Might Not Survive.* Franklin Watts, 2009. ISBN: 978-0-531-21326-1. Gr 4–8. You Wouldn't Want to Be series.

Guiberson, Brenda Z. *Disasters: Natural and Man-Made Catastrophes Through the Centuries.* Henry Holt, 2010. ISBN: 978-0-8050-8170-1. Gr 5–8.

Hartland, Jessie. *How the Sphinx Got to the Museum.* Blue Apple, 2010. ISBN: 978-1-60905-032-0. Gr 2–4.

Hawass, Zahi. *Tutankhamun: The Mystery of the Boy King.* National Geographic, 2005. ISBN: 978-0-7922-8354-6. Gr 5 and up.

Hillenbrand, Laura. *Unbroken: A World War II Story of Survival, Resilience, and Redemption.* Random House, 2010. ISBN: 978-1-4000-6416-8. Adult.

Holzer, Harold. *Father Abraham: Lincoln and His Sons.* Boyds Mills Press, 2011. ISBN: 978-1-59078-303-0. Gr 4–6.

Hopkinson, Deborah. *Titanic: Voices from the Disaster.* Scholastic Press, 2012. ISBN: 978-0-5451-1674-9. Gr 6 and up.

Jestice, Phyllis G. *Ancient Persian Warfare.* Gareth Stevens, 2010. ISBN: 978-1-4339-1973-2. Gr 3–6. Ancient Warfare series.

Jurmain, Suzanne Tripp. *Worst of Friends: Thomas Jefferson, John Adams and the True Story of an American Feud.* Dutton, 2011. ISBN: 978-0-525-47903-1. Gr 3–5.

Kalman, Bobbie. *A Colonial Town: Williamsburg.* Crabtree Publishing Company, 2005. ISBN: 0-86505-489-4. Gr 1 and up. Historic Communities series.

Lessem, Don. *The Ultimate Dinopedia: The Most Complete Dinosaur Reference Ever.* National Geographic, 2010. ISBN: 978-1-4263-0165-0. Gr 3–6.

Levine, Ellen. *Henry's Freedom Box: A True Story from the Underground Railroad.* Scholastic Press, 2007. ISBN: 978-0-4397-7733-9. Gr 2–5.

Levinson, Cynthia Y. *We've Got a Job: The 1963 Birmingham Children's March.* Peachtree, 2013. ISBN: 978-1-5614-5627-7. Gr. 6–12.

Leyson, Leon. *The Boy on the Wooden Box*. Atheneum Books for Young Readers, 2013. ISBN: 978-1-4424-97819-8. YA.

MacDonald, Fiona. *Top 10 Worse Ruthless Warriors You Wouldn't Want to Know*. Gareth Stevens, 2012. ISBN: 978-1-4339-6685-9. Gr 4–7.

MacLeod, Elizabeth. *Monster Fliers: From the Time of the Dinosaurs*. Kids Can, 2010. ISBN: 978-1-55453-199-8. Gr K–3.

McPherson, Stephanie Sammartino. *Iceberg, Right Ahead! The Tragedy of the Titanic*. Twenty-First Century, 2012. ISBN: 978-0-7613-6756-7. Gr 6 and up.

Mountjoy, Shane. *Technology and the Civil War*. Chelsea House, 2009. ISBN: 978-1-60413-037-9. Gr 5–8.

Murphy, Jim. *The Giant and How He Humbugged America*. Scholastic, 2012. ISBN: 978-0-439-69184-0. Gr 6–9.

Murphy, Jim. *Inside the Alamo*. Delacorte, 2003. ISBN: 0-385-32574-6. Gr 6 and up.

Murphy, Jim. *The Day The Soldiers Stopped Fighting*. Scholastic, 2009. ISBN: 978-0-545-13049-3. Gr 5–8.

Murrell, Deborah. *Gladiator*. Black Rabbit, 2010. ISBN: 978-1-5956-6736. Gr 4–7.

Myers, Walter Dean. *Fallen Angels*. Scholastic Paperbacks, 2008. ISBN: 978-0-5450-5576-5. Gr 7 and up.

Naish, Darren. *Dinosaurs Life Size*. Barron's, 2010. ISBN: 978-0-7641-6378-4. Gr 5–7.

O'Brien, Patrick. *Duel of the Ironclads: The Monitor vs. The Virginia*. Walker & Company, 2003. ISBN: 978-0-8027-8843-2. Gr 4–8.

Olson, Tod. *How to Get Rich on a Texas Cattle Drive: In Which I Tell the Honest Truth About Rampaging Rustlers, Stampeding Steers, and Other Fateful Hazards on the Wild Chisolm Trail*. National Geographic, 2010. ISBN: 978-1-4263-0524-5. Gr 3–7.

Osborne, Linda Barrett. *Miles to Go for Freedom: Segregation and Civil Rights in the Jim Crow Years*. Abrams, 2012. ISBN: 978-1-4197-0020-0. Gr. 6–10.

Osborne, Linda Barrett. *Traveling the Freedom Road*. Abrams Books for Young Readers, 2009. ISBN: 978-0-8109-8338-0. Gr 5 and up.

Partridge, Elizabeth. *Marching for Freedom: Walk Together, Children, and Don't You Grow Weary*. Viking, 2009. ISBN: 978-0-670-01189-6. Gr 5 and up.

Rappaport, Doreen. *Beyond Courage: The Untold Story of Jewish Resistance During the Holocaust*. Candlewick, 2012. ISBN: 978-0-7636-2976-2. Gr. 7–12.

Ratliff, Tom. *You Wouldn't Want to Be a Pony Express Rider! A Dusty, Thankless Job You'd Rather Not Do.* Scholastic, 2012. ISBN: 978-0-5312-0872-4. Gr 1 and up.

Raum, Elizabeth. *What Did the Vikings Do For Me?* Heinemann, 2010. ISBN: 978-1-4329-3745-4. Gr 4–7. Linking Past to Present series.

Rice, Rob S. *Ancient Greek Warfare.* Gareth Stevens, 2010. ISBN: 978-1-4339-1972-5. Gr 3–6.

Riggs, Kate. *Gladiators.* Creative Education, 2011. ISBN: 978-1-60818-000-4. Gr K and up.

Ross, Stewart. *Into the Unknown: How Great Explorers Found Their Way by Land.* Candlewick, 2011. ISBN: 978-0-7636-49948-7. Gr 3 and up.

Rumford, James. *From the Good Mountain, How Gutenberg Changed the World.* Roaring Brook, 2012. ISBN: 978-1-59643-542-1. Gr 3–5.

Sanders, Nancy I. *Frederick Douglass for Kids: His Life and Times with 21 Activities.* Chicago Reviews Press, 2012. ISBN: 978-1-5697-6717-7. Gr 4 and up.

Sandler, Martin W. *The Impossible Rescue: The True Story of an Amazing Arctic Adventure.* Candlewick Press, 2012. ISBN: 978-0-7636-5080-3. Gr 5 and up.

Schanzer, Rosalyn. *Witches: The Absolutely True Tale of Disaster in Salem.* National Geographic Children's Books, 2011. ISBN: 978-1-4263-0869-7. Gr 5 and up.

Seiple, Samantha. *Ghosts in the Fog: The Untold Story of Alaska's World War II Invasion.* Scholastic Press, 2011. ISBN: 978-0-5452-9654-0. Gr 6–9.

Sheinkin, Steve. *Bomb: The Race to Build—and Steal—The World's Most Dangerous Weapon.* Roaring Brook, 2012. ISBN: 978-1-5964-3487-5. Gr 5 and up.

Sheinkin, Steve. *Lincoln's Grave Robbers.* Scholastic Press, 2013. ISBN: 978-0-5454-0572-0. Gr 5–9.

Sloan, Christopher. *Mummies: Dried, Tanned, Sealed, Drained, Frozen, Embalmed, Stuffed, Wrapped, and Smoked . . . and We're Dead Serious.* National Geographic, 2010. ISBN: 978-1-4263-0695-2. Gr 4–7.

Stanley, Jerry. *Cowboys and Longhorns: A Portrait of the Long Drive.* Crown, 2003. ISBN: 0-375-81565-1. Gr. 9–12.

Stone, Tanya Lee. *Courage Has No Color: The True Story of the Triple Nickles: America's First Black Paratroopers.* Candlewick, 2013. ISBN: 978-0-7636-5117-6. Gr 5 and up.

Thomson, Ruth. *Terezin: Voices from the Holocaust.* Candlewick Press, 2011. ISBN: 978-0-7636-4963-0. Gr 5 and up.

Turner, Glennette Tilley. *Fort Mose: And the Story of the Man Who Built the First Free Black Settlement in Colonial America.* Abrams Books for Young Readers, 2010. ISBN: 978-0-8109-4056-7. Gr 3–7.

Walker, Sally M. *Blizzard of Glass: The Halifax Explosion of 1917.* Henry Holt and Co., 2011. ISBN: 978-0-8050-8945-5. Gr 5 and up.

Warren, Andrea. *Under Siege! Three Children at the Civil War Battle for Vicksburg.* Farrar Straus Giroux, 2009. ISBN: 978-0-374-31255-8. Gr 5 and up.

Watkins, Angela Farris. *My Uncle Martin's Words for America: Martin Luther King Jr.'s Niece Tells How He Made a Difference.* Abrams, 2011. ISBN: 978-1-4197-0022-4. Gr K–4.

Waxman, Laura Hamilton. *What Are the Articles of Confederation? And Other Questions About the Birth of the United States.* Lerner Publications Company, 2012. ISBN: 978-0-7613-5330-0. Gr 4–6.

Waxman, Laura Hamilton. *Who Were the Accused Witches of Salem? And Other Questions About the Witchcraft Trials.* Lerner, 2012. ISBN: 978-0-7613-5225-9. Gr 3–6.

Weaver, Janice. *Harry Houdini: The Legend of the World's Greatest Escape Artist.* Abrams, 2011. ISBN: 978-1-4197-0014-9. Gr 4–6.

Winters, Kay. *Voices of Ancient Egypt.* National Geographic, 2003. ISBN: 0-7922-7560-8. Gr 2–6.

Yep, Laurence. *The Dragon's Child: A Story of Angel Island.* HarperCollins, 2011. ISBN: 978-0-0620-1815-9. Gr 3–6.

## PICTURE BOOKS

Akbarpour, Ahmad. *Good Night Commander.* Groundwood, 2010. ISBN: 978-0-88899-989-4. Gr 5–8.

Asim, Jabari. *Fifty Cents and a Dream: Young Booker T. Washington.* Little, Brown, 2012. ISBN: 978-0-3160-8657-8. Gr PK–1.

Byrd, Robert. *Electric Ben: The Amazing Life and Times of Benjamin Franklin.* Dial Books for Young Readers, 2012. ISBN: 978-0-8037-3749-5. Gr K–3.

Cole, Henry. *Unspoken: A Story from the Underground Railroad.* Scholastic Press, 2012. ISBN: 978-0-5453-9997-5. Gr PK–3.

Cheney, Lynne. *When Washington Crossed the Delaware: A Wintertime Story for Young Patriots.* Simon and Schuster Books for Young Readers, 2004. ISBN: 978-0-689-87043-4. Gr K–4.

Crowe, Chris. *Just as Good: How Larry Doby Changed America's Game.* Candlewick, 2012. ISBN: 978-0-7636-5026-1. Gr 1–4.

Gilpin, Caroline Crosson. *Abraham Lincoln*. National Geographic, 2012. ISBN: 978-1-4263-1085-0. Gr K–3.

Hyatt, Patricia Rusch. *The Quite Contrary Man: A True American Tale*. Abrams, 2011. ISBN: 978-0-8109-4065-9. Gr K–3.

Jazynka, Kitson. *Martin Luther King, Jr.* National Geographic, 2012. ISBN: 978-1-4263-1087-4. Gr K and up.

King, Martin Luther Jr. *I Have a Dream*. Schwartz & Wade, 2012. ISBN: 978-0-3758-5887-1. Gr K and up.

Lewis, Patrick J. *And the Soldiers Sang*. Creative Editions, 2011. ISBN: 978-1-5684-6220-2. Gr 4 and up.

McKissack, Patricia C. *Never Forgotten*. Schwartz & Wade, 2011. ISBN: 978-0-3758-4384-6. Gr K and up.

Polacco, Patricia. *Just in Time: Abraham Lincoln*. Putnam, 2011. ISBN: 978-0-399-25471-0. Gr 3–5.

Rappaport, Doreen. *We Are the Many: A Picture Book of American Indians*. HarperCollins Publishers, 2002. ISBN: 978-0-688-16559-1. Gr K–4.

Rocco, John. *Fu Finds the Way*. Hyperion, 2009. ISBN: 978-1-4231-0965-5. Gr 3–5.

Rockwell, Anne. *Big George: How a Shy Boy Became President Washington*. Harcourt, Inc., 2009. ISBN: 978-0-15-216583-3. Gr 1–3.

Rosenstock, Barb. *The Camping Trip That Changed America: Theodore Roosevelt, John Muir, and Our National Parks*. Dial, 2012. ISBN: 978-0-8037-3710-5. Gr 1–3.

Rubin, Susan Goldman. *Jean Laffite: The Pirate Who Saved America*. Abrams Books for Young Readers, 2012. ISBN: 978-0-8109-9733-2. Gr 1–4.

Ruelle, Karen Gray. *The Grand Mosque of Paris: A Story of How Muslims Rescued Jews During the Holocaust*. Holiday House, 2009. ISBN: 978-0-8234-2159-6. Gr 3–6.

Sandler, Martin W. *The Impossible Rescue: The True Story of an Amazing Arctic Adventure*. Candlewick, 2012. ISBN: 978-0-7636-5080-3. Gr 5–8.

Schmidt, Gary D. *Martin de Porres: The Rose in the Desert*. Clarion, 2012. ISBN: 978-0-5476-1218-8. Gr 1–4.

Smith, Icy. *Half Spoon of Rice: A Survival Story of the Cambodian Genocide*. East West Discovery Press, 2010. ISBN: 978-0-9821-6758-8. Gr 4–7.

Watson, Renee. *A Place Where Hurricanes Happen*. Random House, 2010. ISBN: 978-0-375-85609-9. Gr 2–5.

## ANNOTATED PROFESSIONAL BOOK

Columba, Lynn, Cathy Y. Kim, and Alden J. Moe. *The Power of Picture Books in Teaching. Math, Science, and Social Studies: Grades PreK-8*. Holcomb Hathaway, 2009.

    The authors share the vitality of stories and especially the power of picture books. They make the case that children's literature along with inquiry-based learning are excellent ways to link related issues and bring life to seemingly isolated and abstract ideas across the subject areas of math, science, and social studies. The authors outline the guiding questions needed to make appropriate selections for the discussed reading audience. They look at various categories of books such as purpose, audience, structure, and content. The lessons are organized by grade level and include several samples from each of three areas: math, science, and social studies. The lessons select a picture book, give a summary, state the standard addressed, give ideas regarding procedure, assessment, and making connections and also list other similar books. The book also includes an appendix with 45 different charts and activity sheets to support learning.

# Chapter 12

# HUMOR AND POETRY

Silly, slapstick stories about taboo subjects are most appealing to boys. The sillier the stories, the more they like them. Boys like to read riddle books and joke books; they love puns and off-the-wall humor. Pranks, mayhem, and bathroom humor are favorite topics. Historically, poetry was written and read by men; oral recitations were a form of their entertainment. Educators today need to introduce boys to a variety of poems that tell stories, make connections to the past, and help boys think in a different way about the world. Boys should read the type of poetry that appeals to them, such as Jack Prelutsky, Ogden Nash, or Shel Silverstein, so they can enjoy the language, word play, and puns.

## FEATURED AUTHORS

Name: Carl Hiaasen

Birth date: March 12, 1953

Place of Birth: Plantation, Florida

Most popular book(s): *Hoot, Flush*

About: A graduate of the University of Florida, Hiaasen joined the *Miami Herald* at age 23 as a general assignment reporter and went on to work for the paper's weekly magazine and later its prize-winning investigative team. Together, Hiaasen's novels have been published in 34 languages, which is 33 more than he is able to read or write. Still, he has reason to believe that all of the foreign translations are brilliantly faithful to the original work.

Web site: http://www.carlhiaasen.com

Name: Jack Prelutsky

Birth date: September 8, 1940

Place of Birth: Brooklyn, New York

Most popular book(s): *The New Kid on the Block, The Dragons are Singing Tonight, The Frogs Wore Red Suspenders*

About: Prelutsky enjoys photography, carpentry, creating games, collages, and found art sculpture. He has been teaching himself how to draw on the computer. He collects art, children's poetry books, and frog miniatures. He eats out a lot.

Web site: http://www.jackprelutsky.com

## ANNOTATIONS

Greenwald, Tommy. *Charlie Joe Jackson's Guide to Extra Credit*. Roaring Brook Press, 2012. ISBN: 978-1-250-01670-6.

Charlie Joe is a smart, funny kid who hates to read, is lazy, and whose homework is always late. When he is threatened with going to an academic summer camp, he makes a deal with his parents. How will he achieve the all As and only one B report card he promised?

Korman, Gordon. *Son of the Mob*. Hyperion Paper, 2004. ISBN: 978-0786815937

Seventeen-year-old Tony Luca's family is in the "vending machine business" and his father is King of the Mob. Tony disassociates himself from the crime organization but the Family interferes with his life. Tony is thrown into jail when it is discovered that the Porsche he received for his sixteenth birthday is "hot." He meets Kendra and falls in love but soon discovers that her father is an FBI agent—actually he is *the* FBI agent who is bugging and wiretapping the Luca family house. In the end, Tony is successful at being part of his family, preserves his self-respect, keeps his conscience clear, and maintains his relationship with Kendra.

Lewis, J. Patrick. *A National Geographic Book of Animal Poetry with Favorites from Robert Frost, Jack Prelutsky, Emily Dickinson, and More*. National Geographic, 2012. ISBN: 978-1-4263-1054-6.

The United States Children's Poet Laureate has wonderful photographs accompanying two hundred poems about animals arranged as: Welcome to the World, The Big Ones, The Little Ones, The Winged Ones, The Water Ones, The Strange Ones, The Noisy Ones, The Quiet Ones, and Final Thoughts. A book meant for browsing.

Kennedy, Caroline. *Poems to Learn by Heart*. Hyperion Books, 2013. ISBN: 978-1-4231-0805-4.

Caroline Kennedy has selected over 100 poems and divided them into sections about nature, sports, monsters, fairies, friendship, and family. She introduces each section and discusses several of the poems in relation to the subject. Beautiful watercolor paintings by Jon J. Muth illustrate the poems.

Prelutsky, Jack. *Pizza, Pigs, and Poetry: How to Write a Poem*. Greenwillow Books, 2008. ISBN: 978-0-06-143449-5.

Jack Prelutsky advises paying attention to what is going on around you, carrying a note-book, and immediately writing down your ideas. For instance, for each poem in this book, he relates the incident in his life that inspired it and provides a corresponding writing tip. There are a total of twenty writing tips.

Scieszka, Jon. *Truckery Rhymes*. Simon & Schuster Books for Young Readers, 2009. ISBN: 978-1-4169-4135-4.
> Jon Scieszka rewrites classic nursery rhymes into "truckery" rhymes; for example, "Wrecker Rosie Sat on a Wall," "The Wheels on the Truck," and "Gabby Had a Little Bear."

## READ ALOUD

Brown, Monica. *Pablo Neruda: Poet of the People*. Holt, 2011. ISBN: 978-0-8050-9198-4.

Buzzeo, Toni. *One Cool Friend*. Dial, 2012. ISBN: 978-0-8037-3413-5.

Fleming, Candace. *Oh, No!* Random, 2012. ISBN: 978-0-3758-4271-9.

Hughes, Langston. *I Too, Am America*. Simon & Schuster Books For Young Readers, 2012. ISBN: 978-1-4442-2008-3.

Newman, Aline Alexander. *National Geographic Kids Chapters: Animal Superstars: And More True Stories of Amazing Animal Talents*. National Geographic Children's Books, 2013. ISBN: 978-1-4263-1092-8.

Singer, Marilyn. *Follow Follow: A Book of Reverso Poems*. Dial, 2013. ISBN: 978-0-8037-3769-3.

## BIBLIOGRAPHY

### Humor

Anderson, M. T. *Zombie Mommy*. Beach Lane Books, 2011. ISBN: 978-1-4442-5440-8. Gr 5 and up.

Angleberger, Tom. *The Secret of The Fortune Wookiee*. Harry N. Abrams, 2012. ISBN: 978-1-4197-0392-7. Gr 3–7.

Applegate, Katherine. *Never Race a Runaway Pumpkin*. HarperCollins, 2009. ISBN: 978-0-0617-8370-8. Gr 1–5. Roscoe Riley Rules series.

Ardagh, Philip. *Dreadful Acts*. Holt, 2003. ISBN: 0-8050-7155-5. Gr 4–7.

Asch, Frank. *The Daily Comet: Boy Saves Earth from Giant Octopus!* Kids Can, 2010. ISBN: 978-1-55453-281-0. Gr 2–4.

Baker, Kimberly. *Pickle: The (Formerly) Anonymous Prank Club of Fountain Point Middle School*. Roaring Brook Press, 2012. ISBN: 978-1-5964-3765-4. Gr 3–7.

Beaty, Andrea. *Attack of the Fluffy Bunnies.* Amulet Books, 2010. ISBN: 978-0-8109-8416-5. Gr 2–8.

Bruel, Nick. *Bad Kitty vs Uncle Murray: The Uproar at the Front Door.* Roaring Brook Press, 2010. ISBN: 978-1-59643-596-4. Gr 2–5.

Bruel, Nick. *Bad Kitty School Daze.* Roaring Brook Press, 2013. ISBN: 978-1-5964-3670-1. Gr 2–5.

Child, Noah. *Diary of a 6th Grade Ninja 3: Rise of the Red Ninjas.* Kindle, 2013. Gr 4 and up.

Cotler, Steve. *Cheesie Mack Is Running Like Crazy.* Random House Books for Young Readers, 2013. ISBN: 978-0-3079-7713-7. Gr 3 and up.

Fleming, Candace. *The Fabled Fifth Graders of Aesop Elementary School.* Random House, 2010. ISBN: 978-0-375-86334-9. Gr 3–5.

Gantos, Jack. *Jack Adrift: Fourth Grade without a Clue.* Farrar Straus Giroux, 2003. ISBN: 0-374-39987-5. Gr 4–7.

Goldblatt, Mark. *Twerp.* Random House, 2013. ISBN: 978-0-3759-714. Gr 4–7.

Griffiths, Andy. *The 13-Story Treehouse.* Feiwel and Friends, 2013. ISBN: 978-1-2500-2690-3. Gr 3–7.

Griffiths, Andy. *Killer Koalas from Outer Space: And Lots of Other Very Bad Stuff That Will Make Your Brain Explode.* Feiwel and Friends, 2011. ISBN: 978-0-312-36789-3. Gr 4–7.

Healy, Christopher. *The Hero's Guide to Saving Your Kingdom (The League of Princes).* Walden Pond Press, 2012. ISBN: 978-0-0621-1743-4. Gr 3 and up.

Hiaasen, Carl. *Chomp.* Knopf Books for Young Readers, 2012. ISBN: 978-0-3758-6842-9. Gr 5 and up.

Keller, Laurie. *Bowling Alley Bandit (Adventures of Arnie the Doughnut).* Henry Holt and Co., 2013. ISBN: 978-0-8050-9076-5. Gr 2–5.

Kinney, Jeff. *Diary of a Wimpy Kid: Cabin Fever.* Abrams, 2011. ISBN: 978-1-4197-0223-5. Gr 5–8.

Kirby, Stan. *Captain Awesome and the Ultimate Spelling Bee.* Little Simon, 2013. ISBN: 978-1-4424-5158-2. Gr K–2. Captain Awesome series.

Korman, Gordon. *Hideout.* Scholastic Press, 2013. ISBN: 978-0-5454-4866-6. Gr 3 and up. Swindle series.

Kowitt, H. N. *The Loser List #3: Jinx of the Loser.* Scholastic Press, 2013. ISBN: 978-0-5455-0794-3. Gr 3 and up.

Krulik, Nancy. *George Brown, Class Clown: What's Black and White and Stinks All Over?* Grosset & Dunlap, 2011. ISBN: 978-0-448-45370-5. Gr 2–4.

Krulik, Nancy. *Trouble Magnet.* Grosset & Dunlap, 2010. ISBN: 978-0-488-45368-2. Gr 2–4.

Lubar, David. *Enter the Zombie.* A Tom Doherty Associates Book, 2010. ISBN: 978-0-7653-2672-0. Gr 3–7.

Lubar, David. *Wizards of the Game.* Philomel, 2003. ISBN: 0-399-23706-2. Gr 6–8.

McCarthy, Meghan. *Pop! The Invention of Bubble Gum.* Simon & Schuster, 2010. ISBN: 978-1-4169-7970-8. Gr 1–3.

McDonald, Megan. *Stink and the Midnight Zombie Walk.* Candlewick, 2012. ISBN: 978-0-7636-5692-8. Gr K–3.

McDonald, Megan. *National Geographic Kids Just Joking 2.* National Geographic, 2012. ISBN: 978-1-4263-1017-1. Gr 2–5.

McDonald, Megan. *National Geographic Kids Just Joking: 300 Hilarious Jokes, Tricked Tongue Twisters, and Ridiculous Riddles.* National Geographic Children's Books, 2012. ISBN: 978-1-4263-0930-4. Gr 2–5.

O'Malley, Kevin. *Once Upon a Royal Super Baby.* Walker, 2010. ISBN: 978-0-8027-2164-8. Gr 3–5.

Pastis, Stephen. *Timmy Failure: Mistakes Were Made.* Candlewick, 2013. ISBN: 978-0-7636-6050-7. Gr 3 and up.

Paulsen, Gary. *Crush: The Theory, Practice and Destructive Properties of Love.* Wendy Lamb Books, 2012. ISBN: 978-0-3857-4230-6. Gr 5–8.

Paulsen, Gary. *Lawn Boy Returns.* Random House, 2010. ISBN: 978-0-385-74662-5. Gr 5–8.

Paulsen, Jim and Gary Paulsen. *Road Trip.* Wendy Lamb Books, 2013. ISBN: 978-0-3857-4191-0. Gr 5 and up.

Pierce, Lincoln. *Big Nate: Game On.* Andrews McMeel, 2013. ISBN: 978-1-4494-2777-1. Gr 2–4. Big Nate series.

Pinkwater, Daniel M. *Looking for Bobowicz: A Hoboken Chicken Story.* HarperCollins, 2004. ISBN: 0-06-053554-7. Gr 3–6.

Rosenthal, Amy Krouse. *Exclamation Mark.* Scholastic Press, 2013. ISBN: 978-0-5454-3679-3. Gr K–3.

Sachar, Louis. *Dogs Don't Tell Jokes.* Sagebrush Education Resources, 1997. ISBN: 0-7857-0133-8. Gr 5–8.

Sachar, Louis. *There's a Boy in the Girl's Bathroom*. Random House, 1997. ISBN: 0-676-76236-0. Gr 3–7.

Scieszka, Jon. *Who Done It?* Soho Teen, 2013. ISBN: 978-1-6169-5152-8. Gr 7 and up.

Scieszka, Jon. *Guys Read: Funny Business*. Walden Pond, 2010. ISBN: 978-0-0619-6373-5. Gr 5–8.

Simon, Francesca. *Horrid Henry and the Zombie Vampire*. Sourcebooks, 2011. ISBN: 978-1-4022-6785-7. Gr 2–5.

Smith, Clete. *Aliens in Disguise*. Disney-Hyperion, 2013. ISBN: 978-1-4231-6598-9. Gr 3 and up. Intergalactic Bed and Breakfast series.

Snicket, Lemony. *The Carnivorous Carnival*. HarperCollins, 2002. ISBN: 0-06-029640-2. Gr 4–8. Others in the series.

Tashjian, Janet. *My Life as a Cartoonist*. Holt, 2013. ISBN: 978-0-8050-9609-5. Gr 4–7.

Van Draanen, Wendelin. *Shredderman: Attack of the Tagger*. Knopf, 2004. ISBN: 0-375-82352-2. Gr 2–5.

Van Draanen, Wendelin. *Shredderman: Meet the Gecko*. Random House, 2005. ISBN: 0-375-82353-0. Gr 2–5.

Van Draanen, Wendelin. *Shredderman: Secret Identity*. Knopf, 2004. ISBN: 0-375-82351-4. Gr 2–5.

Vernon, Ursula. *Nightmare of the Iguana*. Dial Books, 2013. ISBN: 978-0-8037-3846-1. Gr 3–7.

## Poetry

Adoff, Arnold. *Roots and Blues: A Celebration*. Clarion, 2011. ISBN: 978-0-5472-3554-7. Gr 4–8.

Agee, Jon. *Orangutan Tongs: Poems to Tangle Your Tongue*. Hyperion Books, 2009. ISBN: 978-1-4231-0315-8. Gr PK–3.

Black, Michael Ian. *A Pig Parade Is a Terrible Idea*. Simon & Schuster, 2010. ISBN: 978-1-4169-7922-7. Gr PK–2.

Brown, Calef. *Hallowilloween: Nefarious Silliness from Calef Brown*. Houghton Harcourt, 2010. ISBN: 978-0547-21540-2. Gr 2–5.

Brown, Calef. *BowWonders*. Atheneum, 2011. ISBN: 978-1-4169-7877-0. Gr PK–2.

Crawley, Dave. *Reading, Rhyming, and 'Rithmetic*. Boyds Mills, 2010. ISBN: 978-1-59078-565-2. Gr 1–3.

Florian, Douglas. *Shiver Me Timbers! Pirate Poems and Paintings*. Beach Lane Books, 2012. ISBN: 978-1-4424-1321-4. Gr 1–5.

Franco, Betsy, editor. *Falling Hard: 100 Love Poems by Teenagers*. Candlewick Press, 2008. ISBN: 978-0-7636-3437-7. Gr 6–12.

Hale, Christy. *Dreaming Up*. Lee & Low, 2012. ISBN: 978-1-6000-0651-9. Gr K–3.

Heard, Georgia, editor. *The Arrow Finds Its Mark: A Book of Found Poems*. Roaring Brook, 2012. ISBN: 978-1-5964-3665-7. Gr 3–6.

Hoberman, Mary Ann, ed. *Forgot-Me-Nots: Poems to Learn By Heart*. Sourcebooks, 2012, ISBN: 978-0-3161-2947-3. Gr 3–5.

Hopkins, Lee Bennett, selector. *Amazing Faces*. Lee & Low, 2010. ISBN: 978-1-60060-334-1. Gr 2–5.

Hopkins, Lee Bennett. *I Am the Book*. Holiday House, 2011. ISBN: 978-0-8234-2119-0. Gr 2–5.

Jackson, Rob. *Weekend Mischief*. Boyds Mills, 2010. ISBN: 978-1-59078-494-5. Gr 2–5.

Janeczko, Paul B. *A Foot in the Mouth: Poems to Speak, Sing, and Shout*. Candlewick, 2009. ISBN: 978-0-7637-0663-3. Gr 4–7.

Judd, Jennifer Cole. *An Eyeball in My Garden: And Other Pine-tingling Poems*. Marshall Cavendish, 2010. ISBN: 978-0-7614-5655-1. Gr 4–6.

Katz, Susan. *The President's Stuck in the Bathtub: Poems about U.S. Presidents*. Clarion Books, 2012. ISBN: 978-0-547-18221-6. Gr 1–4.

Lear, Edward. *His Shoes Were Far Too Tight*. Chronicle, 2011. ISBN: 978-0-8118-6792-4. Gr 2–5.

Lewis, Jill. *Don't Read This Book*. Tiger Tales, 2010. ISBN: 978-1-58925-094-9. Gr 2–4.

Lewis, J. Patrick. *National Geographic Book of Animal Poetry: 200 Poems with Photographs that Squeak, Soar, and Roar*. National Geographic, 2012. ISBN: 978-1-4263-1054-6. Gr K–3.

Levine, Gail Carson. *Forgive Me, I Meant to Do It*. HarperCollins Publishers, 2012. ISBN: 978-0-06-178725-6. Gr 3–7.

MacLachlan, Patricia. *Cat Talk*. Amistad, 2013. ISBN: 978-0-0602-7978-3. Gr PK–2.

Merchant, Natalie. *Leave Your Sleep: A Collection of Classic Children's Poetry*. Frances Foster Books, 2012. ISBN: 978-0-3743-4368-2. Gr K–3.

Myers, Walter Dean. *We Are America: A Tribute From the Heart*. HarperCollins, 2011. ISBN: 978-0-06-052308-4. Gr 4–8.

Nesbitt, Kenn. *The Tighty Whitey Spider and More Wacky Animal Poems I Totally Made Up*. Sourcebooks, Inc., 2010. ISBN: 978-1-4022-3833-3. Gr 1–6.

Prelutsky, Jack. *My Dog May Be a Genius*. Greenwillow Books, 2008. ISBN: 978-0-06-623862-3. Gr 2–5.

Raczka, Bob. *Lemonade: And Other Poems Squeezed from a Single Word*. Roaring Brook, ISBN: 978-1-59643-541-4. Gr 3 and up.

Raczka, Bob. *Guyku: A Year of Haiku for Boys*. Houghton Harcourt, 2010. ISBN: 978-0-547-24003-9. Gr 1–3.

Shields, Carol Diggory. *Someone Used My Toothbrush! And Other Bathroom Poems*. Dutton, 2010. ISBN: 978-0-525-47937-6. Gr PS–3.

Sidman, Joyce. *Swil by Swirl: Spirals in Nature*. Houghton Mifflin, 2011. ISBN: 978-0-547-31583-6. Gr PS–3.

Silverstein, Shel. *Everything On It*. HarperCollins, 2011. ISBN: 978-0-06-199816-4. Gr 2-7.

Sklansky, Amy E. *Out of This World: Poems and Facts About Space*. Knopf, 2012. ISBN: 978-1-3758-6459-9. Gr 3–5.

Wheeler, Lisa. *The Pet Project: Cute and Cuddly Vicious Verses*. Atheneum Books for Young Readers, 2013. ISBN: 978-1-4169-7595-3. Gr 1–4.

## PICTURE BOOKS

Agee, Jon. *Mr. Putney's Quacking Dog*. Scholastic, 2010. ISBN: 978-0-545-16203-6. Gr K–2.

Bingham, Kelly. *Z Is for Moose*. Greenwillow, 2012. ISBN: 978-0-0607-9984-7. Gr PK–2.

Dahl, Roald. *Roald Dahl's Revolting Rhymes*. Random House, 2002. ISBN: 0-375-81556-2. Gr 1–3.

deGroat, Diane. *Homer*. Scholastic, 2012. ISBN: 978-0-5453-3272-9. Gr 1–3.

Franco, Betsy. *A Dazzling Display of Dogs*. Tricycle, 2011. ISBN: 978-1-58246-343-8. Gr K–3.

Gaiman, Neil. *Instructions*. HarperCollins, 2010. ISBN: 978-0-06-196030-7. Gr K–3.

Gerstein, Mordicai. *Dear Hot Dog: Poems About Everyday Stuff*. Abrams, 2011. ISBN: 978-0-8109-9732-5. Gr K–3.

Gibson, Amy. *Around the World on Eighty Legs*. Scholastic, 2011. ISBN: 978-0-439-58755-6. Gr PK–3.

Hopkins, Lee Bennett. *Marvelous Math: A Book of Poems*. Simon & Schuster, 2001. ISBN: 0-689-80658-2. Gr K–3.

Hopkins, Lee Bennett. *Dizzy Dinosaurs: Silly Dino Poems*. HarperCollins, 2011. ISBN: 978-0-06-135839-5. Gr K–2.

Jarka, Jeff. *Love That Kitty! The Story of a Boy Who Wanted to Be a Cat*. Henry Holt, 2010. ISBN: 978-0-8050-9053-6. Gr PK–2.

Orloff, Karen Kaufman. *I Wanna New Room*. Putnam, 2010. ISBN: 978-0-399-25405-5. Gr PS–2.

Pilkey, Dav. *Dogzilla*. Harcourt, 1993. ISBN: 0-15-223945-6. Gr K and up.

Pilkey, Dav. *Kat Kong*. Harcourt, 1993. ISBN: 0-15-242037-1. Gr K and up.

Sayre, April Pulley. *Vulture View*. Henry Holt, 2007. ISBN: 978-0-8050-7557-1. Gr K and up.

Scieszka, Jon. *The Stinky Cheese Man and Other Fairly Stupid Tales*. Viking, 1992. ISBN: 0-670-84487-X. Gr PK and up.

Scieszka, Jon. *The True Story of the 3 Little Pigs by A. Wolf*. Viking, 1989. ISBN: 0-670-82759-2. Gr K–3.

Seuss, Dr. *Oh, the Places You'll Go*. Random House, 1993. ISBN: 0-679-84736-7. Gr PK–3.

Steig, William. *C D B?* Simon & Schuster, 2003. ISBN: 0-689-85706-3. Gr K–3.

Sierra, Judy. *Tell the Truth*. Knopf, 2010. ISBN: 978-0-375-95620-1. Gr PK–3.

Smith, Lane. *It's a Book*. Roaring Brook, 2010. ISBN: 978-1-59643-606-0. Gr 1–3.

Willems, Mo. *Goldilocks and the Three Dinosaurs*. HarperCollins, 2012. ISBN: 978-0-0621-0418-2. Gr PK–2.

## ANNOTATED PROFESSIONAL BOOK

Scieszka, Jon. *Guys Read: Funny Business*. Walden Pond Press, 2010.
   This book contains ten stories by a variety of well-known authors. They are selected by Jon Scieszka and he claims in the introduction that humor is extremely important to boys and that some authors simply cannot write humor. The selections that he has made for this book include a raging robot, a homicidal turkey, a bloody souvenir, a biker taking over a kid's bedroom, and more—from the best and funniest writers around.

# Chapter 13

# LGBT (LESBIAN, GAY, BISEXUAL, TRANSGENDER)

Research shows that there are an estimated two million children living in lesbian, gay, bisexual, and transgender (LGBT) families. Now more than ever it is important for librarians and educators to find good quality books about these families and the challenges they face. Since colonial times people have been persecuted (even sentenced to death) for their sexual orientation. Scientifically speaking, we know more about sexual orientation now than we ever knew in the past. Leonard Sax, a medical doctor and a psychologist, makes some very clear statements in his book, *Why Gender Matters: What Parents and Teachers Need to Know about the Emerging Science of Sex Differences* (2005). This analogy is clearest: "Some children are destined at birth to be left-handed, and some boys are destined at birth to grow up to be gay."

Despite the scientific support, gays who "come out" often have a difficult time. They are called names and subjected to all sorts of physical violence from beatings to murder. Many Americans believe that homosexuality is wrong and that homosexuals can simply refuse to be that way. This makes it extremely difficult for children in gay families and for children and young adults struggling with homosexual feelings.

## FEATURED AUTHORS

Name: Alex Sanchez
Birth date: 1957
Place of Birth: Mexico City, Mexico
Most popular book(s): *Rainbow Boys*

About: Although Sanchez's novels are widely accepted in thousands of school and public libraries in America, they have faced a handful of challenges and efforts to ban them. In Webster, New York, removal of *Rainbow Boys* from the 2006 summer reading list was met by a counterprotest from students, parents, librarians, and community members resulting in the book being placed on the 2007 summer reading list.

Web site: http://www.alexsanchez.com

Name: David Levithan

Birth date: September 7, 1972

Place of Birth: Short Hills, New Jersey

Most popular book(s): *Boy Meets Boy; Will Grayson, Will Grayson*

About: At 19, Levithan received an internship at Scholastic Corporation where he began working on the The Baby-sitters Club series. Levithan still works for Scholastic as an editorial director. Levithan is also the founding editor of PUSH, a young-adult imprint of Scholastic Press focusing on new voices and new authors. PUSH publishes edgier material for young adults.

Web site: http://www.davidlevithan.com

## ANNOTATIONS

Green, John and David Levithan. *Will Grayson, Will Grayson*. Dutton, 2010. ISBN: 978-0-525-42158-0.

The two main characters, both named Will Grayson, tell their story in the book's alternating chapters. John Green writes the odd-numbered chapters and David Levithan writes the even-numbered chapters. One of the Will Grayson's has an online relationship with what he thought was another boy. The other Will Grayson who has limited friends is on medication for depression. A set of circumstances puts them both in a porn store, where they meet and both of their lives are forever changed.

Hubbard, Jenny. *Paper Covers Rock*. Delacorte Press, 2011. ISBN: 978-0-385-74055-5.

Thomas Broughton dies, while at boarding school, nine days after his seventeenth birthday. Alex, Glenn, and Clay are drinking with Thomas at the river when it is decided, with tragic consequences, to jump into the river to sober up. Clay takes the blame for the accident and is expelled. How will Glenn and Alex cover things up and handle the only other person who happened upon the incident, their young female English teacher?

Levithan, David. *Boy Meets Boy*. Alfred A. Knopf, 2003. ISBN: 0-375-92400-0.

From an early age Paul has known that he is gay. When he was in the third grade he ran for the president of his class as a gay president. His other friends have not been as lucky. Tony has to keep his true identify a secret because of the religious convictions of his parents. Kyle is lost and has feelings for both boys and girls. This book is about Paul's relationship with each of his individual friends, including Joni, but in particular Noah, who is new to the school. Paul makes some mistakes but he bravely shows how he feels to his friends and especially Noah.

Sanchez, Alex. *Rainbow Boys*. Simon and Schuster Books for Young Readers; Reprint edition, 2005. ISBN: 978-0-689-85770-6. Gr 10 and up.

This is the author's first novel and the first of three in the Rainbow series. This story begins with three high school boys, Nelson, who is out and a flamer, has feelings for his best friend Kyle, who is slowly coming out of the closet. Kyle on the other hand likes Jason, a popular jock who has dated Debra for two years but thinks about men and Kyle in particular. A list of support groups with contact information is listed in the back of the book.

Sanchez, Alex. *So Hard to Say*. Simon & Schuster, 2004. ISBN: 0-689-86564-3.

Frederick, thirteen years old, reluctantly moves away from his friends in Wisconsin to California. He meets Xio, who is Mexican American. Gradually they become good friends, but Xio wants to be more than friends, and Frederick is confused because he does not feel the same. Frederick comes to terms with the reality that he may be gay, and Xio learns to accept Frederick as he is. Even though they may not have a sexual relationship, their friendship is recognized and valued.

## BIBLIOGRAPHY

Anderson. M. T. *No Such Thing as the Real World: Stories About Growing Up and Getting a Life*. HarperTeen, 2009. ISBN: 0-06-147058-9. YA.

Bantle, Lee. *David Inside Out*. Holt, 2009. ISBN: 978-0-8090-8122-0. YA.

Bauer, Marion Dane. *Am I Blue?: Coming Out from the Silence*. HarperCollins, 1995. ISBN: 0-06-440587-4. YA.

Beam, Cris. *I am J*. Little, Brown Books for Young Readers, 2011. ISBN: 978-0-3160-5361-9. Gr 9 and up.

Bechard, Margaret. *If It Doesn't Kill You*. Viking, 1999. ISBN: 0-670-99547-9. YA.

Block, Francesca Lia. *Baby Be-Bop*. HarperCollins, 1997. ISBN: 978-0-06-44176-3. YA.

Bray, Libba. *Going Bovine*. Ember; Reissue edition, 2010. ISBN: 978-0-3857-3398-4. Gr 8 and up.

Brezenoff, Steve. *Brooklyn Burning*. Carolrhoda, 2011. ISBN: 978-0-7613-7526-5. YA.

Brooks Kevin. *Black Rabbit Summer*. Scholastic, 2008. ISBN: 978-0-545-05752-3. Scholastic, 2008. YA.

Burd, Nick. *The Vast Fields of Ordinary*. Dial, 2009. ISBN: 978-0-8037-3340-4. YA.

Cameron, Peter. *Someday This Pain Will Be Useful to You*. Farrar, 2007. ISBN: 978-0-374-30989-3. YA.

Cart, Michael, editor. *How Beautiful the Ordinary: Twelve Stories of Identity*. HarperTeen, 2009. ISBN: 978-0-06-115498-0. YA.

Cohn, Rachel. *Naomi and Ely's No Kiss List*. Knopf, 2007. ISBN: 978-0-375-84440-9. YA.

Crutcher, Chris. *Anger Management*. Greenwillow Books; Reprint edition, 2011. ISBN: 978-0-06-0502-485. Gr 9 and up.

Farrey, Brian. *With or Without You*. Simon Pulse, 2011. ISBN: 978-1-4424-0699-5. YA.

Federle, Tim. *Better Nate Than Ever*. Simon & Schuster Books for Young Readers, 2013. ISBN: 978-1-4424-4689-2. Gr 4–8.

Ferguson, Drew. *The Screwed-Up Life of Charlie the Second*. Kensington, 2008. ISBN: 978-0-7582-2708-9. YA.

Freymann-Weyr, Garret. *My Heartbeat*. Houghton, 2002. ISBN: 0-618-14181-2. YA.

Going, K. L. *King of the Screwups*. Harcourt, 2009. ISBN: 978-0-15-206258-3. YA.

Gonzalez, Rigoberto. *The Mariposa Club*. Alyson Books, 2009. ISBN: 978-1-5935-0106-8. Gr 7 and up.

Hartinger, Brent. *Geography Club*. HarperTempest, 2003. ISBN: 0-06-001221-8. YA.

Hartinger, Brent. *Project Sweet Life*. HarperTeen, 2009. ISBN: 978-0-06-082411-2. YA.

Hartinger, Brent. *Shadow Walkers*. Flux; Original edition, 2011. ISBN: 978-0-7387-2364-8. Gr 7 and up.

Higgins, M. G. *Bi-Normal*. Saddleback Educational Publishing, Inc., 2013. ISBN: 978-1-6225-0004-8. YA.

Homes, A. M. *Jack*. Vintage; First edition, 1990. ISBN: 978-0-6797-3221-1.YA.

Hopkins, Ellen. *Tricks*. Margaret K. McElderry Books, 2011. ISBN: 978-1-4169-5008-0. YA.

Howe, James. *The Misfits*. Atheneum Books for Young Readers, 2003.ISBN: 978-0-6898-3956-6. Gr 5 and up.

Hurwin, Davida. *Freaks and Revelations: A Novel*. Little, Brown and Company, 2009. ISBN: 978-0-316-04996-2. YA.

Jacobson, Jennifer. *Stained*. Atheneum, 2005. ISBN: 0-689-86745-X. YA.

Klise, James. *Love Drugged*. Flux, 2010. ISBN: 978-0-7387-2175-0. Gr 7 and up.

Kluger, Steve. *My Most Excellent Year: A Novel of Love, Mary Poppins and Fenway Park*. Dial, 2008. ISBN: 978-0-8037-3227-8. YA.

Koertge, Ron. *Boy Girl Boy*. Harcourt, 2005. ISBN: 0-15-205325-5. YA.

Koja, Kathe. *Talk*. Farrar, 2005. ISBN: 0-374-37382-5. YA.

Kokie, E. M. *Personal Effects*. Candlewick, 2012. ISBN: 978-0-7636-5527-3. YA.

Konigsberg, Bill. *Openly Straight*. Scholastic, 2013. ISBN: 978-0-545-50989-9. YA.

Levithan, David. *Every Day*. Knopf, 2012. ISBN: 978-0-3079-3188-7. Gr. 9–12.

Moore, Perry. *Hero*. Hyperion Book CH, 2009. ISBN: 978-1-4231-0196-3. Gr 9 and up.

Moskowitz, Hannah. *Gone, Gone, Gone*. Simon Pulse, 2012. ISBN: 978-1-4424-5312-8. Gr 9 and up.

Newman, Leslea. *October Mourning: A Song for Matthew Shepard*. Candlewick, 2012. Gr. 9 and up.

Peck, Dale. *Sprout*. Bloomsbury, 2009. ISBN: 978-1-5999-0160-2. YA.

Rapp, Adam. *Punkzilla*. Candlewick, 2009. ISBN: 978-0-7636-3031-7. Gr 9 and up.

Rice-Gonzalez, Charles. *Chulito*. Magnus Books, 2011. ISBN: 978-1-9368-3303-0. YA.

Ryan, Tom. *Way to Go*. Orca Books, 2012. ISBN: 978-1-4598-0077-3-9. Gr 8 and up.

Saenz, Benjamin Alire. *Aristotle and Dante Discover the Secrets of the Universe*. Simon & Schuster, 2012. ISBN: 978-1-4424-0892-0. Gr 7 and up.

Saenz, Benjamin Alire. *Last Night I Sang to the Monster*. Cinco Puntos Press, 2009. ISBN: 978-1-9336-9358-3. Gr 9 and up.

Sanchez, Alex. *Rainbow Road*. Simon, 2005. ISBN: 0-689-86565-1. YA.

Satyal, Rakesh. *Blue Boy*. Kensington Publishing Corporation, 2009. ISBN: 978-0-75823-3136-9. YA.

Telgemeier, Raina. *Drama*. Graphix, 2012. ISBN: 978-0-5453-2699-5. Gr 5 and up.

Walliams, David. *The Boy in the Dress*. Penguin, 2009. ISBN: 978-1-5951-4299-3. Gr 3 and up.

Woodson, Jacqueline. *From the Notebooks of Melanie Sun*. Puffin, 2010. ISBN: 978-0-1424-1641-9. Gr 5 and up.

Wright, Bil. *Putting Makeup on the Fat Boy*. Simon & Schuster, 2012. ISBN: 978-1-4169-4004-3. Gr 7 and up.

Yee, Paul. *Money Boy*. Groundwood Books, 2012. ISBN: 978-1-5549-8094-9. Gr 8 and up.

## INFORMATIONAL

Alsenas, Linas. *Gay America: Struggle for Equality*. Amulet Books, 2008. ISBN: 978-0-8109-9487-4. YA.

Aretha, David. *No Compromise: The Story of Harvey Milk*. Morgan, 2009. ISBN: 978-1-59935-129-2. YA.

Beam, Cris. *Love, Family, and Living the T with Transgender Teenagers*. Mariner Books, 2008. ISBN: 978-0-1560-3377-0. YA.

Cuabcuitti, Jason and Sean Cahill. *LGBT Youth in America's Schools*. The University of Michigan Press, 2012. ISBN: 978-0-4720-3140-5. Adult.

DeWitt, Peter. *Dignity for All: Safeguarding LGBT Students*. Corwin Press, 2012. ISBN: 978-1-4522-0590-8. Adult.

Fakhrid-Deen, Tina. *Let's Get This Straight: The Ultimate Handbook for Youth with LGBTQ Parents*. Seal, 2010. ISBN: 978-1-58005-333-4. Gr 5–10.

Ford, Michael Thomas. *Outspoken: Role Models from the Lesbian and Gay Community*. HarperTrophy, 1998. ISBN: 978-06-8814-897-3. YA.

Garden, Nancy. *Hear Us Out: Lesbian and Gay Stories of Struggle, Progress and Hope, 1950 to the Present*. Farrar, 2007. ISBN: 978-0-374-31759-1. YA.

Greenberg, Keith Elliot. *Zack's Story: Growing Up with Same-Sex Parents*. Lerner, 1996. ISBN: 0-8225-2581-X. Gr 4–7.

Heron, Ann. *Two Teenagers in Twenty: Writings by Gay and Lesbian Youth*. Alyson, 1995. ISBN: 1-55583-229-6. YA.

Hyde, Margaret O. *Know About Gays and Lesbians*. Millbrook Press, 1994. ISBN: 1-56294-298-4. Gr 7 and up.

Jenness, Aylette. *Families: A Celebration of Diversity, Commitment, and Love*. Houghton Mifflin, 1993. ISBN: 0-395-47038-2. Gr 4–6.

Kuklin, Susan. *Families*. Hyperion, 2006. ISBN: 0-7868-0822-5. Gr K–3.

Levithan, David. *How They Met, and Other Stories*. Knopf, 2008. ISBN: 978-0-375-84886-5. YA.

Marcus, Eric. *What If?: Answers to Questions About What It Means to Be Gay and Lesbian*. Simon Pulse, 2013. ISBN: 978-1-4422-8298-2. YA.

Mastoon, Adam. *The Shared Heart: Portraits and Stories Celebrating Lesbian, Gay, and Bisexual Young People*. Morrow, 1997. ISBN: 0-688-14931-6. Gr 7 and up.

Merrel, Billy. *The Full Spectrum: A New Generation of Writing about Gay, Lesbian, Bisexual, Transgender, and Questioning, and Other Identities.* Knopf, 2006. ISBN: 0-375-93290-9. YA.

Moon, Sarah. *The Letter Q: Queer Writers' Notes to Their Younger Selves.* Scholastic, 2012. ISBN: 978-0-545-39932-6. YA.

Peters, Julie Anne. *Grl2grl.* Little, 2007. ISBN: 978-0-316-01343-7. YA.

Pollack, Rachel. *The Journey Out: A Guide For and About Lesbian, Gay, and Bisexual Teens.* Viking, 1995. ISBN: 0-670-85845-5. YA.

Sutton, Roger. *Hearing Us Out: Voices from the Gay and Lesbian Community.* Little, 1994. ISBN: 0-316-82326-0. YA.

Young, Perry Deane. *Lesbians and Gays and Sports.* Chelsea, 1994. ISBN: 0-7910-2951-4. YA.

## PICTURE BOOKS

Bradley, Kimberly Brubaker. *Ballerino Nate.* Dial, 2006. ISBN: 978-0-8037-2954-4. Gr PK and up.

Brannen, Sarah. *Uncle Bobby's Wedding.* Putnam, 2008. ISBN: 978-0-3992-4712-5. Gr PK and up.

de Haan, Linda, and Stern Nijland. *King and King and Family.* Tricycle Press, 2004. ISBN: 978-1-5824-6113-7. Gr K–3.

dePaola, Tomie. *Oliver Button Is a Sissy.* Harcourt Brace Jovanovich, 1979. ISBN: 978-0-8810-3357-1. Gr PK–3. Classic.

Farrell, John. *Dear Child.* Boyds Mills Press, 2008. ISBN: 978-1-5907-8495-2. Gr PK–K.

Fierstein, Harvey. *The Sissy Duckling.* Simon & Schuster, 2002. ISBN: 978-0-6898-3566-7. Gr K–3.

Kilodavis, Cheryl. *My Princess Boy.* Simon & Schuster, 2011. ISBN: 978-0-6153-9594-4. Gr PK and up.

Milgrim, David. *Time to Get Up, Time to Go.* Clarion, 2006. ISBN: 978-0-6185-1998-9. Gr PK–K.

Newman, Leslea. *Donovan's Big Day.* Tricycle, 2011. ISBN: 978-1-58246-332-2. Gr PK–2.

Oelschlager, Vanita. *A Tale of Two Mommies.* Vanita, 2011. ISBN: 978-0-9826-3666-4. Gr PK–2.

Richardson, Justin and Peter Parnell. *And Tango Makes Three.* Simon & Schuster, 2005. ISBN: 978-0-6898-7845-9. Gr PK–3.

Richardson, Justin and Peter Parnell. *Christian, the Hugging Lion.* Simon & Schuster, 2010. ISBN: 978-1-4169-8662-1. Gr PK–3.

Rickards, Lynne. *Pink!* Scholastic, 2008. ISBN: 978-0-5450-8608-0. Gr PK–3.

Valentine, Johnny. *The Duke Who Outlawed Jelly Beans and Other Stories.* Alyson Books, 2004. ISBN: 1-5558-3847-2. Gr K–3.

Zolotow, Charlotte. *William's Doll.* Harper & Row, 1972. ISBN: 978-0-0602-7047-6. Gr K–3. Classic.

## ANNOTATED PROFESSIONAL BOOK

Naidoo, Jamie Campbell. *Rainbow Family Collections: Selecting and Using Children's Books with Lesbian, Gay, Bisexual, Transgender, and Queer Content.* Libraries Unlimited, 2012.
   From the book's back cover, "research shows that an estimated 2 million children are being raised in lesbian, gay, bisexual, and transgender (LGBT) families in the United States; that the number of same-sex couples adopting children is at an all-time high; and that lesbian, gay, bisexual, transgender, and queer/questioning (LGBTQ) couples raising children live in 96% of all counties in the United States." A great resource for librarians and educators, *Rainbow Family Collections* includes a list of award-winning books and gives advice for building a collection of children's materials reflecting LGBYQ content, including picture books, chapter books, and informational books and biographies for LGBTQ children. The last chapter includes resources for educators, librarians, and rainbow families.

# Chapter 14

# MATH AND NUMBERS

Books about math are especially appealing to boys because they provide unusual information about number properties, offer challenging puzzles and games, and give needed insight and practice with problem-solving skills. Numbers and patterns are a good match for boys' natural curiosity, and they also offer practical applications to everyday life. Math can lead to different outcomes and challenges—the sky's the limit and math really is fun!

## FEATURED AUTHORS

Name: Claudia Mills

Birth date: August 21, 1954

Place of Birth: New York City, New York

Most popular book(s): *Fractions = Trouble!*, *How Oliver Olson Changed the World*

About: Mills has always had another job while writing her books. She has two other "jobs" right now: She is a philosophy professor at the University of Colorado at Boulder and the mother of two boys. This means that her writing never seems like a job to her. It is the special, secret work that she loves best.

Web site: http://claudiamillsauthor.com

Name: David Adler

Birth date: April 10, 1947

Place of Birth: New York City, New York

Most popular book(s): *Mystery Math: A First Book of Algebra*, *You Can, Toucan, Math*

About: Cam Jansen is loosely based on a first-grade classmate of David Adler's who everyone envied because they thought he had a photographic memory. Adler has also written many books on the Holocaust including *We Remember the Holocaust*, a book for older readers that incorporates firsthand accounts of the tragedy within the historical context.

Web site: http://www.davidaadler.com

## ANNOTATIONS

Fisher, Valorie. *How High Can a Dinosaur Count and Other Math Mysteries*. Schwartz & Wade, 2012. ISBN: 978-0-3759-3608-1.
    Valorie Fisher has created fifteen unique mysteries with accompanying illustrations. Solutions to the mysteries are included at the end along with additional math mysteries to solve.

Mills, Claudia. *Fractions = Trouble!* Farrar Straus Giroux, 2011. ISBN: 978-1-250-00336-2.
    Nobody is good at all things. Multiplication is hard enough for third-grader Wilson Williams, but now he had fractions to learn and a huge test in three weeks. His parents have hired a math tutor, but Wilson is embarrassed and does not want his friends to know. Read the book to find out how art and hamsters play a role in helping Wilson understand fractions!

Murphy, Stuart J. *Room for Ripley*. HarperCollins Publishers, 1999. ISBN: 978-0-06-446724-7.
    Carlos visits a pet store and makes plans to purchase a fish he calls Ripley. Each time he fills his fish bowl he introduces various units of liquid measure.

Overdeck, Laura. *Bedtime Math: A Fun Excuse to Stay Up Late*. Feiwel and Friends, 2013. ISBN: 978-1-250-03585-1.
    This book introduces math at bedtime with the idea of teaching kids to love math. The math stories are on three levels of challenge: wee ones, little kids, and big ones to accommodate differing math ability. Some of the chapter titles are Exploding Food, Extreme Vehicles, and Sports You Shouldn't Try at Home.

Slade, Suzanne. *The Great Divide*. Sylvan Dell Publishing, 2012. ISBN: 978-1-60718-548-2.
    Each two-page spread illustrates an animal group name while providing an opportunity to practice division skills.

Taylor-Butler, Christine. *Understanding Charts and Graphs*. Children's Press, 2013. ISBN: 978-0-531-26240-5.
    Another name for a chart, table, or graph is a graphic organizer, and they date back thousands of years. Several examples are discussed, such as: flow and prediction charts, spreadsheets, tables, and various line, bar, and scatter plot graphs.

## READ ALOUD

Leedy, Loreen. *Seeing Symmetry*. Holiday House. 2012. ISBN: 978-0-8234-2360-6.

Robbins, Ken. *For Good Measure: The Ways We Say How Much, How Far, How Big, How Old*. Roaring Brook, 2010. ISBN: 978-1-59643-344-1.

Yoder, Eric. *One Minute Mysteries: 65 Short Mysteries You Solve With Math*. Science Naturally, 2010. ISBN: 978-0-9678-0200-8.

## BIBLIOGRAPHY

### Fiction

Barry, David. *The Rajah's Rice: A Mathematical Folktale from India*. Harcourt School Publishers, 2006. ISBN: 978-0-1635-6588-5. Gr 4–6.

Bauer, Joan. *Sticks*. Putnam, 2002. ISBN: 0-399-23752-6. Gr 4–6.

Dodds, Dayle Ann. *Full House: An Invitation to Fractions*. Candlewick, 2009. ISBN: 978-0-7636-4130-6. Gr 1–4.

Dodds, Dayle Ann. *The Great Divide: A Mathematical Marathon*. Candlewick, 2005. ISBN: 978-0-7636-1592-5. Gr K–4.

Enzensberger, Hans Magnus. *The Number Devil: A Mathematical Adventure*. Henry Holt and Co., 1998. ISBN: 0-8050-5770-6. Gr 4–6.

Erskine, Kathryn. *The Absolute Value of Mike*. Philomel, 2011. ISBN: 978-0-399-25505-2. Gr 4–6.

Fienberg, Anna. *Number 8*. Walker Children's, 2007. ISBN: 978-0-8027-9660-8. YA.

Frederick, Heather Vogel. *The Voyage of Patience Goodspeed*. Simon & Schuster Publishing, 2002. ISBN: 0-689-84851-X. Gr 4–6.

Holm, Jennifer L. *Babymouse: Dragonslayer*. Random House Children's Books, 2009. ISBN: 978-0-375-95712-3. Gr 1–3.

Kline, Suzy. *Horrible Harry Cracks the Code*. Viking, 2007. ISBN: 978-0-670-06200-3. Gr 1–3.

Krosoczka, Jarrett J. *Lunch Lady and the Mutant Mathletes*. Random House Children's Books, 2012. ISBN: 978-0-375-87028-6. Gr 4–6.

Latham, Jean Lee. *Carry On, Mr. Bowditch*. Houghton, 2003. ISBN: 0-618-25081-6. YA.

McElligott, Matthew. *Bean Thirteen*. G. P. Putnam's Sons, 2007. ISBN: 978-0-3992-4535-0. Gr K–3.

Mills, Claudia. *7 X 9 = Trouble!* Farrar, Straus and Giroux, 2002. ISBN: 0-374-36746-9. Gr 1–3.

Napoli, Donna Jo. *The Wishing Club: A Story About Fractions*. Henry Holt and Co., 2007. ISBN: 978-0-8050-7665-3. Gr K–3.

Pearsall, Shelley. *All of the Above*. Little, 2006. ISBN: 0-316-11524-X. Gr 4–6.

Schroder, Monika. *Saraswati's Way*. Farrar, Straus and Giroux, 2010. ISBN: 978-0-3743-6411-3. Gr 4–6.

Ward, Rachel. *The Chaos*. Scholastic, 2011. ISBN: 978-0-545-24269-1. YA.

## INFORMATIONAL

Adamson, Thomas K. *How Do You Measure Length and Distance?* Capstone, 2010. ISBN: 978-1-4296-4456-3. Gr PK–2.

Adler, David A. *Perimeter, Area, and Volume*. Holiday House, 2012. ISBN: 978-0-8234-2763-5. Gr 2–5.

Adler, David A. *Time Zones*. Holiday House, 2010. ISBN: 978-0-8234-2385-9. Gr 2 and up.

Adler, David A. *Fun with Roman Numerals*. Holiday House, 2008. ISBN: 978-0-8234-2255-5. Gr 2 and up.

Adler, David A. *Fractions, Decimals, and Percents*. Holiday House, 2010. ISBN: 978-0-8234-2199-2. Gr 3–5.

Adler, David A. *Mystery Math: A First Book of Algebra*. Holiday House, 2011. ISBN: 978-0-8234-2289-0. Gr 2–4.

Anderson, Jill. *Money Math with Sebastian Pig and Friends at the Farmer's Market*. Enslow, 2009. ISBN: 978-0-7660-3364-1. Gr PK and up.

Anderson, Jill. *Finding Shapes with Sebastian Pig and Friends at the Museum*. Enslow, 2009. ISBN: 978-0-7660-3363-4. Gr 1–3.

Arroyo, Sheri L. *How Crime Fighters Use Math*. Chelsea Clubhouse, 2009. ISBN: 978-1-60413-602-9. Gr 4-6. Math in the Real World series.

Ball, Johnny. *Go Figure!: A Totally Cool Book About Numbers*. DK Children, 2005. ISBN: 978-0-7566-1374-7. Gr 4–8.

Ball, Johnny. *Why Pi?* DK Publishing, 2009. ISBN: 978-0-7566-5164-0. Gr 2–5.

Boutin, Chad. *Pierre de Fermat*. Morgan, 2008. ISBN: 978-1-59935-061-5. YA. Profiles in Mathematics series.

Campbell, Sarah C. *Growing Patterns: Fibonacci Numbers in Nature*. Boyds Mills Press, 2010. ISBN: 978-1-59078-752-6. Gr K–3.

Cleary, Brian P. *A Fraction's Goal—Parts of a Whole*. Millbrook, 2011. ISBN: 978-0-8225-7881-9. Gr K–3. Math is CATegorical series.

Cleary, Brian P. *A Dollar, a Penny, How Much and How Many?* Millbrook Press, 2012. ISBN: 978-0-8225-7882-6. Gr K–3.

Clements, Andrew. *A Million Dots.* Simon & Schuster, 2006. ISBN: 978-0-6898-5824-6. Gr 1–4.

D'Agnese, Joseph. *Blockhead: The Life of Fibonacci.* Henry Holt and Co., 2010. ISBN: 978-0-8050-6305-9. Gr 4–6.

D'Amico, Joan. *The Math Chef: Over 60 Math Activities and Recipes for Kids.* J. Wiley, 1997. ISBN: 978-0-4711-3813-6. Gr 4 and up.

Dugan, Christine. *Pack It Up: Surface Area and Volume.* Teacher Created Materials, 2012. ISBN: 978-1-4333-3461-0. Gr 3–5.

Gardner, Robert. *Far-Out Science Projects with Height and Depth: How High Is Up? How Low Is Down?* Enslow, 2003. ISBN: 0-7660-2016-9. Gr K-3. Sensational Science Experiments series.

Goldstone, Bruce. *Greater Estimations.* Holt, 2008. ISBN: 978-0-8050-8315-6. Gr 4–6.

Heiligman, Deborah. *The Boy Who Loved Math: The Improbable Life of Paul Erdos.* Roaring Brook, 2013. ISBN: 978-159643-307-6. Gr K–3.

Hense, Mary. *How Astronauts Use Math.* Chelsea Clubhouse, 2009. ISBN: 978-1-60413-610-4. Gr 4–8.

Hosford, Kate. *Infinity and Me.* Carolrhoda, 2012. ISBN: 978-0-8225-7882-6. Gr K–4.

*Information Everywhere: The World Explained in Facts, Stats, and Graphics.* Dorling Kindersley Limited, 2013. ISBN: 978-1-4654-0257-8. Gr 3 and up.

Irving, Dianne. *Volume and Hot Air Balloons.* Capstone Press, 2011. ISBN: 978-1-4296-6619-0. Gr 4 and up.

Jenkins, Steve. *Just a Second.* Houghton Mifflin, 2011. ISBN: 978-0-6187-0896-3. Gr 4–7.

Larochelle, David. *1+1=5: And Other Unlikely Additions.* Sterling, 2010. ISBN: 978-1-4027-5995-6. Gr K–3.

Lasky, Kathryn. *The Man Who Made Time Travel.* Farrar, Straus and Giroux, 2003. ISBN: 0-374-34788-3. Gr 4–6.

Lewis, J. Patrick. *Edgar Allan Poe's Pie: Math Puzzlers in Classic Poems.* Harcourt, 2012. ISBN: 978-0-5475-1338-6. Gr 3–6.

McCallum, Ann. *Eat Your Math Homework: Recipes for Hungry Minds.* Charlesbridge Pub Inc., 2011. ISBN: 978-1-5709-1780-6. Gr 2–6.

Menotti, Andrea. *How Many Jelly Beans?* Chronicle, 2012. ISBN: 978-1-4521-0206-1. Gr K-4.

Miller, Reagan. *Communication in the Ancient World.* Crabtree, 2011. ISBN: 978-0-7787-1733-1. Gr 5–7.

Nelson, Robin. *Let's Make a Bar Graph.* Lerner Publications, 2013. ISBN: 978-0-7613-8972-9. Gr K–3.

Nelson, Robin. *Let's Make a Rally Chart.* Lerner Publications, 2013. ISBN: 978-0-7613-8975-0. Gr K–3. First Step Nonfiction—Graph It! series.

Noonan, Daina. *Collecting Data in Animal Investigations.* Capstone, 2010. ISBN: 978-1-4296-5237-7. Gr 3–5.

Rosenthal, Amy Krouse. *Wumbers.* Chronicle, 2012. ISBN: 978-1-4521-1022-6. Gr K–4.

Schwartz, David M. *Millions to Measure.* HarperCollins, 2003. ISBN: 0-688-12916-1. Gr K–3.

Schwartz, Joanne. *City Numbers.* Groundwood, 2011. ISBN: 978-1-55498-081-9. Gr 3–7.

Singer, Marilyn. *Mirror Mirror: A Book of Reversible Verse.* Dutton, 2010. ISBN: 978-0-5254-7901-7. Gr 3–6.

Singer, Marilyn. *Follow Follow.* Dutton, 2013. ISBN: 978-0-8037-3769-3. Gr 1 and up.

Woods, Mark and Owen. *Xtreme!: Extreme Sports Facts and Stats.* Gareth, 2011. ISBN: 978-1-4339-5020-9. Gr 4–6. Top Score Math series.

Yolen, Jane. *A Mirror to Nature.* Wordsong, 2009. ISBN: 978-1-5907-8624-6. Gr 3–7.

## PICTURE BOOKS

Axelrod, Amy. *Pigs Will Be Pigs.* S & S, 1994. ISBN: 978-0-7807-7489-6. Gr 2–4.

Beaty, Andrea. *Hide and Sheep.* Simon & Schuster, 2011. ISBN: 978-1-4169-2544-6. Gr PK–2.

Birch, Daid. *The King's Chessboard.* Scott Foresman, 1993. ISBN: 978-0-1405-4880-8. Gr 4–6.

Birtha, Becky. *Lucky Beans.* Albert Whitman & Company, 2010. ISBN: 978-0-8075-4782-3. Gr 2–6.

Burns, Marilyn. *Spaghetti and Meatballs for All!* Scholastic, 1997. ISBN: 978-0-5450-4445-5. Gr 4–6.

Burns, Marilyn. *The Greedy Triangle.* Scholastic, 1994. ISBN: 978-0-5450-4220-8. Gr 2–4.

Calvert, Pam. *Multiplying Menace: The Revenge of Rumpelstiltskin.* Charlesbridge, 2006. ISBN: 1-57091-889-9. Gr K–3.

Cave, Kathryn. *Out for the Count: A Counting Adventure*. Simon & Schuster Children's Publishing. ISBN: 978-0-6717-5591-1. Gr PK–2.

Cuyler, Margery. *Guinea Pigs Add Up*. Walker, 2010. ISBN: 978-0-8027-9795-7. Gr PK–2.

Demi. *One Grain of Rice: A Mathematical Folktale*. Scholastic, 1997. ISBN: 0-590-93998-X. Gr PK–3. Classic.

Dodds, Dayle Ann. *Minnie's Diner: A Multiplying Menu*. Candlewick, 2004. ISBN: 0-7636-1736-9. Gr K–3.

Ellis, Julie. *Pythagoras and the Ratios*. Charlesbridge, 2010. ISBN: 978-1-57091-775-2. Gr 3–7.

Ellis, Julie. *What's Your Angle, Pythagoras? A Math Adventure*. Charlesbridge Publishing, 2004. ISBN: 978-1-5709-1150-7. Gr 3 and up.

Florian, Douglas. *A Pig Is Big*. Greenwillow, 2000. ISBN: 978-06-8817-125-4. Gr K–1.

Franco, Betsy. *Mathematickles!* Simon and Schuster Children's Publishing, 2003. ISBN: 0-689-84357-7. Gr K–5.

Franco, Betsy. *Zero Is the Leaves on the Tree*. Tricycle, 2009. ISBN: 978-1-58246-249-3. Gr K–3.

Fromental, Jean-Luc. *365 Penguins*. Abrams Books for Young Readers, 2006. ISBN: 978-0-8109-4460-2. Gr K–4.

Goldstone, Bruce. *100 Ways to Celebrate 100 Days*. Henry Holt, 2010. ISBN: 978-0-8050-8987-4. Gr PK–2.

Gravett. Emily. *The Rabbit Problem*. Simon and Schuster Children's Publishing, 2010. ISBN: 978-14424-1255-2. Gr 1–5.

Holub, Joan. *Zero the Hero*. Henry Holt and Co., 2012. ISBN: 978-0-8050-9384-1. Gr 1–5.

Hopkins, Lee Bennett. *Marvelous Math: A Book of Poems*. Simon & Schuster, 2001. ISBN: 0-689-80658-2. Gr K–3.

Hutchins, Hazel. *A Second Is a Hiccup*. Arthur A. Levin Bks., 2004. ISBN: 978-0-4398-3106-2. Gr K–1.

Hutchins, Pat. *The Doorbell Rang*. HarperCollins, 1986. ISBN: 978-06-8809-234-4. Gr 2–3.

Jenkins, Emily. *Lemonade in Winter: A Book About Two Kids Counting Money*. Random, 2012. ISBN: 978-0-3758-5883-2. Gr PK–2.

Jenkins, Emily. *Five Creatures*. Farrar, 2001. ISBN: 0-374-32341-0. Gr K–3.

Leedy, Loreen. *It's Probably Penny*. Henry Holt, 2007. ISBN: 978-0-8050-7389-8. Gr K–3.

Lionni, Leo. *Inch by Inch*. HarperTrophy, 1995. ISBN: 978-0-6881-3283-5. Gr K–3.

Long, Ethan. *The Wing Wing Brothers Math Spectacular*. Holiday, 2012. ISBN: 978-0-8234-2320-0. Gr K–1.

Mahy, Margaret. *17 Kings and 42 Elephants*. Dial, 1987. ISBN: 978-0-8037-0458-9. Gr 2–4.

Maloney, Peter. *One Foot Two Feet: An EXCEPTIONal Counting Book*. Putnam, 2011. ISBN: 978-0-399-25446-8. Gr PK–K.

Markel, Michelle. *Tyrannosaurus Math*. Tricycle, 2009. ISBN: 978-1-58246-282-0. Gr PK–2.

Marzollo, Jean. *Help Me Learn Numbers 0-20*. Holiday House, 2011. ISBN: 978-0-8234-2334-7. Gr PK–1.

Merriam, Eve. *Twelve Ways to Get to Eleven*. Simon & Schuster Children's Publishing, 1996. ISBN: 0-671-75544-7. Gr PK and up.

Myller, Rolf. *How Big Is a Foot?* Dell, 1962. ISBN: 978-0-4404-0495-8. Gr 2–3.

Pinczes, Elinor J. *A Remainder of One*. Houghton, 2002. 978-0-6182-5077-6. Gr 3–6.

Pinczes, Elinor J. *One Hundred Hungry Ants*. Houghton, 1993. ISBN: 978-0-3959-7013-9. Gr 2–4.

Rosenthal, Amy Krouse. *Wumbers*. Chronicle, 2012. ISBN: 978-1-4521-1022-6. Gr K–3.

Ross, Tony. *Centipede's 100 Shoes*. Holt, 2003. ISBN: 978-0-8050-7298-3. Gr 3–4.

Rumford, James. *Nine Animals and the Well*. Houghton, 2003. ISBN: 0-618-30915-2. Gr K–3.

Scieszka, Jon. *Math Curse*. Viking, 1995. ISBN: 0-670-86194-4. Gr PK and up.

Sebe, Masayuki. *Let's Count to 100!* Kids Can, 2011. ISBN: 978-1-55453-661-0. Gr PK–2.

Shulevitz, Uri. *One Monday Morning*. Farrar, 2003. ISBN: 978-0-3744-5648-1. Gr K–1.

## ANNOTATED PROFESSIONAL BOOK

Fraser, Elizabeth. *Reality Rules II: A Guide to Teen Nonfiction Reading Interests.* Libraries Unlimited, 2012.

Fraser's book is a great resource for teen nonfiction. The introduction provides information about trends, purpose, scope, and selection criteria. The book is divided into three parts. Nonfiction genres include: true adventure and true crime. Life stories include: memoirs, autobiographies, and biographies. Nonfiction subject interests include: history, science, math, and the environment, sports, all about you, how to, the arts, and understanding and changing the world. The appendix includes resources, review journals, online sources, and book awards and selection lists. Each section contains the definition, the appeal, and the organization of the chapter. There is a complete summary of each book listed, including keywords and fiction read-alikes.

# Chapter 15

# MECHANICS AND TECHNOLOGY

Mechanics and technology are fascinating fields for boys. Information about technology tools and how they work as well as software programs are always appealing. Boys are interested in creating Web sites and apps as well as developing their own digital music and movies. They have always been interested in how things work and there are many books that share that information on a large scale. Boys like taking things apart and books can show them how to do it!

## FEATURED AUTHORS

Name: Scott Westerfeld

Birth date: May 5, 1963

Place of Birth: Dallas, Texas

Most popular book(s): *The Uglies Series, The Leviathan Series*

About: Westerfeld is the author of thirteen young adult novels. He is a vegetarian, has a telescope, and never wears jeans. Never!

Web site: http://www.scottwesterfeld.com

Name: David Macaulay

Birth date: December 2, 1946

Place of Birth: Lancashire, United Kingdom

Most popular book(s): *The Way Things Work, Building Big: Bridges*

About: Macaulay is a British-born American illustrator and writer. His most famous works have been graphic, nonfiction children's books about architecture and engineering.

Web site: http://hmhbooks.com/davidmacaulay/

## ANNOTATIONS

Brush, Jim. *Roller Coasters*. Sea-to-Sea, 2012. ISBN: 978-1-59771-329-0.
During most of the ride, the train of the roller coaster is moved along by gravity. Initially the train is pulled up the lift hill by motors and then gravity takes over. Includes many pictures, facts, and Web sites.

Hammond, Richard. *Car Science*. DK Publishing, 2008. ISBN: 978-0-75664-026-2.
Four chapters titled Power; Speed; Handling; and Technology cover everything one needs to be a real driving expert. It also includes what cars we might be driving in the future.

Isaacs, Sally Senzell. *Stagecoaches and Railroads*. Kingfisher, 2012. ISBN: 978-0-7534-6516-5.
Each topic about the development and growth of transportation in the United States is covered on a two-page spread, along with panels that include photographs, paintings, and engravings depicting the time. Some of the topics included are the first locomotives, stagecoaches out West, the Pony Express, linking the continent, and railroads after the frontier days.

Woodroffe, David. *Making Paper Airplanes: Make Your Own Aircraft and Watch Them Fly!* Skyhorse Publishing, 2012. ISBN: 978-1-62087-168-3.
"Thrust and lift are the forces that make a paper plane fly, whereas gravity and drag are the forces that will eventually bring it back to earth." The book contains approximately 175 proven planes and three kites. The planes to be copied are on the right page and instructions are found on the left page. They are best flown inside or on a very still day.

Westerfeld, Scott. *Leviathan*. Simon Pulse, Reprint edition, 2009. ISBN: 978-1-4169-7173-3.
In *Leviathan* there are two opposing factions. The Clanker nations in the industrial north use steam iron machines. The Darwinists in the agricultural south use living fabricated animals and have the *Leviathan*, a large whale ship. The beginning of the trilogy starts with the people of the Austro-Hungarian Empire turning on Alexander, the heir to their throne. The opposing nations begin arming for the start of World War I.

Woog, Adam. *You Tube*. Norwood House Press, 2009. ISBN: 978-1-59953-198-4.
Chad Hurley, Steve Chen, and Jawed Karim worked together at PayPal since it began in 2000. When PayPal was sold in 2002, they earned a lot of money and decided to start another Internet company. In 2005, they designed a site where people of all computer skills could post and watch their videos. The name, "YouTube" and the motto, "Broadcast Yourself" became the "symbols of their hope to let anyone and everyone freely use the site."

Zimmermann, Karl. *The Stourbridge Lion*. Boyd Mills Press, 2012. ISBN: 978-1-59078-859-2.
Horatio Allen was sent to Stourbridge, England, to purchase steam locomotives to help deliver coal from the coal fields to the Delaware Hudson Canal. A lion was painted on its front, thus the Stourbridge Lion would be the first locomotive to run on a real railroad in America on August 8, 1829.

## READ ALOUD

Berger, Lee R. *The Skull in the Rock: How a Scientist, a Boy, and Google Earth Opened a New Window on Human Origins*. National Geographic Books, 2012. ISBN: 978-1-4263-1010-2.

Cassidy, John. *The Klutz Book of Inventions*. Klutz, 2010. ISBN: 978-0-545-61114-5.

Gurstelle, William. *The Art of the Catapult: Build Greek Ballistae, Roman Onagers, English Trebuchets, and More Ancient Artillery*. Chicago Review Press, 2004. ISBN: 978-1-5565-2526-1.

Johnson, D. B. *Pelazzo Inverso*. Houghton Mifflin Books for Children, 2010. ISBN: 978-0-547-23999-6.

## BIBLIOGRAPHY

### Fiction

Asch, Frank. *Star Jumper: Journal of a Cardboard Genius*. Kids Can, 2006. ISBN: 1-55337-887-3. Gr 1–3.

Buckley, Michael. *NERDS 2!: M Is for Mama's Boy*. Abrams, 2010. ISBN: 978-0-8109-8986-3. Gr 4–6.

Buckley, Michael. *NERDS 3: The Cheerleaders of Doom*. Abrams, 2011. ISBN: 978-1-4197-0024-8. Gr 4–6.

Clayton, Emma. *The Whisper*. Scholastic, 2012. ISBN: 978-0-545-31772-6. YA.

Carlson, Drew. *Attack of the Turtle*. Eerdmans, 2007. ISBN: 978-0-8028-5308-0. Gr 4–6.

Cohen, Rich. *Alex and the Amazing Time Machine*. Holt, 2012. ISBN: 978-0-8050-9418-3. Gr 4–6.

Cohn, Rachel. *Very LeFreak*. Knopf, 2010. ISBN: 978-0-375-85758-4. YA.

Colfer, Eoin. *Airman*. Hyperion, 2008. ISBN: 978-1-4231-0750-7. YA.

Cusick, John M. *Girl Parts*. Candlewick, 2010. ISBN: 978-0-7636-4930-2. YA.

Doctorow, Cory. *Little Brother*. TOR, 2008. ISBN: 978-0-7653-1985-2. YA.

Gagnon, Michelle. *Don't Turn Around*. HarperCollins, 2012. ISBN: 978-0-06-21090-4. YA.

Grant, Michael. *BZRK*. Egmont, 2012. ISBN: 978-1-60684-312-3. YA.

Haseley, Dennis. *The Amazing Thinking Machine*. Dial, 2002. ISBN: 0-8037-2609-0. Gr 4–6.

Horowitz, Anthony. *Alex Rider: The Gadgets*. Philomel, 2006. ISBN: 0-399-24486-7. YA.

Houtman, Jacqueline. *The Reinvention of Edison Thomas*. Front, 2010. ISBN: 978-1-59078-708-3. Gr 4–6.

Jinks, Catherine. *Genius Squad*. Harcourt, 2008. ISBN: 978-0-05-205985-9. YA.

Jinks, Catherine. *The Paradise Trap*. Egmont, 2012. ISBN: 978-1-60684-273-7. Gr 4–6.

Karp, Jesse. *Those That Wake*. Harcourt, 2011. ISBN: 978-0-547-55311-5. YA.

Kincaid, S. J. *Insignia*. HarperCollins, 2012. ISBN: 978-0-06-209299-1. YA.

McGann, Oisin. *Daylight Runner*. HarperCollins, 2008. ISBN: 978-0-06-134058-1. YA.

Reeve, Philip. *A Web of Air*. Scholastic, 2011. ISBN: 978-0-545-22213-7. YA.

Reeve, Philip. *Fever Crumb*. Scholastic, 2010. ISBN: 978-0-545-20719-5. YA.

Reeve, Philip. *Scrivener's Moon*. Scholastic, 2012. ISBN: 978-0-545-22218-1. YA.

Seidler, Tor. *Brainboy and the Deathmaster*. HarperCollins, 2003. ISBN: 0-06-029182-6. Gr 4–6.

Selznick, Brian. *The Invention of Hugo Cabret*. Scholastic, 2007. ISBN: 978-0-439-81378-5. Gr 4–6.

Smibert, Angie. *The Forgetting Curve*. Cavendish, 2012. ISBN: 978-0-7614-6265-1. YA.

Teague, Mark. *The Doom Machine*. Scholastic, 2009. ISBN: 978-0-545-15142-9. Gr 4–6.

Walden, Mark. *H.I.V.E.: Zero Hour*. Simon and Schuster Children's Publishing, 2012. ISBN: 978-1-4422-2188-2. Gr 4–6.

Webb, Philip. *Six Days*. Scholastic, 2011. ISBN: 978-0-545-31767-2. Gr 4–6.

Westerfeld, Scott. *Behemoth*. Simon Pulse, 2010. ISBN: 978-1-4169-7175-7. YA.

Westerfeld, Scott. *The Manual of Aeronautics: An Illustrated Guide to the Leviathan Series*. Simon Pulse, 2012. ISBN: 978-1-4169-7179-5. YA.

Wolf, Allan. *The Watch That Ends the Night: Voices from the Titanic*. Candlewick, 2011. ISBN: 978-0-7636-3703-3. YA.

Young, E. L. *STORM: The Infinity Code*. Dial, 2008. ISBN: 978-0-8037-3265-0. Gr 4–6.

## INFORMATIONAL

Allen, Thomas B. *Mr. Lincoln's High-Tech War*. National Geographic Books, 2008. ISBN: 978-1-4263-0379-1. Gr 4–6.

Alvarez, Carlos. *AC-130H/U Gunships*. Children's Press, 2010. ISBN: 978-1-6001-4493-6. Gr 4–6.

Arato, Rona. *Design It! The Ordinary Things We Use Every Day and the Not-So-Ordinary Ways They Come to Be*. Tundra Paper, 2010. ISBN: 978-0-88776-846-0. Gr 4–6.

Becker, Helaine. *What's the Big Idea: Inventions That Changed Life on Earth*. Maple Tree, 2009. ISBN: 978-1-8973-4960-1. Gr 3–6.

Benoit, Peter. *The Hindenburg Disaster*. Children's Press, 2011. ISBN: 978-0-531-20626-3. Gr 3–5.

Bidner, Jenni. *The Kid's Guide to Digital Photography: How to Shoot, Save, Play with & Print Your Digital Photos*. Lark Books, 2004. ISBN: 1-57990-604-4. Gr 4 and up.

Blackburn, Ken. *Kids' Paper Air Plane Book*. Workman, 1996. ISBN: 978-0-7611-0478-0. Gr 2 and up.

Blumenthal, Karen. *Steve Jobs: The Man Who Thought Different*. Feiwel and Friends, 2012. ISBN: 978-1-2500-1557-0. Gr 7–10.

Bodden, Valerie. *Carousels*. Creative Education, 2012. ISBN: 978-1-6081-8112-4. Gr K–3.

Bortz, Fred. *Wonders of Space Technology*. Twenty-First Century, 2011. ISBN: 978-0-7613-5453-6. YA.

Bow, James. *Aston Martin*. Crabtree Publishing Company, 2012. ISBN: 978-0-7787-2099-7. Superstar Cars series.

Bridgman, Roger. *Electronics*. DK Children, 2000. ISBN: 978-0-7894-5598-7. Gr 4–6.

Briggs, Jason R. *Python for Kids: A Playful Introduction to Programming*. No Starch Press, 2012. ISBN: 978-1-5932-7407-8. Gr 5 and up.

Callery, Sean. *Victor Wouk: The Father of the Hybrid Car*. Crabtree Publishing Company, 2009. ISBN: 978-0-7787-4664-5. Gr 4 and up. Voices for Green Choices series.

Carter, David. *The Elements of Pop-Up: A Pop-Up Book for Aspiring Paper Engineers*. Scholastic, 1999. ISBN: 0-689-82224-3. Gr 4–7.

Cerullo, Mary M. *Shipwrecks: Exploring Sunken Cities Beneath the Sea*. Dutton, 2009. ISBN: 978-0-525-47968-0. Gr 5–8.

Claybourne, Anna. *Who Split the Atom?* Arcturus, 2010. ISBN: 978-1-84837-683-0. Gr 4–6.

Cooper. Ilene. *The Dead Sea Scrolls*. HarperCollins, 1997. ISBN: 0-688-14300-8. Gr 4–8.

DiPiazza, Francesca Davis. *Friend Me! 600 Years of Social Networking in America*. Twenty-First Century, 2012. ISBN: 978-0-7613-4607-4. Gr 5–8.

Egan, Erin. *Hottest Race Cars.* Enslow, 2007. ISBN: 978-0-7660-2871-5. Gr 4–6. Wild Wheels series.

Finkelstein, Norman H. *Three Across: The Great Transatlantic Air Race of 1927.* Boyds Mills, 2008. ISBN: 978-1-5907-8462-4. Gr 5–8.

Firestone, Mary. *Nintendo: The Company and Its Founders.* ABDO, 2011. ISBN: 978-1-61714-809-5. YA. Technology Pioneers series.

Gifford, Clive. *Things That Go.* Kingfisher, 2011. ISBN: 978-0-7534-6593-6. Gr 3–5.

Gigliotti, Jim. *Hottest Dragsters and Funny Cars.* Enslow Publishers, 2008. ISBN: 978-0-7660-2870-8. Gr 5–9. Wild Wheels series.

Goldfish, Meish. *Amazing Amusement Park Rides.* Bearport, 2011. ISBN: 978-1-6177-2304-9. Gr 1–5.

Goldfish, Meish. *Spectacular Skyscrapers.* Bearport, 2011. ISBN: 978-1-6177-2303-2. Gr 1–5.

Grabowski, John. *Television.* Lucent, 2011. ISBN: 978-1-4205-0169-8. YA.

Graham, Ian. *Amazing Stadiums.* Amicus, 2010. ISBN: 978-1-60753-131-9. Gr 5–7.

Graham, Ian. *Fabulous Bridges.* Amicus, 2010. ISBN: 978-1-60753-132-6. Gr 5–7.

Graham, Ian. *Robot Technology.* Smart Apple, 2011. ISBN: 978-1-59920-533-5. YA.

Gutelle, Andrew. *Stock Car Kings.* Penguin Group, 2001. ISBN: 978-0-44842-4897. Gr 2–3. All Aboard Reading series.

Jackson, Kay. *Navy Submarines in Action.* PowerKids Press, 2009. ISBN: 978-1-4358-2751-6. Gr 2 and up.

Josefowicz, Chris. *Video Game Developer.* Gareth Stevens, 2010. ISBN: 978-1-4339-1958-9. Gr 4–6. Cool Careers: Cutting Edge series.

Hamen, Susan E. *Google: The Company and Its Founders.* ABDO, 2011. ISBN: 978-1-61714-808-8. YA. Technology Pioneers series.

Hillstrom, Laurie Collier. *Global Positioning Systems.* Lucent, 2011. ISBN: 978-1-4205-0325-8. YA. Technology 360 series.

Kent, Peter. *Technology.* Kingfisher, 2009. ISBN: 978-0-7534-6307-9. Gr 4–7.

Kinney, Jeff. *The Wimpy Kid Movie Diary: How Greg Heffley Went Hollywood.* Abrams, 2010. ISBN: 978-0-8109-9616-8. Gr 4–8.

Laroche, Giles. *What's Inside?* Houghton Mifflin Books for Children, 2009. ISBN: 978-0-618-86247-4. Gr 1–4.

Lee, Dora. *Biomimicry: Inventions Inspired by Nature*. Kids Can, 2011. ISBN: 978-1-55453-467-8. Gr 3–6.

Macaulay, David with Sheila Keenan. *Castle: How It Works*. Square Fish, 2012. ISBN: 978-1-5964-3744-9. Gr 2–3.

Macaulay, David with Sheila Keenan. *Built to Last*. HMH Books for Young Readers, 2010. ISBN: 978-0-5473-4240-5. Gr 5 and up.

Mann, Elizabeth. *The Brooklyn Bridge*. Mikaya, 2006. ISBN: 0-9650493-0-2. Gr 4–6.

McClafferty, Carla Kilough. *Tech Titans: One Frontier, Six Bios*. Scholastic Paper, 2012. ISBN: 978-0-5453-6577-2. Gr 5–7.

McKendry, Joe. *Beneath the Streets of Boston: Building America's First Subway*. Godine, 2005. ISBN: 1-56792-284-8. Gr 4–6.

Mills, J. Elizabeth. *Creating Content: Maximizing Wikis, Widgets, Blogs, and More*. The Rosen Publishing Company, 2011. ISBN: 978-1-4488-1322-3. YA.

Mitchell, Don. *Driven: A Photobiography of Henry Ford*. National Geographic, 2010. ISBN: 978-1-4263-0155-1. Gr 4–7.

Mitchell, Susan K. *Spy Tech: Digital Dangers*. Enslow, 2011. ISBN: 978-0-7660-3712-0. Gr 4–6.

Mooney, Carla. *The Industrial Revolution: Investigate How Science and Technology Changed the World with 25 Projects*. Nomad, 2011. ISBN: 978-1-9363-1381-5. Gr 4–7.

Mooney, Carla. *Pilotless Planes*. Norwood, 2010. ISBN: 978-1-59953-381-0. Gr 5–7.

O'Neill, Joseph. *Movie Director*. Cherry Lake Publishing, 2010. ISBN: 978-1-60279-499-3. YA. New Technology series.

Oxlade, Chris. *Gaming Technology*. Smart Apple, 2011. ISBN: 978-1-59920-531-1. YA.

Pollack, Pam. *Who Was Steve Jobs?* Grosset & Dunlap, 2012. ISBN: 978-0-4484-7940-8. Gr 3 and up. Who Was . . .? series.

Ross, Stewart. *Sports Technology*. Smart Apple, 2011. ISBN: 978-1-59920-534-2. YA

Rubalcaba, Jill. *I. M. Pei: Architect of Time, Space, and Purpose*. Marshall Cavendish, 2011. ISBN: 978-0-7614-5973-6. YA.

Samuels, Charlie. *The Rise of Industry (1700–1800)*. Gareth Stevens Publishing, 2011. ISBN: 978-1-4339-4145-0. YA. Science Highlights series.

Shea, Therese. *Robotics Club: Teaming Up to Build Robots*. The Rosen Publishing Group, 2011. ISBN: 978-1-4488-1237-0. Gr 5 and up. Robotics series.

Sobey, Ed. *The Motorboat Book: Build & Launch 20 Jet Boats, Paddle Wheelers, Electric Submarines & More*. Chicago Review Press, 2013. ISBN: 978-1-6137-4447-5. Gr 4 and up.

Sobey, Ed. *Robot Experiments*. Enslow, 2011. ISBN: 978-0-7660-3303-0. YA. Cool Science Projects with Technology series.

Steele. Philip. *Trains: The Slide-out, See-Through Story of World-Famous Trains and Railroads*. Kingfisher, 2010. ISBN: 978-0-7534-6465-6. Gr K–6.

Sullivan, George. *Built to Last: Building America's Amazing Bridges, Dams, Tunnels, and Skyscrapers*. Scholastic Nonfiction, 2005. ISBN: 0-439-51737-0. Gr 4–7.

Swanson, Jennifer. *How Hybrid Cars Work*. Child's World, 2011. ISBN: 978-1-6097-3217-2. Gr 4–6.

The LEAD Project. *Super Scratch Programming Adventure: Learn to Program by Making Cool Games*. No Starch Press, 2012. ISBN: 978-1-5932-7409-2. YA.

Venezia, Mike. *Steve Jobs and Steve Wozniak: Geek Heroes Who Put the Personal in Computers*. Scholastic, 2010. ISBN: 978-0-531-23730-4. Gr 2–4.

Verstraete, Larry. *Surviving the Hindenburg*. Sleeping Bear, 2012. ISBN: 978-1-5836-6787-0. Gr 1–4.

Weitzman, David. *Skywalkers: Mohawk Ironworkers Build the City*. Flash Point, 2010. ISBN: 978-1-5964-3162-1. Gr 4–7.

Woods, Michael. *Ancients Machine Technology: From Wheels to Forges*. Twenty-First Century, 2011. ISBN: 978-0-7913-6523-5. YA. Technology in Ancient Cultures series.

Wyckoff, Edwin Brit. *The Guy Who Invented Home Video Games: Ralph Baer and His Awesome Invention*. Enslow, 2010. ISBN: 978-0-7660-3450-1. Gr 3–5.

Zaunders, Bo. *Feathers, Flaps, and Flops: Fabulous Early Fliers*. Dutton, 2001. ISBN: 0-525-46466-2. Gr 4–6.

## PICTURE BOOKS

Ammon, Richard. *Conestoga Wagons*. Holiday, 2000. ISBN: 0-8234-1475-2. Gr K–3.

Baker, Keith. *On the Go with Mr. and Mrs. Green*. Harcourt, 2006. ISBN: 0-15-205762-5. Gr K–3.

Buller, Don Hillestad. *F Is for Firefighting*. Pelican, 2007. ISBN: 978-1-58980-420-3. Gr K–3.

Cordell, Matthew. *Hello! Hello!* Hyperion, 2012. ISBN: 978-1-4231-5906-3. Gr K–3.

Dodds, Dayle Ann. *Henry's Amazing Machine*. Farrar, 2004. ISBN: 0-374-32953-2. Gr K–3.

Fleming, Candace. *Papa's Mechanical Fish*. Margaret Ferguson, 2013. ISBN: 978-0-374-39908-5. Gr 2–4.

Gall, Chris. *Awesome Dawson*. Little, Brown and Company, 2013. ISBN: 978-0-3162-1330-1. Gr PK–1.

Garland, Sarah. *Eddie's Toolbox and How to Make and Mend Things*. Frances Lincoln Children's Books, 2010. ISBN: 978-1-84780-053-4. Gr PK–2.

Geisert, Arthur. *Lights Out*. Houghton, 2005. ISBN: 0-618-47892-2. Gr K–3.

Glover, David. *Pulleys and Gears*. Heinemann, 2006. ISBN: 1-4034-8564-X. Gr K–3. Simple Machines series.

Griffith, Victoria. *The Fabulous Flying Machines of Alberto Santos-Dumont*. Abrams, 2011. ISBN: 978-1-4197-0011-8. Gr K–3.

Jungman, Ann. *The Most Magnificent Mosque*. Frances Children's Books, 2007. ISBN: 978-1-8450-7085-4. Gr 1–4.

Kamkwamba, William. *The Boy Who Harnessed the Wind: Young Readers Edition*. Dial, 2012. ISBN: 978-0-8037-3511-8. Gr 1 and up.

Kulling, Monica. *Going Up!: Elisha Otis's Trip to the Top*. Tundra, 2012. ISBN: 978-1-77049-240-0. Gr K–3.

Laroche, Giles. *If You Lived Here: Houses of the World*. Houghton Mifflin, 2011. ISBN: 978-0-547-23892-0. Gr K–3.

Lord, Cynthia. *Hot Rod Hamster*. Scholastic Press, 2010. ISBN: 978-0-545-03530-9. Gr PK–1.

Low, William. *Machines Go to Work in the City*. Holt, 2012. ISBN: 978-0-8050-9050-5. Gr PK–1.

Masiello, Ralph. *Ralph Masiello's Robot Drawing Book*. Charlesbridge, 2011. ISBN: 978-1-57091-536-9. Gr K–3.

Mezzanotte, Jim. *Giant Bulldozers*. Gareth, 2005. ISBN: 0-8368-4910-8. Gr K–3. Giant Vehicles series.

O'Brien, Patrick. *Steam, Smoke, and Steel: Back in Time with Trains*. Charlesbridge, 2000. ISBN: 0-88106-972-8. Gr K–3.

O'Brien, Patrick. *The Hindenburg*. Holt, 2000. ISBN: 0-8050-6415-X. Gr K–3.

O'Sullivan, Robyn. *The Wright Brothers Fly*. National Geographic Books, 2007. ISBN: 978-1-4263-0188-9. Gr K–3.

Oxlade, Chris. *Flight*. Kingfisher, 2012. ISBN: 987-0-7534-6881-4. Gr K–3.

Rinker, Sherri Duskey. *Goodnight, Goodnight Construction Site*. Chronicle Books, 2011. ISBN: 978-0-8118-7782-4. Gr K–2.

Rubin, Adam. *Those Darn Squirrels Fly South*. Clarion, 2012. ISBN: 978-0-547-67823-8. Gr K–3.

Sarcone-Roach, Julia. *Subway Story*. Knopf, 2011. ISBN: 978-0-375-85859-8. Gr 1–3.

Simon, Seymour. *Out of Sight: Pictures of Hidden Worlds*. North-South, 2000. ISBN: 1-58717-011-6. Gr K–3.

Smith, Lane. *It's a Book*. Roaring Brook, 2010. ISBN: 978-1-59643-606-0. Gr K–3.

Sobel, June. *B Is for Bulldozer: A Construction ABC*. Sandpiper, 2006. ISBN: 0-1520-2250-3. Gr K and up.

Sutton, Sally. *Demolition*. Candlewick Press, 2012. ISBN: 978-0-7636-5830-4. Gr PK–2.

Tanaka, Shelley. *New Dinos: The Latest Finds! The Coolest Dinosaur Discoveries*. Simon & Schuster, 2003. ISBN: 0-689-85183-9. Gr K–3.

Tougas, Chris. *Mechanimals*. Orca, 2007. ISBN: 978-1-55143-628-9. Gr K–3.

Walker, Sally M. *Investigating Electricity*. Lerner, 2011. ISBN: 978-0-7613-5772-8. Gr K–3. How Does Energy Work series.

Williams, Treat. *Air Show*. Hyperion, 2010. ISBN: 978-1-4231-1185-6. Gr PK–2.

## ANNOTATED PROFESSIONAL BOOK

Beers, Kylene and Robert Probst. *Notice & Note: Strategies for Close Reading*. Heinemann, 2013.

> The first part of the book is organized by questions. What is the role of talk, what is close reading, do text-dependent questions foster engagement, must everyone read the same book, how does one judge complexity of the text, and are we creating life-long learners? The second part describes the signposts found: notices and notes—the important book features and characteristics such as contrasts and contradictions, aha moments, tough questions, words of the wiser, again and again, and memory moments. The reader must not only notice and question the signposts they find as they read independently but they also need to learn from them.

# Chapter 16

# NATURE, ENVIRONMENT, AND ANIMALS

The environment and nature, including animals and natural resources, have always held a strong interest for boys. They are fascinated by such things as global warming and climate change and the aftereffects. The plight of endangered species in nature and the importance of sustainable fuels for the future are also compelling topics. Boys might have close encounters with nature when hiking and camping and turn to books for additional information. Books offer an endless supply of facts and pictures that help boys find answers and get involved!

## FEATURED AUTHORS

Name: Steve Jenkins

Birth date: 1952

Place of Birth: Hickory, North Carolina

Most popular book(s): *The Beetle Book, Animals Upside Down, Animals in Flight*

About: Jenkins's father was in the military and the family moved often. As a child he kept a small menagerie of lizards, turtles, spiders, and other animals. He collected rocks and fossils and blew up things in his small chemistry lab. He went to school to study graphic design and eventually opened his own graphic design business.

Web site: http://www.stevejenkinsbooks.com

Name: Jim Arnosky

Birth date: September 1, 1946

Place of Birth: New York City, New York

Most popular book(s): *Thunder Birds, Monster Hunt*

About: Arnosky has written and illustrated 86 books on nature subjects and has illustrated 46 other books written by various authors. Jim loves to fish, boat, and play his guitar.

Web site: http://www.jimarnosky.com

## ANNOTATIONS

Arnosky, Jim. *Shimmer & Splash: The Sparkling World of Sea Life*. Sterling Children's Books, 2013. ISBN: 978-1-4027-8623-5.

The featured sea life can be seen in the shallow waters near the beach or in the deep water offshore. There are several foldout pages that accompany the text, which detail almost 200 sea creatures and many are painted life size.

Bauer, Michael Gerard. *Just a Dog*. Scholastic, Inc., 2010. ISBN: 978-0-5453-7452-1.

Mister Mosely was never just a dog; he was Corey's entire world from puppyhood until he passed one night. Each chapter tells a unique story about Mister Mosely, the one trick he could perform, his fears, and how patient and kind he was with Corey's younger sister. Mister Mosely also taught Corey one trick: how to wait. "Wait for stuff to happen or stop happening, for things to heal up and get better . . ."

Berger, Lee R. and Marc Aronson. *The Skull in the Rock: How a Scientist, a Boy, and Google Earth Opened a New Window on Human Origins*. National Geographic, 2012. ISBN: 978-1-4263-1010-2.

In August 2008, on a fossil-hunting mission, a boy, Matthew Berger, and his scientist dad, Dr. Lee Berger, made an amazing discovery. They were near Johannesburg, South Africa, with their two Rhodesian ridgebacks. Matthew found a fossil of a clavicle from a young male about 11 to 13 years old. Using Google Earth, Lee discovered interesting features of the area where the clavicle was found, which led to further discoveries. Fantastic photographs and a companion web site, www.scimania.org, make this a great read for future archeologists!

Gregory, Josh. *The Superstorm: Hurricane Sandy*. Scholastic, Inc., 2013. ISBN: 978-0-531-23751-9.

A timeline, track, and photos of Hurricane Sandy as it made its way out at sea along the coast and then headed west and made landfall October 29, 2012, with 80 mile-per-hour winds. It was dubbed a superstorm because powerful winds extended 420 miles from its center. The damage caused by Hurricane Sandy is estimated to be $25 billion.

Jenkins, Steve. *The Beetle Book*. Houghton Mifflin Books for Children, 2012. ISBN: 978-0-547-68084-2.

There are over 350,000 different kinds of beetles. One out of every four plants and animals on our earth is a beetle. Beetles are insects and most of them share the same basic blueprint. Colorful, detailed illustrations accompany the descriptions of the life of the beetle and what makes it special.

*National Geographic Kids World Atlas*. National Geographic, 2013. ISBN: 978-1-4263-1403-2.

   The *World Atlas* is divided by continents represented by a color that include maps of the regions, illustrations, photographs, charts, and basic facts. Explore or browse places in the world, oceans, flags, or statistics, and geo facts and figures. Download the free NG Kids scanner app for digital extras.

Strauss, Rochelle. *Tree of Life: The Incredible Biodiversity of Life on Earth*. Kids Can Press, 2013. ISBN: 978-1-55453-961-1.

   Scientists have discovered and named 1,750,000 different species, and a problem with one may affect all other species. Life can be divided into five branches or kingdoms, and they are all related, some closely and others more distantly. Each kingdom is discussed, along with changes to the tree of life, some species at risk, and becoming guardians of the tree of life.

## READ ALOUD

Carnesi, Monica. *Little Lost Dog: The True Story of a Brave Dog Named Baltic*. Nancy Paulsen Books, 2012. ISBN: 978-0-3992-5666-0.

French, Vivian. *T. Rex*. Candlewick Press, 2004. ISBN: 978-0-7636-3999-0.

Hoose, Phillip. *Moonbird: A Year on the Wind with the Great Survivor B95*. Farrar. 2012. ISBN: 978-0374304683.

Jenkins, Martin. *Can We Save the Tiger?* Candlewick, 2011. ISBN: 978-0-7636-4909-8.

*National Geographic Kids Ultimate Weird but True 2*. National Geographic Society, 2013. ISBN: 978-1-4263-1358-5.

## BIBLIOGRAPHY

Applegate, Katherine. *The One and Only Ivan*. HarperCollins, 2012. ISBN: 978-0-0619-9225-4. Gr 3 and up.

Bauer, Michael Gerard. *Just a Dog*. Scholastic Press, 2010. ISBN: 978-0-545-37452-1. Gr 3–5.

Bodeen, S. A. *The Compound*. Feiwel, 2008. ISBN: 978-0-312-37015-2. YA.

Bradman, Tony, ed. *Under the Weather: Stories About Climate Change*. Candlewick, 2010. ISBN: 978-1-84507-930-7. Gr 4–7.

Broach, Elise. *Masterpiece*. Holt, 2008. ISBN: 978-0-8050-8270-8. Gr 4–6.

Byars, Betsy. *Tornado*. Perfection Learning, 1997. ISBN: 978-0-7807-6962-5. Gr 3–5.

Connor, Leslie. *Crunch*. HarperCollins, 2010. ISBN: 978-0-06-169229-1. Gr 4–6.

Cooling, Wendy. *All the Wild Wonders: Poems of Our Earth*. Frances Lincoln, 2010. ISBN: 978-1-84780-073-2. Gr 2–5.

Crossan, Sarah. *Breathe*. HarperCollins, 2012. ISBN: 978-0-06-211869-1. YA.

Gipson, Fred. *Old Yeller*. Perennial Modern Classics, 2009. ISBN: 978-0-5900-2310-8. Gr 5 and up. Classic.

Hiaasen, Carl. *Chomp*. Knopf, 2012. ISBN: 978-0-375-86842-9. Gr 4–6.

Hiaasen, Carl. *Flush*. Knopf, 2005. ISBN: 0-375-82182-1. Gr 5 and up.

Hobbs, Will. *The Maze*. Morrow, 1998. ISBN: 0-688-15092-6. Gr 6 and up.

Hunter, Erin. *Survivors: The Empty City*. Harper, 2012. ISBN: 978-0-06-210256-0. Gr 3–7.

Ibbotson, Eva. *One Dog and His Boy*. Scholastic, 2012. ISBN: 978-0-5453-5196-6. Gr 3–6.

Jennings, Patrick. *Guinea Dog*. Egmont, 2010. ISBN: 978-1-60684-053-5. Gr 3–5.

Kehret, Peg. *Ghost Dog Secrets*. Dutton, 2010. ISBN: 978-0-525-42178-8. Gr 5–7.

Korman, Gordon. *Showoff*. Scholastic, 2012. ISBN: 978-0-545-32059-7. Gr 3–6.

Kurtz, Chris. *The Adventures of South Pole Pig: A Novel of Snow and Courage*. Harcourt Children's Books, 2013. ISBN: 978-0-5476-3455-5. Gr 4–7.

Laybourne, Emmy. *Monument 14: Sky on Fire*. Feiwel, 2013. ISBN: 978-0-312-56904-4. YA.

Lloyd, Saci. *Momentum*. Holiday, 2012. ISBN: 978-0-8234-2414-6. YA.

London, Jack. *The Call of the Wild*. Simon & Brow, 2013. ISBN: 978-1-6138-2349-1. Gr 5 and up.

Paley, Jane. *Hooper Finds a Family: A Hurricane Katrina Dog's Survival Tale*. HarperCollins, 2011. ISBN: 978-0-06-201103-9. Gr 3–7.

Rawls, Wilson. *Where the Red Fern Grows*. Random House Children's Books, 1961. ISBN: 978-0-5532-7429-5. Gr 3–7.

Sidman, Joyce. *Dark Emperor and Other Poems of the Night*. Houghton Mifflin, 2010. ISBN: 978-0-547-15228-8. Gr 3–6.

Tellegen, Toon. *Far Away Across the Sea*. Boxer, 2010. ISBN: 978-1-907152-37-5. Gr K–4.

Vacco, Corina. *My Chemical Mountain*. Delacorte, 2013. ISBN: 978-0-385-74242-9. YA.

## INFORMATIONAL

Alderfer, Jonathan. *National Geographic Kids Bird Guide of North America: The Best Birding Book for Kids from National Geographic's Bird Experts*. National Geographic Children's Books, 2013. ISBN: 978-1-4263-1094-2. Gr 2–4.

Arnosky, Jim. *Thunder Birds: Nature's Flying Predators*. Sterling, 2011. ISBN: 978-1-4027-5661-0. Gr 4–6.

Bang, Molly and Penny Chisholm. *Ocean Sunlight: How Tiny Plants Feed the Seas*. Blue Sky, 2012. ISBN: 978-0-5452-7322-0. Gr K–3.

Barr, Brady. *Crocodile Encounters: and More True Stories of Adventures with Animals*. National Geographic Children's Books, 2012. ISBN: 978-1-4263-1028-5. Gr 2–5. National Geographic Kids Chapters series.

Becker, Helaine. *The Big Green Book of the Big Blue Sea*. Kids Can, 2012. ISBN: 978-1-55453-746-4. Gr 4–6.

Benoit, Peter. *The BP Oil Spill*. Children's Press, 2011. ISBN: 978-0-531-28999-0. Gr 3–5.

Bishop, Nic. *Spiders*. Scholastic Nonfiction, 2007. ISBN: 978-0-4398-7756-5. Gr 6–8.

Bryson, Bill. *A Really Short History of Nearly Everything*. Delacorte, 2009. ISBN: 978-0-385-73810-1. Gr 5–8.

Burnie, David. *How Animals Work: Why and How Animals Do the Things They Do*. DK, 2010. ISBN: 978-0-7566-5897-7. Gr 5 and up.

Caduto, Michael J. *Catch the Wind, Harness the Sun: 22 Super-Charged Science Projects for Kids*. Storey, 2011. ISBN: 978-1-60342-794-4. Gr 5–8.

Carson, Mary Kay. *Inside Hurricanes*. Sterling, 2010. ISBN: 978-1-4027-5880-5. Gr 3–6.

Carson, Mary Kay. *Inside Tornadoes*. Sterling, 2010. ISBN: 978-1-4027-5879-9. Gr 4–6.

Cate, Annette LeBlanc. *Look Up! Bird-Watching in Your Own Backyard*. Candlewick Press, 2013. ISBN: 978-0-7636-4561-8. Gr 3–7.

Chin, Jason. *Island: A Story of the Galapagos*. Roaring Brook, 2012. ISBN: 978-1-5964-3716-6. Gr K–4.

Clark, Willow. *Green Tree Pythons*. PowerKids Press, 2012. ISBN: 978-1-4488-6187-3. Gr 1 and up.

Cole, Joanna. *The Magic School Bus and the Climate Change*. Scholastic, 2010. ISBN: 978-0-590-10826-3. Gr K–3.

Connolly, Sean. *The Book of Potentially Catastrophic Science: 50 Experiments for Daring Young Scientists*. Workman, 2010. ISBN: 978-0-7611-5687-1. Gr 5–8.

Corwin, Jeff. *Jeff Corwin: A Wild Life: The Authorized Biography*. Puffin Paper, 2009. ISBN: 978-0-14-241403-3. Gr 4–8.

Davies, Nicola. *Poop: A Natural History of the Unmentionable*. Candlewick, 2004. ISBN: 978-0-7636-3437-8. Gr 3–5.

Davies, Nicola. *Talk, Talk, Squawk!* Candlewick, 2011. ISBN: 978-0-7636-5088-9. Gr 3–5.

Esbaum, Jill. *Angry Birds Playground: Animals: An Around-the-World Habitat Adventure*. National Geographic Children's Books, 2012. ISBN: 978-1-4263-1266-3. Gr K–3.

Fradin, Judith Bloom. *Tornado! The Story Behind These Twisting, Turning, Spinning and Spiraling Storms*. National Geographic, 2011. ISBN: 978-1-4263-0779-9. Gr 4–6.

*Friends of the Earth: A History of American Environmentalism with 21 Activities*. Chicago Review Press, 2013. ISBN: 978-1-5697-6718-1. Gr 4–8.

Frydenborg, Kay. *Wild Horse Scientists*. Houghton, 2012. ISBN: 978-0-5475-1831-2. Gr. 7–9.

George, Jean Craighead. *The Wolves Are Back*. Dutton, 2008. ISBN: 978-0-525-47947-5. Gr K–3.

Gerstein, Mordicai. *The Camping Trip That Changed America: Theodore Roosevelt, John Muir, and Our National Parks*. Dial Books, 2012. ISBN: 978-0-8037-3710-5. Gr 1–3.

Gish, Melissa. *Zebras*. Creative Education, 2013. ISBN: 978-1-60818-173-3. Gr 5 and up. Living Wild series.

Grubman, Steve. *Orangutans Are Ticklish: Fun Facts from an Animal Photographer*. Random House, 2010. ISBN: 978-0-375-85886-4. Gr 2–4.

Gutman, Dan, editor. *Recycle This Book: 100 Top Children's Book Authors Tell You How to Go Green*. Random House paper, 2009. ISBN: 978-0-385-73721-0. Gr 5–9.

Haas, Robert. *I Dreamed of Flying Like a Bird: My Adventures Photographing Wild Animals from a Helicopter*. National Geographic Children's Books, 2010. ISBN: 978-1-4263-0693-8. Gr 6 and up.

Halls, Kelly Milner. *Saving the Baghdad Zoo: A True Story of Hope and Heroes*. Greenwillow Books, 2009. ISBN: 978-0-06-177202-3. Gr 6–9.

Hearst, Michael. *Unusual Creatures: A Mostly Accurate Account of Some of Earth's Strangest Animals*. Chronicle Books, 2012. ISBN: 978-1-4521-0467-6. Gr 3 and up.

Hirsch, Rebecca E. *Protecting Our Natural Resources.* Cherry Lake, 2010. ISBN: 978-1-60279-661-4. Gr 3–7.

Jenkins, Steve. *The Animal Book: A Collection of the Fastest, Fiercest, Toughest, Cleverest, Shyest—and Most Surprising.* HMH Books for Young Readers, 2013. ISBN: 978-0-5475-5799-1. Gr 1–4.

Johnson, J. Angelique. *The Eco-Student's Guide to Being Green at School.* Picture Window, 2010. ISBN: 978-1-4048-6027-8. Gr 2–4.

Johnson, Jinny. *Polar Sea Life.* Smart Apple, 2011. ISBN: 978-1-59920-505-2. Gr 4–6. Watery Worlds series.

Johnson, Rebecca L. *Zombie Makers: True Stories of Nature's Undead.* Millbrook Press, 2012. ISBN: 978-0-7613-8633-9. Gr 5–8.

Kainen, Dan and Carol Kaufmann. *Safari: A Photicular Book.* Workman Publishing, 2012. ISBN: 978-0-7611-6380-0. All ages.

Kent, Peter. *Peter Kent's City Across Time: From the Stone Age to the Distant Future.* Kingfisher, 2010. ISBN: 978-0-7534-6400-7. Gr 2–4.

Kirk, Ellen. *Human Footprint.* National Geographic Paper, 2011. ISBN: 978-1-4263-0767-6. Gr 3–7.

Kosara, Tori. *Hibernation.* Scholastic Inc., 2011. ISBN: 978-0-545-36582-6. Gr 2–3.

Kurlansky, Mark. *World Without Fish.* Workman, 2011. ISBN: 978-0-7611-5607-9. YA.

Landau, Elaine. *Oil Spill! Disaster in the Gulf of Mexico.* Millbrook, 2011. ISBN: 978-0-7613-7485-5. Gr 3–5.

Lasky, Kathryn. *John Muir: America's First Environmentalist.* Candlewick, 2006. ISBN: 0-7636-1957-4. Gr 4–6.

Marsh, Laura. *Weird Sea Creatures.* National Geographic, 2012. ISBN: 978-1-4263-1048-5. Gr K–2.

Marsh, Laura. *Amazing Animal Journeys.* National Geographic, 2010. ISBN: 978-1-4263-0742-3. Gr 2–4.

McAllister, Ian. *The Sea Wolves: Living Wild in the Great Bear Rainforest.* Orca Books, 2010. ISBN: 978-1-5546-9206-4. Gr 6–9.

McGinty, Alice B. *Darwin.* Houghton, 2009. ISBN: 978-0-618-99531-8. Gr 4–6.

McLeish, Ewan. *Population Explosion.* Rosen, 2010. ISBN: 978-1-4358-5356-0. Gr 4–8.

Miller, Debbie S. *Survival at 40 Below*. Walker, 2010. ISBN: 978-0-8027-9816-9. Gr 2–4.

Minden, Cecilia. *Reduce, Reuse, and Recycle*. Cherry Lake, 2010. ISBN: 978-1-60279-662-1. Gr 3–7.

*Monkeys*. DK Publishing, 2012. ISBN: 978-0-7566-9277-3. Gr PK.

Montgomery, Sy. *Saving the Ghost of the Mountain: An Expedition Among Snow Leopards in Mongolia*. Houghton, 2009. ISBN: 978-0-628-91645-0. Gr 4–6.

Montgomery, Sy *Kakapo Rescue: Saving the World's Strangest Parrot*. Houghton Mifflin Books for Children, 2010. ISBN: 978-0-6184-9417-0. Gr 6–12.

Montgomery, Sy *The Tapir Scientist: Saving South America's Largest Mammal*. Houghton Mifflin Books for Children, 2013. ISBN: 978-0-5478-1548-0. Gr 3 and up.

Munro, Roxie. *EcoMazes: Twelve Earth Adventures*. Sterling, 2010. ISBN: 978-1-4027-6393-9. Gr 1–3.

Newman, Aline Alexander. *National Geographic Kids Chapters: Ape Escapes!: and More True Stories of Animals Behaving Badly*. National Geographic Children's Books, 2012. ISBN: 978-1-4263-0936-6. Gr 2–5.

Nivola, Claire A. *Life in the Ocean: The Story of Oceanographer Sylvia Earle*. Farrar, Straus & Giroux, 2012. ISBN: 978-0-3743-8068-7. Gr. K–3.

O'Connell, Caitlin. *The Elephant Scientist*. Houghton Mifflin Books for Children, 2011. ISBN: 978-0-5470-5344-8. Gr 5 and up.

Patent, Dorothy Hinshaw. *The Horse and the Plains Indians: a Powerful Partnership*. Clarion Books, 2012. ISBN: 978-0-547-12551-0. Gr 4–6.

Patent, Dorothy Hinshaw. *Dogs on Duty*. Walker, 2012. ISBN: 978-0-8027-2845-6. Gr 2 and up.

Phillips, Dee. *Groundhog's Burrow*. Bearport Publishing, 2012. ISBN: 978-1-6177-2410-7. Gr 1–3.

Pringle, Laurence. *Billions of Years, Amazing Changes: The Story of Evolution*. Boyds Mills Press, 2011. ISBN: 978-1-5907-8723-6. Gr 3 and up.

Richardson, Gillian. *Kaboom! Explosions of All Kinds*. Annick, 2009. ISBN: 978-1-55451-204-1. Gr 4–7.

Salisbury, Graham. *Night of the Howling Dogs*. Random, 2007. ISBN: 978-0-385-73122-5. Gr 4–6.

Sayre, April Pulley. *Here Comes the Humpbacks*. Charlesbridge, 2013. ISBN: 978-1-58089-405-0. Gr K–3.

Schwartz, David M. *What in the Wild? Mysteries of Nature Concealed . . . and Revealed.* Tricycle, 2010. ISBN: 978-1-58246-310-0. Gr 2–4.

Simon, Seymour. *Global Warming.* HarperCollins, 2010. ISBN: 978-0-06-114251-2. Gr 3–5.

Simon, Seymour. *Seymour Simon's Extreme Earth Records.* Chronicle Books, 2012. ISBN: 978-1-4521-0785-1. Gr 1–4.

Smith, Miranda. *Sharks.* Kingfisher Paper, 2010. ISBN: 978-0-7534-6405-2. Gr 4–7.

Spangler, Steve. *Naked Eggs and Flying Potatoes: Unforgettable Experiments That Make Science Fun.* Greenleaf paper, 2010. ISBN: 978-1-6083-2060-8. Gr 3–6.

Stewart, Melissa. *Inside Earthquakes.* Sterling, 2011. ISBN: 978-1-4027-5877-5. Gr 5–8.

Suzuki, David. *You Are the Earth: Know Your World So You Can Help Make It Better.* Greystone Paper, 2011. ISBN: 978-1-55365-476-6. Gr 4–8.

Thomas, Keltie. *Animals That Changed the World.* Annick, 2010. ISBN: 978-1-55451-242-3. Gr 4–8.

Turner, Pamela S. *A Life in the Wild: George Shaller's Struggle to Save the Last Great Beasts.* Farrar, Straus and Giroux, 2008. ISBN: 978-0-3743-4578-5. Gr 6–9.

Webb, Barbara L. *What Does Green Mean?* Rourke Paper, 2011. ISBN: 978-1-6174-1973-7. Gr 1–3.

Winter, Jonah. *Here Comes the Garbage Barge!* Random House, 2010. ISBN: 978-0-375-95218-0. Gr 1–3.

Yezerski, Thomas F. *Meadowlands: A Wetland Survival Story.* Farrar, Straus and Giroux, 2011. ISBN: 978-0-3743-4913-4. Gr K–3.

## PICTURE BOOKS

Agee, Jon. *My Rhinoceros.* Scholastic 2011. ISBN: 978-0-545-29441-6. Gr PK–2.

Arnold, Caroline. *A Warmer World: From Polar Bears to Butterflies. How Climate Change Affects Wildlife.* Charlesbridge, 2012. ISBN: 978-1-5808-9266-7. Gr 3–7.

Arnosky, Jim. *At This Very Moment.* Dutton, 2011. ISBN: 978-0-525-42252-5. Gr PK–3.

Arnosky, Jim. *Slow Down for Manatees.* Putnam, 2010. ISBN: 978-0399-24170-3. Gr 1–3.

Belton, Robyn. *Herbert: The True Story of a Brave Sea Dog.* Candlewick, 2010. ISBN: 978-0-7636-4741-4. Gr PK–2.

Berk, Ari. *Nightsong.* Simon and Schuster Books for Young Readers, 2012. ISBN: 978-1-4169-7886-2. Gr K and up.

Bingham, Kelly. *Z Is for Moose*. Greenwillow Books, 2012. ISBN: 978-0-0607-9984-7. Gr K and up.

Bishop, Nic. *Lizards*. Scholastic, 2010. ISBN: 978-0-545-20634-1. Gr 2–4.

Blake, Robert J. *Painter and Ugly*. Philomel, 2011. ISBN: 978-0-399-24323-3. Gr K–3.

Campbell, Eileen. *Charlie and Kiwi: An Evolutionary Adventure*. Atheneum, 2011. ISBN: 978-1-4424-2112-7. Gr K–3.

Chin, Jason. *Redwoods*. Roaring Brook Press, 2009. ISBN: 978-1-59643-430-1. Gr PK–3.

Cole, Joanna. *The Magic School Bus and the Climate Change*. Scholastic, 2010. ISBN: 978-0-590-10826-3. Gr 2–4.

Crump, Marty. *Mysteries of the Komodo Dragon: The Biggest, Deadliest Lizard Gives Up Its Secrets*. Boyd Mills, 2010. ISBN: 978-1-5907-8757-1. Gr 3–5.

de la Bedoyere, Camilla. *100 Things You Should Know About Nocturnal Animals*. Mason Crest, 2009. ISBN: 978-1-4222-1523-4. Gr 4–6. Remarkable Man and Beast: Facing Survival series.

Ehlert, Lois. *RRRalph*. Simon & Schuster, 2011. ISBN: 978-1-4424-1305-4. Gr PK–3.

Fogliano, Julie. *And Then It's Spring*. Roaring Brook, 2012. ISBN: 978-1-5964-3624-4. Gr PK–2.

Fogliano, Julie. *If You Want to See a Whale*. Roaring Brook Press, 2013. ISBN: 978-1-5964-3731-9. Gr PS-2.

Fox, Mem. *Two Little Monkeys*. Simon & Schuster, 2012. ISBN: 978-1-4169-8687-4. Gr PK-K.

French, Vivian. *Yucky Worms*. Candlewick Press, 2010. ISBN: 978-0-7636-4446-8. Gr K–3.

Hamilton, Sue. *Attacked by a Crocodile*. ABDO, 2010. ISBN: 978-1-60453-929-5. Gr 4–7. Close Encounters of the Wild Kind series.

Harris, Trudy. *Say Something, Perico*. Millbrook, 2011. ISBN: 978-0-7613-5231-0. Gr PK–2.

Hartland, Jessie. *How the Dinosaur Got to the Museum*. Blue Apple Books, 2011. ISBN: 978-1-6090-5090-0. Gr 1–4.

Hatkoff, Craig. *Leo the Snow Leopard: The True Story of an Amazing Rescue*. Scholastic, 2010. ISBN: 978-0-545-22927-2. Gr PK–3.

Heilbroner, Joan. *A Pet Named Sneaker*. Random House Children's Books, 2013. ISBN: 978-0-3759-7116-7. Gr K–3.

Helm, Zebedee. *Kit & Willy's Dogs of the World*. Pucci Books, 2011. ISBN: 978-0-9560-2843-3. Gr K–2.

Hills, Tad. *Rocket Writes a Story*. Schwartz & Wade, 2012. ISBN: 978-0-3758-7086-6. Gr K and up.

Hills, Tad *How Rocket Learned to Read*. Schwartz & Wade, 2010. ISBN: 978-0-3758-5899-4. Gr PK–2.

Hulbert, Laura. *Who Has These Feet?* Henry Holt, 2011. ISBN: 978-0-8050-8907-3. Gr PK–2.

Ipcizade, Catherine. *Big Predators*. Capstone, 2009. ISBN: 978-1-4296-3316-1. Gr K–2.

Jeffers, Oliver. *This Moose Belongs to Me*. Philomel, 2012. ISBN: 978-0-3991-6103-2. Gr PK and up.

Jenkins, Martin. *The Emperor's Egg*. Candlewick Press, 2002. ISBN: 978-0-7636-1871-1. Gr K–3.

Jenkins, Martin. *Can We Save the Tiger?* Candlewick, 2011. ISBN: 978-0-7636-4909-8. Gr K–3.

Jenkins, Steve. *My First Day*. Houghton Mifflin Books for Children, 2013. ISBN: 978-0-5477-3851-2. Gr PK–3.

Jenkins, Martin. *Living Color*. Houghton Mifflin, 2007. ISBN: 978-0-6187-0897-0. Gr 1–4.

Jenkins, Martin. *Time to Eat*. Houghton Mifflin, 2011. ISBN: 978-0-547-25032-8. Gr PK–3.

Kirby, Pamela F. *What Bluebirds Do*. Boyds Mills Press, 2009. ISBN: 978-1-5907-8614-7. Gr K–2.

Klassen, Jon. *This Is Not My Hat*. Candlewick, 2012. ISBN: 978-0-7637-5599-0. Gr K and up.

Kooser, Ted. *Bag in the Wind*. Candlewick, 2010. ISBN: 978-0-7636-3001-0. Gr 1–3.

Knudsen, Michelle. *Big Mean Mike*. Candlewick, 2012. ISBN: 978-0-7636-4990-6. Gr K and up.

Levine, Ellen. *Seababy*. Walker, 2012. ISBN: 978-0-8027-9808-4. Gr PK–3.

Marceau, Fani. *Panorama: A Foldout Book*. Abrams, 2009. ISBN: 978-0-8109-8332-8. Gr K–3.

Markle, Sandra. *Race the Wild Wind: A Story of the Sable Island Horses*. Walker, 2011. ISBN: 978-0-8027-9766-7. Gr K–3.

McCarthy, Meghan. *City Hawk: The Story of Pale Male*. Simon, 2007. ISBN: 978-1-4169-3359-5. Gr K–3.

McCully, Emily Arnold. *Wonder Horse: The True Story of the World's Smartest Horse*. Henry Holt, 2010. ISBN: 978-0-8050-8793-2. Gr PK–2.

McGuirk, Leslie. *If Rocks Could Sing: A Discovered Alphabet*. Tricycle Press, 2011. ISBN: 978-1-5824-6370-4. Gr K–3.

Napoli, Donna Jo. *Mama Miti: Wangari Maathai and the Trees of Kenya*. Simon & Schuster, 2010. ISBN: 978-1-4169-3505-6. Gr K–3.

Nelson, Marilyn. *Snook Alone*. Candlewick, 2010. ISBN: 978-0-7636-2667-9. Gr K–3.

Raschka, Chris. *Hip Hop Dog*. HarperCollins, 2010. ISBN: 978-0-06-123963-2. Gr PK–2.

Reed, Lynn Rowe. *Roscoe and the Pelican Rescue*. Holiday House, 2011. ISBN: 978-0-8234-2352-1. Gr PK–2.

Riggs, Kate. *Alligators*. Creative Education, 2012. ISBN: 978-1-6081-8104-9. Gr K–3.

Riggs, Kate. *Gorillas*. Creative Education, 2012. ISBN: 978-1-6081-8107-0. Gr K–3.

Rubin, Adam. *Those Darn Squirrels Fly South*. Clarion Books, 2012. ISBN: 978-05476-7823-8. Gr K and up.

Seeger, Laura Vaccaro. *First the Egg*. Roaring Brook Press, 2007. ISBN: 978-1-5964-3272-7. Gr PK–1.

Sidman, Joyce. *Swirl by Swirl: Spirals in Nature*. Houghton Mifflin, 2011. ISBN: 978-0-5473-1583-6. Gr K–2.

Wardlaw, Lee. *Woon Ton: A Cat Tale Told in Haiku*. Henry Holt, 2011. ISBN: 978-0-8050-8995-0. Gr K–3.

Willems, Mo. *City Dog, Country Frog*. Hyperion, 2010. ISBN: 978-1-4231-0300-4. Gr PK–2.

## ANNOTATED PROFESSIONAL BOOK

Littlejohn, Carol. *Book Clubbing! Successful Book Clubs for Young People*. Linworth, 2011. Littlejohn examines the research on book clubs and their effectiveness and discusses the importance of having just the right adult leader. She believes that care should be taken with the setting and the ambience, and suggestions for post–book club meeting activities are included. The last two chapters include a list of good reads and numerous resources for teachers.

# Chapter 17

# REALISTIC FICTION AND SOCIAL ISSUES

It is comforting to know that we are not alone when we experience challenges and dilemmas. Boys can strengthen character and develop understanding of peers, teachers, parents, and siblings by reading realistic stories set in recent times. Seeing how others deal with issues and realizing that they, too, will overcome their problems helps boys to be more understanding and feel better about themselves. The American Library Association provides many resources for bibliotherapy, or using books to help students understand the issues they have or that they are experiencing with family and friends. The Carnegie Library of Pittsburgh (http://www.carnegielibrary.org/kids/books/bibtherapy.cfm) offers a Bibliography Bookshelf that includes links to titles in these sample categories: adoption, AIDS & HIV, appreciating the elderly, bullies, death, divorce, homelessness, illness, parents in prison, thumb sucking, and even toilet training!

## FEATURED AUTHORS

Name: Walter Dean Myers

Birth date: August 12, 1937

Place of Birth: Martinsburg, West Virginia

Most popular book(s): *Kick, We Are America, Looking for the Easy Life, Carmen*

About: As a baby, Walter was given to a man named Herbert Dean who lived in Harlem. He does not know why. He was raised by Herbert and his wife, Florence. Herbert was African American. Florence was German and Native American and wonderful and loved him very much. He was smart but did not do well in school.

He wrote well in high school and a teacher (bless her!) recognized this and also knew he was going to drop out. She advised him to keep on writing no matter what happened.

Web site: http://www.walterdeanmyers.net

Name: Don Brown

Birth date: June 3, 1960

Place of Birth: Plymouth, North Carolina

Most popular book(s): *Odd Boy Out, Mack Made Movies, Rare Treasure*

About: Don Brown is the award-winning author and illustrator of many picture book biographies. He has been widely praised for his resonant storytelling and his delicate watercolor paintings that evoke the excitement, humor, pain, and joy of lives lived with passion.

Web site: http://www.booksbybrown.com

## ANNOTATIONS

Brimner, Larry Dane. *Birmingham Sunday*. Calkins Creek, 2010. ISBN: 978-1-59078-613-0.
> On September 4, 1963, Birmingham reluctantly allowed black students into some of its white schools, complying with a federal court order. The National States Rights Party and the Ku Klux Klan threatened violence. On September 15, 10 to 19 sticks of dynamite were placed under the basement church stairs. At 10:22, a blast rocked the building and four girls and two boys would die. It would take thirty-nine years before justice would finally be served.

Brown, Don. *Odd Boy Out: Young Albert Einstein*. HMH Books for Young Readers; Reprint edition, 2008. ISBN: 978-0547014357.
> This is a picture book biography of Albert Einstein who as a small boy was different looking and often misunderstood because of his intelligence. He was allowed to wander and explore by his permissive parents but often had major temper tantrums. He had few friends and spent his time working on puzzles and scientific problems.

Cormier, Robert. *The Chocolate War*. Pantheon Books, 1974. ISBN: 0-394-82805-4.
> Jerry has a poster of a solitary man standing upright on the beach, mounted inside his locker. Inscribed on the poster is the slogan: "Do I Dare Disturb the Universe." Jerry comes to understand the poster when he defies a teacher; the Vigils, an underground organization; and ultimately the entire school. He sadly learns that people let you do your own thing only when it happens to be their own thing.

Cousins, Dave. *15 Days Without a Head*. Flux, 2013. ISBN: 978-0-7387-3642-6.
> Fifteen-year-old Laurence Roach lives in a household with no money and no Mum and is responsible for his younger brother, Jay, who thinks he is Scooby. Laurence's mother is a depressed alcoholic, and one day she does not come home from the two jobs she works. Laurence's solution is that if he can win the prized luxury vacation being given away by a radio show that his Mum will come home and life will be normal once again.

Key, Watt. *Fourmile*. Farrar Straus Giroux, 2010. ISBN: 978-0-3743-5095-6.
After the accidental death of his father, Foster shows no interest in anything except his dog, Joe. Foster's lonely mother briefly gets involved with Dax, a jealous, troubled drunk who threatens Joe, Foster, and even his mother. A mysterious stranger, Gary, with a past of his own, befriends Foster and his mother and gets in the middle of an ensuing violent situation.

Myers, Walter Dean. *Darius & Twig*. HarperCollins 2013. ISBN: 978-0-06-172823-8.
Darius and Twig each have a special talent; however, to develop it and win a scholarship, they will have to dig within and find the better person. Through their strong bond of friendship they survive gangs, bullies, and letting others define who they are.

Wright, Simeon with Herb Boyd. *Simeon's Story: An Eyewitness Account of Kidnapping of Emmett Till*. Lawrence Hill Books, 2010. ISBN: 978-1-55652-783-8.
Simeon Wright, 12, cousin of Emmett Till, or Bobo, 14, vividly portrays the everyday life of the black population in Mississippi in the 1940s and 1950s. Simeon (with four others in the car) was with Bobo when he whistled at Carolyn Bryant at the Bryant grocery store. Bobo was a comedian and Simeon thought he was trying to make the other boys laugh when he whistled, nothing more. Later on in the week, Simeon was sleeping in the same bed with Bobo when Roy Bryant, with gun in hand, and J. W. Milan came for Emmett in the middle of the night. Emmett was found several days later badly beaten and left for dead in the Tallahatchie River. Simeon clears up many misconceptions and lies surrounding this terrible crime and gives further advice to anyone working in the communications field, "if you want an accurate account of any story, go to the primary sources."

## READ ALOUD

Pinkney, Andrea Davis. *Sit-In: How Four Friends Stood Up by Sitting Down*. Little Brown Books for Young Readers, 2010. ISBN: 978-0-3160-7016-4.

Seeger, Laura Vaccaro. *Bully*. Roaring Brook Press, 2013. ISBN: 978-1-5964-3630-5.

Sundem, Garth. *Real Kids, Real Stories, Real Change: Courageous Actions Around the World*. Free Spirit Publishing, 2010. ISBN: 978-1-5754-2350-0.

Woodson, Jacqueline. *Each Kindness*. Nancy Paulsen Books, 2012. ISBN: 978-0-399-24652-4.

## BIBLIOGRAPHY

Allen, Crystal. *How Lamar's Bad Prank Won a Bubba-Sized Trophy*. HarperCollins, 2011. ISBN: 978-0-06-199272-8. Gr 5–8.

Amato, Mary. *Invisible Lines*. Egmont, 2009. ISBN: 978-1-60684-010-8. Gr 5–8.

Asher, Jay. *Thirteen Reasons Why*. Razorbill, Reprint, 2011. ISBN: 978-1-5951-4188-0. Gr 7 and up.

Avi. *Nothing But the Truth: A Documentary Novel.* Orchard, 1991. ISBN: 0-531-08559-7 Gr. 7–10 Classic.

Baker, Kim. *Pickle: The (Formerly) Anonymous Prank Club of Fountain Point Middle School.* Roaring Brook, 2012. ISBN: 978-1-59643-765-4. Gr 4–6.

Baskin, Nora Raleigh. *Anything But Typical.* Simon & Schuster Books for Young Readers, 2010. ISBN: 978-1-4169-9500-5. Gr 4–7.

Booth, Coe. *Bronxwood.* Push, 2011. ISBN: 978-0-4399-2534-1. YA.

Bunting, Eve. *So Far from the Sea.* Clarion Books, 2009. ISBN: 0-395-72095-8. Gr 1–3.

Buyea, Rob. *Because of Mr. Terupt.* Yearling, 2011. ISBN: 978-0-3758-5824-6. Gr 4–6.

Cart, Michael (editor). *Love and Sex.* Simon & Schuster, 2003. ISBN: 0-689-85668-7. YA.

Child, Noah. *Diary of a 6th Grade Ninja: Private Invasion.* Amazon Digital Services. 2012. ISBN: 1-4936-2501-2. Gr 4 and up.

Clements, Andrew. *Troublemaker.* Atheneum Books for Young Readers, 2013. ISBN: 978-1-4169-4932-9. Gr 3–7.

Clements, Andrew. *Lost and Found.* Atheneum, 2008. ISBN: 978-1-4169-0985-9. Gr 4–6.

Clinton, Lutricia. *Freaky Fast Frankie Joe.* Holiday House, 2012. ISBN: 978-0-8234-2367-5. Gr 4–6.

Connelly, Neil. *St. Michael's Scales.* Scholastic, 2002. ISBN: 0-439-194445-8. YA.

DeFelice, Cynthia. *Wild Life.* Farrar, Straus and Giroux, 2011. ISBN: 978-0-3743-8001-4. Gr 3 and up.

Deutsch, Stacia. *Hot Pursuit: Murder in Mississippi.* Lerner, 2010. ISBN: 978-0-7613-3955-7. Gr 5–8.

Divakaruni, Chitra Banerjee. *The Conch Bearer.* Roaring Brook, 2003. ISBN: 0-77613-1935-2. Gr 5–9.

Doctorow, Cory. *Little Brother.* Tor, 2008. ISBN: 978-0-7653-1985-2. YA.

Doctorow, Cory. *Homeland.* Tor Teen, 2013. ISBN: 978-0-7653-3369-8. YA.

Gantos, Jack. *Joey Pigza Loses Control.* Farrar, 2000. ISBN: 0-374-39989-1 Gr. 4–7.

Gantos, Jack. *Joey Pigza Swallowed the Key.* Farrar, 1998. ISBN: 0-374-33664-4. Gr 4–8.

Gantos, Jack. *Jack Adrift: Fourth Grade Without a Clue.* Farrar, 2003. ISBN: 0-374-39987-5. Gr 4–6.

Grant, Vicki. *Hold the Pickles*. Orca, 2012. ISBN: 978-1-5546-9921-6. Gr 5–8.

Grimes, Nikki. *Rich*. Putnam, 2009. ISBN: 978-0-3992-5176-4. Gr 2–4.

Harris, Nathaniel. *The Rise of Hitler*. Heinemann, 2004. ISBN: 1-4034-5526-0. Gr 4–6.

Hinton, S. E. *That Was Then, This Is Now*. Puffin Books, 1998. ISBN: 978-0-1403-8966-1. Gr 7 and up.

Hinton, S. E. *The Outsiders*. Penguin Group, 1995. ISBN: 9780140385724. Gr 7 and up.

Houtman, Jacqueline. *The Reinvention of Edison Thomas*. Front Street, 2010. ISBN: 978-1-59078-708-3. Gr 5–8.

Jacobson, Jennifer Richard. *Small as an Elephant*. Candlewick, 2011. ISBN: 978-0-7636-4155-9. Gr 4–6.

Knowles, John. *A Separate Peace*. Random House Publishing, 1994. ISBN: 978-0-5532-8041-8. YA.

Korman, Gordon. *The Juvie Three*. Hyperion Book, 2008. ISBN: 978-1-4231-0158-1. Gr 7 and up.

Korman, Gordon. *Jake, Reinvented*. Hyperion, 2003. ISBN: 0-7868-1957-X. YA.

Lee, Harper. *To Kill a Mockingbird*. Grand Central Publishing, 1988. ISBN: 978-0-4463-1078-9. YA.

Levithan, David. *Every Day*. Knopf Books for Young Readers, 2012. ISBN: 978-0-3079-3188-7. Gr 7 and up.

Mullin, Mike. *Ashfall*. Tanglewood Press, 2011. ISBN: 978-1-9337-1855-2. YA.

Myers, Walter Dean. *Dope Sick*. Amistad, 2010. ISBN: 978-0-0612-1479-0. YA.

Myers, Walter Dean. *Monster*. Amistad; Reprint edition, 2004. ISBN: 978-0-0644-0731-1. YA.

Naylor, Phyllis Reynolds. *Walker's Crossing*. Simon & Schuster, 1999. ISBN: 0-689-82939-6. YA.

Neri, G. and Randy DuBurke. *Yummy: The Last Days of a Southside Shorty*. Lee & Low, 2010. ISBN: 978-1-5843-0267-4. YA.

Nolan, Han. *When We Were Saints*. Harcourt, 2003. ISBN: 0-15-216371-9. Gr 7–10.

Patterson, James. *Middle School, The Worst Years of My Life*. Little, Brown, 2011. ISBN: 978-0-316-10187-5. Gr 3–5.

Paulsen, Gary. *Flat Broke: The Theory, Practice and Destructive Properties of Greed*. Yearling, 2012. ISBN: 978-0-3758-6612-8. Gr 3 and up.

Preller, James. *Bystander*. Feiwel & Friends, 2009. ISBN: 978-0-312-37906-3. Gr 5–8.

Rupp, Rebecca. *After Eli*. Candlewick, 2012. ISBN: 978-0-7636-5810-6. Gr 4 and up.

Saenz, Benjamin Alire. *Aristotle and Dante Discover Secrets of the Universe*. Simon & Schuster Books for Young Readers, 2012. ISBN: 978-1-4424-0892-0. Gr 7 and up.

Schmidt, Gary. *Okay for Now*. HMH Books for Young Readers, 2013. ISBN: 978-0-5440-2280-5. Gr 5 and up.

Scieszka, Jon. *Guys Write for Guys Read: Boys' Favorite Authors Write About Being Boys*. Viking Juvenile, 2008. ISBN: 978-0-6700-1144-5. Gr 6–9.

Seidler, Tor. *The Dulcimer Boy*. HarperCollins, 2003. ISBN: 0-06-023609-6. Gr 4–8.

Senzai, N. H. *Shooting Kabul*. Simon & Schuster, 2011. ISBN: 978-1-4424-0195-2. Gr 5–8.

Sheth, Kashmira. *Boys Without Names*. Balzer + Bray, Reprint edition, 2011. ISBN: 978-0-0618-5762-1. Gr 4–7.

Spinelli, Jerry. *Jake and Lily*. Balzer + Bray, 2013. ISBN: 978-0-0644-7198-5. Gr 3 and up.

Spinelli, Jerry. *Wringer*. HarperCollins, 1998. ISBN: 0-06-644057-8. Gr 4–6.

Springer, Nancy. *Blood Trail*. Holiday, 2003. ISBN: 0-8234-1723-8. Gr 6–8.

Stead, Rebecca. *Liar & Spy*. Wendy Lamb Books, 2012. ISBN: 978-0-3857-3743-2. Gr 4 and up.

Stine, R. L. *It's the First Day of School . . . Forever!* Feiwel & Friends, 2011. ISBN: 978-0-312-64954-8. Gr 4–6.

Strasser, Todd. *If I Grow Up*. Simon & Schuster Books for Young Readers, Reprint, 2010. ISBN: 978-1-4169-9443-5. Gr 8–10.

Tashjian, Janet. *Fault Line*. Holt, 2003. ISBN: 0-8050-7200-4. YA.

Tolan, Stephanie. *Wishworks, Inc*. Scholastic, 2009. ISBN: 978-0-545-03154-7. Gr 4–6.

Wallace, Rich. *Benched*. Knopf, 2010. ISBN: 978-0-3759-5756-7. Gr 2–4.

Weissman, Elissa Brent. *Nerd Camp*. Atheneum. 2011. ISBN: 978-1-4424-1703-8. Gr 4–6.

Weissman, Elissa Brent. *The Trouble with Mark Hopper*. Dutton, 2009. ISBN: 978-0-525-42067-5. Gr 4–6.

Wilson, Jacqueline. *The Worry Web Site*. Delacorte, 2003. ISBN: 0-385-73083-7. Gr 3–7.

Yoo, David. *The Detention Club*. HarperCollins, 2011. ISBN: 978-0-06-178378-4. Gr 4–6.

## INFORMATIONAL

Aronson, Marc. *Race: A History Beyond Black and White*. Atheneum, 2007. ISBN: 978-0-689-86554-1. YA.

Atkins, S. Beth. *Voices from the Streets: Young Former Gang Members Tell their Stories*. Little Brown and Company. 1996. ISBN: 0-316-05634-0. Gr 4–6.

Barber, Nicola. *Coping with Population Growth: Express Edition*. Raintree, 2011. ISBN: 978-1-4109-4317-0. Gr 4–6.

Brown, Don. *America Is Under Attack: September 11, 2001: The Day the Towers Fell*. Flash Point, 2011. ISBN: 978-1-5964-3694-7. Gr 1–5.

Hampton, Wilborn. *September 11, 2001: Attack on New York City*. Candlewick, 2011. ISBN: 978-0-7636-5767-3. Gr 6–9.

Haskins, James. *The March on Washington*. HarperCollins, 2004. ISBN: 0-06-021289-6. Gr 4–6.

Hopkinson, Deborah. *Shutting Out the Sky: Life in the Tenements of New York, 1880–1924*. Scholastic, 2003. ISBN: 0-439-37590-8. Gr 3–7.

Kallen, Stuart A. *The Aftermath of the Sandinista Revolution*. Twenty-First Century, 2009. ISBN: 978-0-8225-9091-0. YA. Aftermath of History series.

Mastoon, Adam. *The Shared Heart: Portraits and Stories Celebrating Lesbian, Gay, and Bisexual Young People*. Morrow, 1997. ISBN: 0-688-14931-6. Gr 7 and up.

Moore, Wes. *Discovering Wes Moore: Chances, Choices, Changes*. Delacorte, 2012. ISBN: 978-0-3759-9018-2. Gr 7 and up.

Robinson, J. Dennis. *Striking Back: The Fight to End Child Labor Exploitation*. Compass Point, 2010. ISBN: 978-0-7565-4297-9. Gr 5–8.

Schmit, Gary D. *The Wednesday Wars*. Sandpiper, Reprint, 2009. ISBN: 978-0-5472-4760-2. Gr 5 and up.

Seidler, Tor. *The Dulcimer Boy*. HarperCollins, 2003. ISBN: 0-06-023609-6. Gr. 4–8.

Slade, Suzanne. *Climbing Lincoln's Steps*. Whitman, 2010. ISBN: 978-0-8075-1204-3. Gr 2–5.

Son, John. *Finding My Hat*. Scholastic, 2003. ISBN: 0-439-43538-2. Gr 4–8.

Wilson, Janet. *One Peace: True Stories of Young Activists*. Orca, 2008. ISBN: 978-1-55143-892-4 Gr 4–7.

Woof, Alex. *Why Are People Terrorists?* Raintree, 2004. ISBN: 978-0-7398-6686-9. Gr 4–6. Exploring Tough Issues series.

## PICTURE BOOKS

Arnold, Tedd. *Fly Guy vs. the Fly Swatter!* Scholastic, 2011. ISBN: 978-0-545-31286-8. Gr PK–2.

Asch, Frank. *The Daily Comet: Boy Saves Earth from Giant Octopus*. Kids Can, 2010. ISBN: 978-1-55453-281-0. Gr 2–4.

Barton, Chris. *Shark vs. Train*. Little, Brown, 2010. ISBN: 978-0-316-00762-7. Gr PK–1.

Brennan, Eileen. *Dirtball Pete*. Random House, 2010. ISBN: 978-0-375-83425-7. Gr 1–3.

Carle, Eric. *The Artist Who Painted a Blue Horse*. Philomel, 2011. ISBN: 978-0-399-25713-1. Gr PK-K.

Castellucci, Cecil. *Odd Duck*. First-Second, 2013. ISBN: 978-1-5964-3557-5. Gr 2–4.

Chocolate, Debbi. *El Barrio*. Henry Holt, 2009. ISBN: 0-8050-7457-0. Gr K–3.

Cook, Lisa Broadie. *Peanut Butter and Homework*. Putnam, 2011. ISBN: 978-0-399-24533-6. Gr K–2.

Folgueira, Rodrigo. *Ribbit!* Alfred A. Knopf, 2013. ISBN: 978-0-307-98146-2. Gr PK–2.

Gaiman, Neil. *The Wolves in the Walls*. HarperCollins, 2003. ISBN: 0-380-97827-X. Gr 1 and up.

Grandits, John. *Ten Rules You Absolutely Must Not Break If You Want to Survive the School Bus*. Clarion, 2011. ISBN: 978-0-618-78822-4. Gr K–3.

Gutman, Dan. *Miss Laney Is Zany*. HarperCollins, 2010. ISBN: 978-0-06-155415-5. Gr 2–5. My Weird School series.

Hanlon, Abby. *Ralph Tells a Story*. Amazon Children's Publishing, 2012. ISBN: 978-0-7614-6180-7. Gr 1–3.

Heller, Alyson. *Time for T-Ball*. Aladdin paper, 2010. ISBN: 978-1-4169-9412-1. Gr PK–1.

Johnson, Stephen T. *As the City Sleeps*. Viking, 2002. ISBN: 0-670-88940-7. Gr 2–4.

Juster, Norton. *Neville*. Random House, 2011. ISBN: 978-0-375-86765-1. Gr PK–3.

Meng, Cece. *I Will Not Read This Book.* Clarion, 2011. ISBN: 978-0-547-04971-7. Gr K–2.

Peete, Holly Robinson. *My Brother Charlie.* Scholastic Press, 2010. ISBN: 978-0-5450-9466-6. Gr 2–5.

Say, Allen. *Grandfather's Journey.* Houghton, 1993. ISBN: 0-395-57035-2. Gr PK–3.

Schneider, Josh. *Tales for Very Picky Eaters.* Clarion, 2011. ISBN: 978-0-547-14956-1. Gr K–3.

Spalding, Andrea. *Secret of the Dance.* Orca, 2006. ISBN: 1-55143-396-6. Gr K–3.

Taback, Simms. *Postcards from Camp.* Penguin, 2011. ISBN: 978-0-399-23973-3. Gr 1–3.

Uhlberg, Myron. *A Storm Called Katrina.* Peachtree, 2011. ISBN: 978-1-56145-591-1. Gr 1–4.

Wells, Rosemary. *Hands Off, Harry!* HarperCollins, 2011. ISBN: 978-0-06-192112-4. Gr PK–K.

## ANNOTATED PROFESSIONAL BOOK

Wadham, Rachel and Jon Osterson. *Integrating Young Adult Literature through the Common Core Standards.* Libraries Unlimited, 2013.

> This book provides a compelling template for teachers using young adult literature and inquiry learning to meet students' needs and the demands of the English Language Arts Common Core Standards. The book is divided into two parts: defining the complexity of young adult literature using the Common Core Standards and planning instruction using young adult literature and the Common Core Standards. The first chapter gives an overview of young adult literature: its history, dispelling some myths about it, using young adult literature in the classroom, and embracing young adult literature. There are four chapters on the dimensions of text complexity. There is a chapter on inquiry learning and then a chapter that serves as a model unit plan. The appendix includes an analysis form, a raw materials planning sheet, and model unit materials.

# Chapter 18

# SCIENCE AND SPACE

Science and space are of great interest to boys. Most boys love to read about outer space—both fiction and nonfiction! In their imaginations they can plan future space travel, or at least a visit to the Kennedy Space Center or the Smithsonian National Air and Space Museum. Science is a unique subject because it piques boys' curiosity, it teaches them to look at the world in a different way, and to ask that important question, "Why?", as many times as possible and to search for answers. Science is action-based, fascinating, practical, and centered in factual knowledge. Boys can read about how science is changing and how those changes are making a difference in many areas. With books in hand, they can plan and dream of the contributions they can make.

## FEATURED AUTHORS

Name: Seymour Simon

Birth date: August 9, 1931

Place of Birth: New York City, New York

Most popular book(s): *Coral Reefs, Sharks, The Impossible Shrinking Machine*

About: Simon has written nearly 300 books. He was once a science teacher in a New York City middle school. When his first book was published, Simon proudly showed it to his mother, especially because he had dedicated it to her.

Web site: http://www.seymoursimon.com

Name: Philip Reeve

Birth date: February 28, 1966

Place of Birth: Brighton, United Kingdom

Most popular book(s): *Mortal Engines, Fever Crumb*

About: Reeve wrote his first story at the tender age of five; it was about a spaceman called Spike and his dog Spook. His 2009 novel, *Fever Crumb*, returns to the world of Mortal Engines. Along with its sequels *A Web of Air* and *Scrivener's Moon*, it tells the story of how the Traction Era began.

Web site: http://www.philip-reeve.com/

# ANNOTATIONS

Dakin, Glenn. *Star Wars the Clone Wars: Who Are the Jedi?* DK, 2013. ISBN: 978-0-7566-9795-2.
    With colorful graphics and numerous side bars, each two-page spread poses a question and proceeds to answer it. Includes an index and glossary.

Griffiths, Andy. *What Body Part Is That?* Feiwel and Friends, 2011. ISBN: 978-0-312-36790-9.
    All you ever need to know about your body with fun facts, clever illustrations, and novel information about your body. A Quick Reference Guide numbers the parts of the body and that number also refers to the two-page spread of information and accompanying illustration.

Jemison, Mae. *The 100 Year Starship*. Children's Press, 2013. ISBN: 978-0-531-24060-1.
    The 100YSS proposal was initiated by Dr. Mae Jemison, former NASA astronaut. Her plan brings people from all walks of life to work together to make human travel to other stars possible in the next 100 years.

Schyffert, Bea Uusma. *The Man Who Went to the Far Side of the Moon: The Story of Apollo 11 Astronaut Michael Collins*. Chronicle Books, 2003. ISBN: 0-8118-4007-7.
    Michael Collins circles the moon in a small spacecraft while Neil Armstrong and Buzz Aldrin land the lunar module. He circles the moon 14 times and is out of communication for 48 minutes each time he is on the far side. This is a creative documentary of his experience with photos, diagrams, personal notes, and interesting facts.

Simon, Seymour. *Coral Reefs*. HarperCollins, 2013. ISBN: 978-0-06-191495-9.
    This book describes the different types of coral reefs and their inhabitants with great photos and simple language. Simon tells about the environmental changes such as global warming and toxic waste that are harming the reefs. There is a helpful glossary included. Seymour Simon has written over 250 books for children.

Siy, Alexandra. *Cars on Mars: Roving, the Red Planet*. Charlesbridge, 2009. ISBN: 978-1-57091-462-1.
    Two rovers, Spirit and Opportunity, are about the size of golf carts, and they began exploring Mars, the Red Planet, in January 2004. Spectacular photographs (217,000) document five years of exploring and traveling a combined total of about 12 miles.

Van Vleet, Carmella. *Explore Electricity with 25 Great Projects*. Nomad Press, 2013. ISBN: 978-1-61930-180-1.

A practical introduction to electricity with many experiments and projects aimed at the six-through nine-year-old. Some of the projects included are a solar oven, anemometer, simple motor, and a night light.

## READ ALOUD

Burns, Loree Griffin. *Tracking Trash: Flotsam, Jetsam, and the Science of Ocean Motion.* Houghton, 2007. ISBN: 978-0-61858-131-3.

Cusick, Dawn. *Get the Scoop on Animal Poop: From Lions to Tapeworms: 251 Cool Facts about Scat, Frass, Dung, and More.* Imagine Publishing, 2012. ISBN: 978-1-62354-104-2.

Kudlinski, Kathleen V. *Boy, Were We Wrong About Dinosaurs!* Dutton. 2005. ISBN 978-0-52546-978-0.

## BIBLIOGRAPHY

### Fiction

Anderson, M. T. *The Suburb Beyond the Stars.* Scholastic, 2010. ISBN: 978-0-545-13882-6. Gr 4–6.

Arnston, Steven. *The Wikkeling.* Running, 2011. ISBN: 978-0-7624-3903-4. Gr 4–6.

Asch, Frank. *Gravity Buster: Journal of a Cardboard Genius.* Kids Can, 2007. ISBN: 978-1-55453-068-7. Gr 1–3.

Barnes, John. *Losers in Space.* Viking, 2012. ISBN: 978-0-670-06156-3. YA.

Beaty, Andrea. *Attack of the Fluffy Bunnies.* Abrams, 2010. ISBN: 978-0-8109-8416-5. Gr 4–6. Beaty.

Bransford, Nathan. *Jacob Wonderbar and the Cosmic Space Kapow.* Dial, 2011. ISBN: 978-0-8037-3537-8. Gr 4–6.

Bransford, Nathan. *Jacob Wonderbar and the Interstellar Time Warp.* Dial, 2013. ISBN: 978-0-8037-3703-7. Gr 4–6.

Brooks, Walter R. *Freddy and the Space Ship.* Overlook, 2001. ISBN: 1-58567-105-3. Gr 4–6.

Cottrell Boyce, Frank. *Cosmic.* HarperCollins, 2010. ISBN: 978-0-06-183683-1. Gr 4–6.

Dakin, Glenn. *What Is a Sith Warrior?* DK Publishing, 2013. ISBN: 978-0-7566-9794-5. Gr 2 and up.

Daley, Michael J. *Rat Trap.* Holiday, 2008. ISBN: 978-0-8234-2093-3. Gr 4–6.

Dashner, James. *The 13th Reality: The Journal of Curious Letters.* Aladdin, 2009. ISBN: 0-8234-1866-9. Gr 4–6.

Dowell, Frances O'Roark. *Phineas L. MacGuire . . . Blasts Off!* Atheneum, 2008. ISBN: 978-1-4169-9152-6. Gr 1–3.

Eldred, Tim. *Grease Monkey.* Tor, 2006. ISBN: 0-765-31325-1. Gr 4–6.

Fearing, Mark. *Earthling.* Chronicle, 2012. ISBN: 978-1-8118-7106-8. Gr 4–6.

Feig, Paul. *Ignatius MacFarland: Frequenaut!* Little, 2008. ISBN: 978-0-316-16663-8. Gr 4–6.

Gauthier, Gail. *Club Earth.* Putnam, 1999. ISBN: 0-399-23373-3. Gr 4–6.

Griffiths, Andy. *Killer Koalas from Outer Space: And Lots of Other Very Bad Stuff That Will Make Your Brain Explode.* Feiwel, 2011. ISBN: 978-0-312-36789-3. Gr 4–6.

Haddon, Mark. *Boom!* Random, 2010. ISBN: 978-0-385-75187-2. Gr 4–6.

Hatke, Ben. *Zita the Spacegirl.* Roaring Brook, 2011. ISBN: 978-1-59343-695-4. Gr 4–6.

Jeffrey, Mark. *Max Quick: The Pocket and the Pendant.* HarperCollins, 2011. ISBN: 978-0-06-198892-9. Gr 4–6.

Jinks, Catherine. *Living Hell.* Harcourt, 2010. ISBN: 978-0-15-206193-7. YA.

Kahn, Hena. *Mars!* Chronicle Books, 2011. ISBN: 978-0-8118-7124-2. Gr 4 and up. Worst Case Scenario Ultimate Adventure series.

Kerr, P. B. *One Small Step.* Margaret K. McElderry Books, 2008. ISBN: 978-1-4169-4213-9. Gr 7–9.

Kline, Suzy. *Horrible Harry Goes to the Moon.* Viking, 2000. ISBN: 0-670-88764-1. Gr 1–3.

Lennon, Joan. *Questors.* McElderryBooks, 2007. ISBN: 978-0-1-4169-3658-9. Gr 4–6.

Mackel, Kathy. *Alien in a Bottle.* HarperCollins, 2004. ISBN: 0-06-029281-4. Gr 4–6.

Mahy, Margaret. *The Greatest Show Off Earth.* Viking, 1994. ISBN: 0-670-85736-X. Gr 4–6.

Mass, Wendy. *Pi in the Sky.* Little, 2013. ISBN: 978-0-316-08916-6. Gr 4–6.

McElligott, Matthew. *Benjamin Franklinstein Lives!* Putnam, 2010. ISBN: 978-0-399-2529-7. Gr 4–7.

McNamee, Eoin. *City of Time.* Random, 2008. ISBN: 978-0-375-83912-2. Gr 4–6.

Nix, Garth. *Sir Thursday.* Scholastic, 2006. ISBN: 0-439-70087-6. Gr 4–6. Keys to the Kingdom series.

Oppel, Kenneth. *Starclimber*. HarperCollins, 2009. ISBN: 978-0-06-085057-9. YA.

Ottaviani, Jim. *T-Minus: The Race to the Moon*. Simon, 2009. ISBN: 978-1-4169-8682-9. Gr 4–6.

Parker, Jake. *Missile Mouse: The Star Crusher*. Scholastic, 2010. ISBN: 978-0-545-11714-2. Gr 4–6.

Pilkey, Dav. *Captain Underpants and the Invasion of the Incredibly Naughty Cafeteria Ladies from Outer Space (and the Subsequent Assault of the Equally Evil Lunchroom Zombie Nerds)*. Scholastic, 1999. ISBN: 0-439-04995-4. Gr 4–6.

Pinkwater, Daniel. *Mush's Jazz Adventure*. Simon, 2002. ISBN: 0-689-84576-6. Gr 1–3.

Reeve, Philip. *Larklight: A Rousing Tale of Dauntless Pluck in the Farthest Reaches of Space*. Bloomsbury, 2006. ISBN: 1-59990-020-3. Gr 4–6.

Revis, Beth. *Shades of Earth*. Penguin, 2013. ISBN: 978-1-59514-399-0. YA.

Schooley, Bob. *Liar of Kudzu*. Simon, 2007. ISBN: 978-1-4169-1488-4. Gr 4–6.

Scroggs, Kirk. *Hair Ball from Outer Space*. Little, 2007. ISBN: 978-0-316-05951-0. Gr 1–3.

Smith, Clete Barrett. *Aliens on Vacation*. Hyperion, 2011. ISBN: 978-1-4231-3363-6. Gr 4–6.

Spires, Ashley. *Binky Takes Charge*. Kids Can, 2012. ISBN: 978-1-55453-703-7. Gr 1–3.

Teague, Mark. *The Doom Machine*. Scholastic, 2011. ISBN: 978-0-545-15142-9. Gr 4–6.

Thompson, Kate. *Origins*. Bloomsbury, 2007. ISBN: 978-1-58234-652-6. Gr 4–6.

Trine, Greg. *Invasion from Planet Dork*. Holt, 2010. ISBN: 978-0-8050-8165-7. Gr 1–3.

Webb, Philip. *Six Days*. Scholastic, 2011. ISBN: 978-0-545-31767-2. Gr 4–6.

Wilson, N. D. *100 Cupboards*. Random, 2007. ISBN: 978-0-375-83881-1. Gr 4–6. 100 Cupboard series.

Yaccarino, Dan. *First Day on a Strange New Planet*. Hyperion, 2000. ISBN: 0-7868-2499-9. Gr 1–3.

Young, E. L. *STORM: The Infinity Code*. Dial, 2008. ISBN: 978-0-8037-3265-0. Gr 4–6.

## INFORMATIONAL

Bardoe, Cheryl. *Mammoths and Mastodons: Titans of the Ice Age*. Abrams, 2010. ISBN: 978-0-8109-8413-4. Gr 4–6.

Becker, Tom. *A Zombie's Guide to the Human Body*. Scholastic Reference, 2010. ISBN: 978-0-5452-4979-9. Gr 3–7.

Benson, Michael. *Beyond: A Solar System Voyage*. Abrams Books for Young Readers, 2009. ISBN: 978-0-8109-8322-9. Gr 3–9.

Berger, Lee R. and Marc Aronson. *The Skull in the Rock: How a Scientist, a Boy, and Google Earth Opened a New Window on Human Origins*. National Geographic, 2012. ISBN: 978-1-4263-1053-9. Gr 5 and up.

Bjorklund, Ruth. *Venus*. Marshall Cavendish, 2010. ISBN: 978-0-7614-4251-6. Gr 4–8. Space! series.

Bortz, Fred. *Seven Wonders of Space Technology*. Lerner, 2011. ISBN: 978-0-7613-5453-6. Gr 5–8.

Brake, Mark. *Really, Really Big Questions About Space and Time*. Kingfisher, 2010. ISBN: 978-0-7534-6502-8. Gr 4–7.

Brown, Jordan D. *Crazy Concoctions: A Mad Scientist's Guide to Messy Mixtures*. Imagine, 2012. ISBN: 978-1-9361-4051-0. Gr 4–7.

Bryson, Bill. *A Really Short History of Nearly Everything*. Delacorte, 2009. ISBN: 978-0-385-73810-1. Gr 5–8.

Burns, Loree Griffin. *Citizen Scientists: Be a Part of Scientific Discovery from Your Own Backyard*. Henry Holt, 2012. ISBN: 978-0-8050-9062-8. Gr 3–5.

Chaikin, Andrew. *Mission Control, This Is Apollo: The Story of the First Voyages to the Moon*. Penguin Group, 2009. ISBN: 978-0-6700-1156-8. Gr 6–9.

DeCristofano, Carolyn Cinami. *A Black Hole Is Not a Hole*. Charlesbridge, 2012. ISBN: 978-1-5709-1783-7. Gr 5–8.

Deem, James M. *Bodies From the Ice: Melting Glaciers and the Recovery of the Past*. Houghton Mifflin, 2008. ISBN: 978-0-6188-0045-2. Gr 5–8.

Dingle, Adrian. *How to Make a Universe with 92 Ingredients*. Owl Kids Books, 2013. ISBN: 978-0-7714-7008-7. Gr 4 and up.

Donovan, Sandy. *Does It Really Take Seven Years to Digest Swallowed Gum? And Other Questions You've Always Wanted to Ask*. Lerner, 2010. ISBN: 978-0-8225-9085-9. Gr 4–6.

Floca, Brian. *Moonshot: The Flight of Apollo 11*. Atheneum Books for Young Readers, 2009. ISBN: 978-1-4169-5046-2. Gr PK–5.

Florian, Douglas. *Comets, Stars, the Moon, and Mars: Space Poems and Paintings*. Harcourt, 2007. ISBN: 978-0-15-205372-7. Gr K–5.

Goodman, Susan E. *Gee Whiz! It's All About Pee.* Viking, 2006. ISBN: 978-0-670-06064-1. Gr 3–5.

Goodman, Susan E. *The Truth About Poop.* Puffin; Reprint edition, 2007. ISBN: 978-0-1424-0930-5. Gr 3–5.

Hicks, Terry Allan. *Earth and the Moon.* Marshall Cavendish, 2010. ISBN: 978-0-7614-4254-7. Gr 4–8.

Hillman, Ben. *How Weird Is It? A Freaky Book All About Strangeness.* Scholastic, 2009. ISBN: 978-0-4399-1868-8. Gr 6–9.

Hughes, Catherine D. *National Geographic Little Kids First Big Book of Space.* National Geographic Books, 2012. ISBN: 978-1-4263-1014-0. Gr K–3.

Johnson, Rebecca L. *Journey into the Deep: Discovering New Ocean Creatures.* Millbrook, 2010. ISBN: 978-0-7613-4148-2. Gr 4–6.

Johnson, Rebecca L. *Zombie Makers: True Stories of Nature's Undead.* Millbrook Press, 2012. ISBN: 978-0-7613-8633-9. Gr 5–8.

Kortenkamp, Steve. *Space Robots.* Capstone Press, 2009. ISBN: 978-1-4296-2322-3. Gr 3 and up.

Lourie, Peter. *Whaling Season: A Year in the Life of an Arctic Whale Scientist.* Houghton Mifflin, 2009. ISBN: 978-0-618-77709-9. Gr 4–8.

Miller, Ron. *Seven Wonders of Space Technology.* Twenty-First Century Books, 2011. ISBN: 978-0-7613-5454-3. Gr 6–9. Seven Wonders series.

Murphy, Glenn. *Stuff That Scares Your Pants Off! The Science Scoop on More than 30 Terrifying Phenomena.* Roaring Book Press, 2011. ISBN: 978-1-5964-3633-6. Gr 6–9.

Murphy, Glenn. *How Loud Can You Burp? More Extremely Important Questions (and Answers!).* Flash Point Paper, 2009. ISBN: 978-1-59643-506-3. Gr 4–7.

Nardo, Don. *Destined for Space: Our Story of Exploration.* Capstone, 2012. ISBN: 978-1-4296-7540-6. Gr 3–5.

O'Meara, Stephen Jones. *Are You Afraid Yet? The Science Behind Scary Stuff.* Kids Can Press, 2009. ISBN: 978-1-5545-3294-0. Gr 6–9.

Parker, Steve. *What About . . . Science and Technology.* Mason Crest, 2009. ISBN: 978-1-4222-1565-4. Gr 5–8.

Richardson, Gillian. *Kaboom! Explosions of All Kinds.* Annick, 2009. ISBN: 978-1-55451-204-1. Gr 4–7.

Rusch, Caroline Starr. *Mighty Mars Rovers: The Incredible Adventures of Spirit and Opportunity*. Houghton, 2012. ISBN: 978-0-5474-7881-4. Gr 5 and up.

Scott, Elaine. *Space, Stars, and the Beginning of Time: What the Hubble Telescope Saw*. Clarion Books, 2011. ISBN: 978-0-5472-4189-0. Gr 4 and up.

Soloway, Andrew. *Sports Science*. Heinemann-Raintree, 2009. ISBN: 978-1-4329-2480-5. Gr 4–9. Why Science Matters series.

Sparrow, Giles. *Night Sky*. Scholastic, 2013. ISBN: 978-0-545-38374-5. Gr 3–7.

Stone, Jerry. *One Small Step: Celebrating the First Men on the Moon*. Flash Point, 2009. ISBN: 978-1-5964-3491-0. Gr 1–5.

Timmesh, Catherine. *Lucy Long Ago: Uncovering the Mystery of Where We Came From*. Houghton Mifflin Books for Children, 2010. ISBN: 978-0-5470-5199-4. Gr 5 and up.

Walker, Sally M. *Written in Bone: Buried Lives of Jamestown and Colonial Maryland*. Carolrhodda Books, 2009. ISBN: 978-0-822-57135-3. Gr 6–12.

## PICTURE BOOKS

Adler, David. *Bones and the Dinosaur Mystery*. Viking 2005. ISBN: 0-670-06010-0. Gr K–3.

Arnold, Tedd. *Green Wilma, Frog in Space*. Dial, 2009. ISBN: 978-0-8037-2698-7. Gr K–3.

Bahr, Mary. *My Brother Loved Snowflakes: The Story of Wilson A. Bentley, the Snowflake Man*. Boyds Mills Press, 2002. ISBN: 1-56397-689-7. Gr K–3.

Barnett, Mac. *Oh No! (Or How My Science Project Destroyed the World)*. Hyperion, 2010. ISBN: 978-1-4231-2312-5. Gr K–3.

Bauer, Marion Dane. *Wind*. Simon, 2003. ISBN: 0-689-85442-0. Gr K–3.

Cassino, Mark. *The Story of Snow: The Science of Winter's Wonder*. Chronicle, 2009. ISBN: 978-0-8118-6866-2. Gr K–3.

Chin, Jason. *Island: A Story of the Galapagos*. Roaring Brook, 2012. ISBN: 978-1-59643-716-6. Gr K–3.

Cole, Joanna. *The Magic School Bus and the Science Fair Expedition*. Scholastic, 2006. ISBN: 0-590-10824-7. Gr K–3.

Cole, Joanna. *The Magic School Bus Lost in the Solar System*. Scholastic, 1992. ISBN: 0-590-41426-3. Gr K–3.

Collins, Andrew. *Violent Weather: Thunderstorms, Tornadoes, and Hurricanes*. National Geographic Books, 2006. ISBN: 0-7922-5947-5. Gr K–3.

Davies, Nicola. *Ice Bear: In the Steps of the Polar Bear*. Candlewick, 2005. ISBN: 0-7636-2759-3. Gr K–3.

Floca, Brian. *Moonshot: The Flight of Apollo 11*. Atheneum, 2009. ISBN: 978-1-4169-5046-2. Gr K–3.

Gerstein, Mordicai. *How to Bicycle to the Moon to Plant Sunflowers: A Simple but Brilliant Plan in 24 Easy Steps*. Roaring Brook Press, 2013. ISBN: 978-1-5964-3512-4. Gr PK–2.

Goldsmith, Mike. *Everything You Need to Know About Science*. Kingfisher, 2009. ISBN: 978-0-7534-6302-4. Gr K–3.

Grey, Mini. *Toys in Space*. Alfred A. Knopf, 2013. ISBN: 978-0-3079-7815-8. Gr K–2.

Guiberson, Brenda Z. *The Emperor Lays an Egg*. Holt, 2001. ISBN: 0-8050-6204-1. Gr K–3.

Harrison, James. *Space*. Kingfisher, 2012. ISBN: 978-0-7534-6883-8. Gr K–3.

Hopkins, Lee Bennett. *Blast Off!: Poems About Space*. HarperCollins, 1995. ISBN: 978-0-0602-4261-9. Gr 1–3.

Jenkins, Steve. *Life on Earth: The Story of Evolution*. Houghton, 2002. ISBN: 0-618-16476-6. Gr K–3.

Karas, G. Brian. *On Earth*. Putnam, 2005. ISBN: 0-399-24025-X. Gr K–3.

Kolar, Bob. *Astroblast: Code Blue*. Scholastic, 2010. ISBN: 978-0-545-12104-0. Gr K–3.

Kops, Deborah. *Exploring Space Robots*. Lerner, 2011. ISBN: 978-0-7613-5445-1. Gr K–3.

Lauber, Patricia. *You're Abroad Spaceship Earth*. HarperCollins, 1996. ISBN: 0-06-024407-0. Gr K–3.

Markle, Sandra. *Outside and Inside Sharks*. Aladdin, 1999. ISBN: 978-0-6898-2683-2. Gr K–3.

Markle, Sandra. *Growing Up Wild: Penguins*. Atheneum, 2002. ISBN: 0-689-81887-4. Gr K–3.

McNulty, Faith. *If You Decide to Go to the Moon*. Scholastic, 2005. ISBN: 0-590-48359-5. Gr K–3.

Micucci, Charles. *The Life and Times of the Ant*. Houghton, 2003. ISBN: 0-618-00559-5. Gr K–3.

Naujore Akaitis, Pranas. *Balloon Toons: Dinosaurs in Space*. Blue Apple Books, 2012. ISBN: 978-1-6090-5253-9. Gr 1–4.

O'Brien, Patrick. *You Are the First Kid on Mars*. Putnam Juvenile, 2009. ISBN: 978-0-3992-4634-0. Gr K and up.

Offill, Jenny. *Eleven Experiments That Failed*. Random House, 2011. ISBN: 978-0-375-84762-2. Gr K–2.

Pfeffer, Wendy. *Life in a Coral Reef*. HarperCollins, 2009. ISBN: 978-0-06-029553-0. Gr K–3.

Pinkney, Brian. *Cosmo and the Robot*. Greenwillow, 2000. ISBN: 0-688-15940-0. Gr K–3.

Raab, Brigitte. *Where Does Pepper Come From?* North-South, 2006. ISBN: 0-7358-2070-8. Gr K–3.

Reinhart, Matthew. *Star Wars: A Galactic Pop-Up Adventure*. Scholastic, 2012. ISBN: 978-0-545-17616-3. Gr K–3.

Rockwell, Anne. *Clouds: Let's-Read-and-Find-Out Science*. Collins, 2008. ISBN: 978-0-06-445220-4. Gr PK–1.

Schlein, Miriam. *The Puzzle of the Dinosaur-Bird: The Story of Archaeopteryx*. Dial, 1996. ISBN: 0-8037-1282-0. Gr K–3.

Scieszka, Jon. *Science Verse*. Viking, 2004. ISBN: 0-670-91057-0. Gr K–3.

Shields, Amy. *Little Kids First Big Book of Why*. National Geographic Books, 2011. ISBN: 978-1-4263-0793-5. Gr K–3.

Simon, Seymour. *Oceans*. Morrow, 2006. ISBN: 0-688-09453-8. Gr K–3.

Waxman, Laura Hamilton. *Exploring the International Space Station*. Lerner, 2011. ISBN: 978-0-7613-5443-7. Gr K–3.

## ANNOTATED PROFESSIONAL BOOK

Owocki, Gretchen. *The Common Core Lesson Book, K-5: Working with Increasingly Complex Literature, Informational Text, and Foundational Reading Skills*. Heinemann, 2012.
   The Owocki book is divided into two sections: one for literature and one for informational text. The strategies are organized by the nine reading anchors, and there are examples of activities to do to strengthen each area. The activities are engaging and easy to use in any classroom situation. They utilize most all of the important aspects of the English Language Arts Common Core Standards.

# Chapter 19

# SPORTS

Being good at a sport is very important to many boys. In the news today they see the influential lives that many professional athletes lead. Unfortunately, professional athletes are not always good role models. In any case, most boys like sports and want to succeed and be accepted by their peers. Stories that depict the trials and tribulations of those who want to participate help boys to understand that they are not alone in the things they are experiencing. By reading about athletes and different kinds of sports, they can learn statistics, history, terminology, issues, and be more knowledgeable about the process.

## FEATURED AUTHORS

Name: Mike Lupica

Birth date: May 11, 1952

Place of Birth: Oneida, New York

Most popular book(s): *QB1, True Legend, The Underdogs, Hero*

About: Lupica began his newspaper career covering the New York Knicks for the *New York Post* at age 23. He became the youngest columnist ever at a New York paper with the *New York Daily News*, which he joined in 1977. Lupica is also what he describes as a "serial Little League coach," a youth basketball coach, and a soccer coach for his four children, three sons and a daughter.

Web site: http://www.mikelupicabooks.com

Name: Chris Oxlade

Birth date: January 3, 1961

Place of Birth: England

Most popular book(s): *Sports (The Science Behind), Cricket (Know Your Sport)*

About: Oxlade has written over 200 titles. Apart from writing books, he also works as a rock-climbing instructor. Most of his spare hours are spent rock climbing, playing tennis, taking photographs, and trying to keep track of ever-changing technology. Web site: http://www.oxgan.pwp.blueyonder.co.uk/author

## ANNOTATIONS

Adamson, Thomas K. *The Technology of Baseball*. Capstone Press, 2013. ISBN: 978-1-62065-906-9.

> Computers, statistics, and review of videos help players and managers make the best game-day decisions. The book includes the technology that provides the best and safest equipment, helps prepare the players, and the apps and video boards for fans to watch and enjoy the game.

Cain, Patrick G. *Skateboarding Vert*. Lerner, 2013. ISBN: 978-1-4677-1085-5.

> Skateboarding began in the early 1950s and evolved to building greater speeds and getting airborne to do tricks, thus the sport of vert or vertical skateboarding. The book discusses safety, parts of the skateboard, the moves, and going pro.

Deuker, Carl. *High Heat*. Houghton Mifflin, 2003. ISBN: 0-618-31117-3.

> Within six months it was all gone—the big house, Lexus cars, and private school education. Shane would never know if his father was a criminal or not; however, after his father committed suicide, it did not matter. Now Shane waits at the public school bus stop with his head down while his former friends drive by. In his previous life, Shane was the closing pitcher at Shorelake, now he isn't sure if he even wanted to play ball. Before long, Shane is in trouble with the police and part of his rehabilitation is to work on conditioning the local baseball field. He meets Coach Cornelius Grandison, who is also the coach at the public high school. Shane has a spot on the high school baseball team; however, when he meets his former teammates in an unofficial game, his anger and resentment come out. Shane tricks the batter into stepping closer to the plate then throws a fast ball on the inside, hits the batter, and sends him to the hospital. Neither pitcher nor batter will ever be the same, and one year later they will meet in a playoff game.

Lupica, Mike. *The Underdogs*. Puffin Books, 2011. ISBN: 978-0-1424-2139-0.

> Will Tyler, 12 years old, loved the game of football and as a running back he could fly when his teammates opened up a hole for him and the end zone was in sight. Only this year, the city of Forbes had no money to sponsor his team. Will takes it upon himself to find a national sponsor, teammates, and coach. They were the bulldogs as well as underdogs when the season begins and they want "another shot at Castle Rock in another West River championship game."

Smith, Charles R. *Twelve Rounds to Glory: The Story of Muhammad Ali*. Candlewick Press, 2007. ISBN: 978-0-7636-1692-2.

> Bryan Collier illustrates the rap-inspired verse that accompanies the twelve rounds beginning with birth, January 17, 1943, and ending with Muhammad on the mountain.

"God gave me Parkinson's syndrome to show me I'm not 'The Greatest'—he is. To show me I have human frailties like everyone else does. That's all I am; a man."

## READ ALOUD

Osborne, Mary Pope. *Ancient Greece and the Olympics: A Nonfiction Companion to Hour of the Olympics*. Random House, 2004. ISBN: 0-375-92378-0.

Riggs, Kate. *Gladiators*. Creative Education, 2011. ISBN: 978-1-60818-000-4.

Sports Illustrated Kids. *Sports Illustrated Kids Big Book of Why Sports Edition*. Sports Illustrated for Kids, 2012. ISBN: 978-1-6189-3035-4.

Tavares, Matt. *Henry Aaron's Dream*. Candlewick, 2010. ISBN: 978-0-7636-3224-3.

Torres, John Albert. *Top 25 Basketball Skills, Tips, and Tricks*. Enslow Publishers, Inc., 2012. ISBN: 978-1-59845-356-0.

## BIBLIOGRAPHY

Alexie, Alexie Sherman. *The Absolutely True Diary of a Part-Time Indian*. Little, Brown, 2009. ISBN: 978-0-3160-1369-7. Gr 7 and up.

Barber, Tiki and Ronde. *End Zone*. Simon & Schuster, 2012. ISBN: 978-1-4169-9097-0. Gr 3–7. Kickoff series.

Barber, Tiki and Ronde. *Wild Card*. Simon & Schuster, 2012. ISBN: 978-1-4169-6859-7. Gr 3–7.

Bowen, Fred. *Perfect Game*. Peachtree Publishers, 2013. ISBN: 978-1-5614-5625-3. Gr 3 and up. Fred Bowen Sports Story series.

Bowen, Fred. *The Golden Glove*. Peachtree Publishers; Reissue edition, 2009. ISBN: 978-1-5614-5505-8. Gr 3 and up. The All-Star Sports Story series.

Bruchac, Joseph. *The Warriors*. Darby Creek, Reprint edition; 2004. ISBN: 1-58196-002-8. Gr 5–8.

Coy, John. *Take Your Best Shot*. Feiwel & Friends, 2012. ISBN: 978-0-3123-7332-0. Gr 3 and up. 4 for 4 series.

Coy, John. *Box Out*. Scholastic Press, 2008. ISBN: 978-0-4398-7032-0. Gr 7 and up.

Crutcher, Chris. *Period 8*. Greenwillow, 2013. SBN: 978-0-0619-1480-5. YA.

Crutcher, Chris. *Whale Talk*. Greenwillow Books; Reprint edition, 2009. ISBN: 0-0617-7131-7. YA.

Crutcher, Chris. *Deadline.* Greenwillow Books, Reprint edition, 2009. ISBN: 978-0-0608-5091-4. Gr 9 and up.

Deuker, Carl. *Payback Time.* Graphia; Reprint edition, 2012. ISBN: 978-0-5475-7733-3. Gr 7 and up.

Feinstein, John. *Rush for the Gold: Mystery at the Olympics.* Knopf Books for Young Readers, 2012. ISBN: 978-0-3758-6963-1. Gr 5 and up.

Feinstein, John. *Change-Up: Mystery at the World Series.* Knopf, 2009. ISBN: 978-0-375-85636-5. Gr 5–8.

Green, Tim. *Force Out.* HarperCollins, 2013. ISBN: 978-0-0620-8959-5. Gr 3–7.

Green, Tim. *Deep Zone.* HarperCollins, 2012. ISBN: 978-0-0620-1245-6. Gr 3–7. Football Genius series.

Green, Tim. *Perfect Season.* HarperCollins, 2013. ISBN: 978-0-0622-0869-9. Gr 3–7.

Gutman, Dan. *Roberto and Me.* HarperCollins, 2012. ISBN: 978-0-0612-3486-6. Gr 3 and up. Baseball Card Adventure series.

Heldring, Thatcher. *The League.* Delacorte Books for Young Readers, 2013. ISBN: 978-0-3857-4181-1. Gr 5 and up.

Hicks, Betty. *Doubles Troubles.* Roaring Brook Press, 2010. ISBN: 978-1-5964-3489-9. Gr 2–4. Gym Shorts series.

Jones, Gareth. *Ninja Meerkats (#1): The Clan of the Scorpion.* Square Fish, 2013. ISBN: 978-1-2500-1664-5. Gr 2–4.

Kelly, David A. *The Wrigley Riddle.* Random House Books for Young Readers, 2013. ISBN: 978-0-3079-7776-2. Gr 1–3. Baseball Mysteries series.

Knudson, Mike. *Raymond and Graham: Bases Loaded.* Viking, 2010. ISBN: 978-0-670-01205-3. Gr 3–5.

Lipsyte, Robert. *Raiders Night.* HarperTeen; Reprint edition, 2007. ISBN: 978-0-0605-9948-5. Gr 10–12.

Lipsyte, Robert. *The Twinning Project.* Clarion Books, 2012. ISBN: 978-0-5476-4571-1. Gr 5–8.

Lupica, Mike. *True Legend.* Puffin; Reprint edition, 2013. ISBN: 978-0-1424-2650-0. Gr 5–8.

Lupica, Mike. *Play Makers.* Scholastic Press, 2013. ISBN: 978-0-5453-8183-3. Gr 3 and up. Game Changers series.

Lupica, Mike. *QB 1*. Philomel, 2013. ISBN: 978-0-3992-5228-0. Gr 5 and up.

Mack, W. C. *Athlete vs. Mathlete*. Bloomsbury, 2013. ISBN: 978-1-5999-0915-8. Gr 3–6.

Maddox, Jake. *Hockey Meltdown*. Stone Arch Books, 2011. ISBN: 978-1-4342-3426-1. Gr 4 and up. Jake Maddox Sports Story series.

Maddox, Jake. *Lacrosse Attack*. Stone Arch Books, 2008. ISBN: 978-1-4342-0872-9. Gr 4 and up. Jake Maddox Sports Story series.

Markey, Kevin. *Rainmaker*. HarperCollins, 2012. ISBN: 978-0-0611-5228-3. Gr 3 and up. The Super Sluggers series.

Myers, Walter Dean. *The Greatest: Muhammad Ali*. Scholastic, 2001. ISBN: 0-590-54343-1. Gr. 7 and up.

Myers, Walter Dean. *Slam*. Scholastic Paperbacks, 2008. ISBN: 978-0-5450-5574-1. Gr 8 and up.

Myers, Walter Dean. *Kick*. HarperTeen, 2012. ISBN: 978-0-0620-0491-8. Gr 6–9.

Northrup, Michael. *Plunked*. Scholastic Press, 2012. ISBN: 978-0-5452-9714-1. Gr 3 and up.

Paulsen, Gary. *How Angel Peterson Got His Name and Other Outrageous Tales about Extreme Sports*. Yearling, 2004. ISBN: 978-0-4402-2935-3. Gr 5–8.

Ripken Jr, Cal. *Wild Pitch*. Hyperion Books CH, 2013. ISBN: 978-1-4231-4002-3. Gr 3 and up. Cal Ripken, Jr's All-Stars series.

Ritter, John H. *Fenway Fever*. Puffin; Reprint edition, 2013. ISBN: 978-0-1424-2491-9. Gr 5 and up.

Scieszka, Jon. *Guys Read the Sports Page*. Walden Pond, 2012. ISBN: 978-0-0619-6377-3. Gr 3 and up.

Smith, Andrew. *Winger*. Simon & Schuster Books for Young Readers, 2013. ISBN: 978-1-4424-4492-8. YA.

Tharp, Tim. *Knights of the Hill Country*. Laurel Leaf; Reprint edition, 2008. ISBN: 978-0-5534-9513-3. Gr 8 and up.

Tooke, Wes. *King of the Mound: My Summer with Satchel Paige*. Simon & Schuster Books for Young Readers, 2013. ISBN: 978-1-4424-3347-2. Gr 3 and up.

Volponi, Paul. *The Final Four*. Viking, 2012. ISBN: 978-0-6700-1264-0. Gr 9–12.

Wallace, Rich. *Game-Day Jitters*. Yearling, 2012. ISBN: 978-0-3758-5095-0. Gr 2–5. Kickers series.

Weaver, Will. *Checkered Flag Cheater: A Motor Novel*. Farrar, Straus and Giroux, 2010. ISBN: 978-0-3743-5062-8. Gr 7 and up. Motor Novels series.

## INFORMATIONAL

Aaseng, Nathan. *African-American Athletes*. Facts on File, 2003. ISBN: 0-8160-4805-3. Gr 8–12

Batten, Jack. *The Man Who Ran Faster Than Everyone: The Story of Tom Longboat*. Tundra Paper, 2002. ISBN: 0-88776-507-6. Gr 7–12.

Berman, Len. *The Greatest Moments in Sports: Upsets and Underdogs*. Sourcebooks, 2012. ISBN: 978-1-4022-7226-4. Gr 4–6.

Bonnet, Robert L. *Home Run!: Science Projects with Baseball and Softball*. Enslow, 2009. ISBN: 978-0-7660-3365-8, Gr 4–6. Score! Sports Science Projects series.

Breton, Marcos. *Home Is Everything: The Latino Baseball Story*. Cinco Puntos Paper, 2003. ISBN: 0-938317-70-9. Gr 7–12.

Buckley, James Jr. *The Ultimate Guide to Football*. Scholastic, 2010. ISBN: 978-0-531-20752-9. Gr 4 and up.

Buckley, James Jr. *The Ultimate Guide to Baseball*. Scholastic, 2010. ISBN: 978-0-531-20750-5. Gr 4 and up.

Carpenter, Tom. *Small Game Hunting: Bear, Deer, Elk, Sheep, and More*. Lerner, 2012. ISBN: 978-1-4677-0222-5. Gr 4–6. Great Outdoors Sports Zone series.

Catel, Patrick. *Surviving Stunts and Other Amazing Feats*. Heinemann, 2011. ISBN: 978-1-4109-3969-2. Gr 4–7.

Christopher, Matt. *On the Field with . . . Peyton and Eli Manning*. Little, Brown Books for Young Readers, 2008. Gr 3 and up. Matt Christopher Sports Biographies series.

Christopher, Matt. *On the Court with Dwight Howard*. Little, Brown Books for Young Readers, 2010. Gr 3 and up. Matt Christopher Sports Biographies series.

Clifford, Clive. *The Kingfisher Soccer Encyclopedia: The Facts the Goals the Superstars*. Kingfisher, 2006. ISBN: 978-0-7534-6397-0. Gr 3 and up.

Cole, Steve. *Kids' Easy Bike Care: Tune-Ups, Tools and Quick Fixes*. Williamson Paper, 2003. ISBN: 1-885593-86-4. Gr 5–9.

Crossingham, John. *Lacrosse in Action*. Crabtree, 2002. ISBN: 0-7787-0329-0. Gr 4–7.

Crossingham, John. *Wrestling in Action*. Crabtree, 2003. ISBN: 0-7787-0336-3. Gr 4–7.

Crossingham, John. *Cycling in Action*. Crabtree, 2002. ISBN: 0-7787-0118-2. Gr 4–7.

Crowther, Nicky. *The Ultimate Mountain Bike Book: The Definitive Illustrated Guide to Bikes, Components, Techniques, Thrills and Trails*. Firefly Paper, 2002. ISBN: 1-55297-653-X. Gr 7–12.

David, Jack. *Big Air Skateboarding*. Bellwether Media, 2008. ISBN: 978-1-60014-121-8. Gr 3 and up.

Doeden, Matt. *The World's Greatest Soccer Players*. Capstone Press, 2010. ISBN: 978-1-4296-3925-5. Gr 3 and up.

Doeden, Matt. *The Greatest Baseball Records*. Capstone Press, 2009. ISBN: 978-1-4296-2005-5. Gr 3 and up.

Doeden, Matt. *Kevin Durant: Basketball Superstar*. Capstone Press, 2012. ISBN: 978-1-4296-8004-2. Gr 1–3. Superstar Athletes series.

Dunning, Mark. *Basketball*. Sterling Paper, 2003. ISBN: 0-8069-9372-3. Gr 4–8.

Gifford, Clive. *From Tee to Green—The Essential Guide for Young Golfers*. Kingfisher, 2010. ISBN: 978-0-7534-6399-4. Gr 5–8.

Gigliotti, Jim. *Barefoot Waterskiing*. Child's World, 2011. ISBN: 978-1-6097-3177-9. Gr 5–8.

Goldblatt, David. *The Soccer Book: The Sport, the Teams, the Tactics, the Cups*. DK, 2009. ISBN: 978-0-7566-5098-8. Gr 6–12.

Goldner, John. *Hockey Talk: The Language of Hockey from A–Z*. Fitzhenry & Whiteside, 2010. ISBN: 978-1-5545-5092-0. Gr 6–9.

Grabowski, John F. *The Boston Celtics*. Gale, 2003. ISBN: 1-56006-937-6. Gr 7–9.

Haney-Withrow, Anna. *Tae Kwon Do*. Marshall Cavendish, 2012. ISBN: 978-0-7614-4940-9. Gr 4 and up.

Hill, Anne E. *LeBron James*. Twenty-First Century Books, 2012. ISBN: 978-0-7613-8641-4.

Hon, Shek. *BMX Riding Skills: The Guide to Flatland Tricks*. Firefly Books, 2010. ISBN: 978-1-5540-7400-6. Gr 6–12.

Hornby, Hugh. *Eyewitness Soccer*. DK, 2010. ISBN: 978-0-7566-6294-3. Gr 3–7.

Howes, Chris. *Caving*. Heinemann, 2003. ISBN: 1-58810-626-8. Gr 4–8.

Iggulden, Conn. *The Dangerous Book for Boys*. William Morrow, 2012. ISBN: 978-0-0622-0897-2. Gr 4–8.

Johnstone, Mike. *NASCAR*. Lerner, 2002. ISBN: 0-8225-0389-1. Gr 5–8.

Kalman, Bobbie. *Bowling in Action*. Crabtree, 2003. ISBN: 0-7787-0335-5. Gr 4–7.

King, Daniel. *Chess: From First Moves to Checkmate*. Houghton, 2000. ISBN: 0-7534-5279-0. Gr 4–6.

Kingsbury, Robert. *Roberto Clemente*. Rosen, 2003. ISBN: 0-8239-3602-3. Gr 4–7.

Krasner, Steven. *Play Ball Like the Pros: Tips for Kids from 20 Big League Stars*. Peachtree Paper, 2002. ISBN: 1-56145-261-0. Gr 5–9.

Lewis, Michael. *The Blind Side*. W. W. Norton and Company, 2006. ISBN: 978-0-3930-6123-9. Gr 9–12.

Mason, Paul. *Skiing*. Heinemann, 2003. ISBN: 1-58810-628-4. Gr 4–8.

Mattern, Joanne. *Basketball Greats. ISBN: 98-0-7868-0832-8*. Gale, 2003. ISBN: 1-59018-228-6. Gr 6–10.

MTV Overground. *Boards: The Art and Design of the Skateboard*. Universe Publishing, 2003. ISBN: 0-7893-0977-7. Adult.

Nelson, Kadir. *We Are the Ship: The Story of Negro League Baseball*. Hyperion, 2008. ISBN: 978-0-7868-0832-8. Gr 3 and up.

Oxlade, Chris. *Rock Climbing*. Lerner, 2003. ISBN: 0-8225-1240-8. Gr 3–6.

Pimm, Nancy Roe. *The Daytona 500: The Thrill and Thunder of the Great American Race*. Millbrook, 2011. ISBN: 978-0-7613-6677-5. Gr 5–8.

Roberts, Jeremy. *Tiger Woods: Golf's Master*. Lerner, 2008. ISBN: 978-1-5801-3569-9-6. Gr 5–8.

Robinson, Laura. *Cyclist Bikelist: The Book for Every Rider*. Tundra Paper, 2010. ISBN: 978-0-8877-6784-5. Gr 4–6.

Sandler, Michael. *Super Surfers*. Bearport, 2009. ISBN: 978-1-5971-6953-0. Gr 3–6.

Savage, Jeff. *Dale Earnhardt Jr*. Lerner Publications Company, 2009. ISBN: 978-1-4395-9177-2. Gr 2 and up. Amazing Athletes series.

Savage, Jeff. *Top 10 Physically Challenged Athletes*. Enslow, 2000. ISBN: 0-7660-1272-7. Gr 4–7.

Scandiffio, Laura. *The Martial Arts Book*. Annick Press, 2010. ISBN: 978-1-5503-7776-7. Gr 6 and up.

Scheppler, Bill. *The Ironman Triathlon*. Rosen, 2002. ISBN: 0-8239-3556-6. Gr 7–10.

Schlegel, Elfi. *The Gymnastics Book: The Young Performer's Guide to Gymnastics*.

Firefly Books, 2012. ISBN: 978-1-7708-5133-7. Gr 3–9.

Schwartz, Heather E. *Snowboarding.* Lucent, 2011. ISBN: 978-1-4205-0322-7. Gr 5–10.

St. John, Warren. *Outcasts United: The Story of a Refugee Soccer Team That Changed a Town.* Delacorte, 2012. ISBN: 978-0-385-74194-1. Gr 9–12.

Stewart, Mark. *Dale Earnhardt Jr.: Driven by Destiny.* Millbrook, 2003. ISBN: 0-7613-2908-0. Gr 5–8.

Stewart, Mark. *Daunte Culpepper: Command and Control.* Millbrook, 2002. ISBN: 0-7613-2613-8. Gr 4–7.

Stewart, Mark. *Score! The Action and Artistry of Hockey's Magnificent Moment.* Millbrook, 2010. ISBN: 978-0-8225-8753-8. Gr 5–8.

Stock, Charlotte and Ben Powell. *Skateboarding Step-By-Step.* Rosen Central, 2010. ISBN: 978-1-4358-3365-4. Gr 5 and up.

Stock, Charlotte and Ben Powell. *Tom Brady: Heart of the Huddle.* Millbrook, 2003. ISBN: 0-7613-2907-2. Gr 4–7.

Stutt, Ryan. *The Skateboarding Field Manual.* Firefly Books, 2009. ISBN: 978-1-5540-7467-9. Gr 6–12.

Sullivan, George. *Baseball's Boneheads, Bad Boys, and Just Plain Crazy Guys.* Millbrook, 2003. ISBN: 0-7613-2321-X. Gr 5–8.

Weekes, Don. *Explosive Hockey Trivia: Puzzles, Quizzes.* Douglas & McIntyre Paper, 2004. ISBN: 1-55-54-851-4. Adult.

Weekes, Don. *The Best and Worst of Hockey Firsts: The Unofficial Guide.* Douglas & McIntyre Paper, 2004. ISBN: 1-55-54-860-3. Adult.

Wells, Garrison. *Amateur Wrestling: Combat on the Mat.* Lerner Publications Company, 2012. ISBN: 978-0-7613-8460-1. Gr 4–8.

Woods, Bob. *Motorcross History.* Crabtree Publishing Company, 2008. ISBN: 978-0-7787-4000-1. Gr 4 and up.

Zeigler, Heidi. *Hang Gliding.* Children's, 2003. ISBN: 0-516-24320-9. Gr 4–8.

## PICTURE BOOKS

Adler, David A. *Joe Louis: America's Fighter.* Harcourt, 2005. ISBN: 0-15-216480-4. Gr K–3.

Bildner, Phil. *The Unforgettable Season: The Story of Joe DiMaggio, Ted Williams and the Record-Setting Summer of '41.* Putnam, 2011. ISBN: 978-0-399-25501-4. Gr K–3.

Blake, Robert J. *Swift*. Philomel, 2007. ISBN: 978-0-399-23383-8. Gr K–3.

Bolden, Tonya. *The Champ: The Story of Muhammad Ali*. Knopf, 2004. ISBN: 0-375-82401-4. Gr K–3.

Boone, Mary. *Tim Lincecum*. Mitchell Lane, 2011. ISBN: 978-1-6122-8058-5. Gr 2–4.

Borden, Louise. *The Greatest Skating Race: A World War II Story from the Netherlands*. McElderry, 2004. ISBN: 0-689-84502-2. Gr K–3.

Bruchac, James. *Raccoon's Last Race: A Traditional Abenaki Story*. Dial, 2004. ISBN: 0-8037-2977-4. Gr K–3.

Buitrago, Jairo. *Jimmy the Greatest*. Groundwood, 2012. ISBN: 978-1-5549-8178-6. Gr PS–2.

Cline-Ransome, Lesa. *Young Pele: Soccer's First Star*. Random, 2007. ISBN: 978-0-375-93599-2. Gr K–3.

Compestine, Ying Chang. *Crouching Tiger*. Candlewick, 2011. ISBN: 978-0-7636-4642-4. Gr K–3.

Cooper, Floyd. *Jump!: From the Life of Michael Jordan*. Philomel, 2004. ISBN: 0-399-24230-9. Gr K–3.

Coy, John. *Hoop Genius: How a Desperate Teacher and a Rowdy Gym Class Invented Basketball*. Carolrhoda, 2013. ISBN: 978-0-7613-6617-1. Gr K–3.

Crowe, Chris. *Just as Good: How Larry Doby Changed America's Game*. Candlewick, 2012. ISBN: 978-0-7636-5026-1. Gr 1–3.

De La Pena, Matt. *A Nation's Hope: The Story of Boxing Legend Joe Louis*. Dial, 2011. ISBN: 978-0-8037-3167-7. Gr 1–3.

DiPrimio, Pete. *Dwayne Wade*. Mitchell Lane, 2011. ISBN: 978-1-6122-8063-9. Gr 2–4.

Foreman, Michael. *Wonder Goal*. Farrar, 2003. ISBN: 0-374-38500-9. Gr K–3.

Gagne, Tammy. *LeBron James*. Mitchell Lane, 2010. ISBN: 978-1-5841-5858-5. Gr 1–3.

Gantos, Jack. *Three Strikes for Rotten Ralph*. Farrar, 2011. ISBN: 978-0-374-36354-3. Gr 1–3.

Gutman, Dan. *Casey Back at Bat*. HarperCollins, 2007. ISBN: 978-0-06-056025-6. Gr K–3.

Hubbard, Crystal. *Game Set Match Champion Arthur Ashe*. Lee & Low, 2010. ISBN: 978-1-60060-366-2. Gr 4–7.

Jenkins, Steve. *The Top of the World: Climbing Mount Everest*. Houghton, 1999. ISBN: 0-395-94218-7. Gr K–3.

Lester, Helen. *Tacky and the Winter Games*. Houghton, 2005. ISBN: 0-618-55659-1. Gr K–3.

Lewin, Ted. *Horse Song: The Naadam of Mongolia*. Lee, 2008. ISBN: 978-1-58430-277-3. Gr K–3.

Michelson, Richard. *Lipman Pike: America's First Home Run King*. Sleeping Bear, 2011. ISBN: 978-1-58536-465-7. Gr 2–4.

Mochizuki, Ken. *Be Water, My Friend: The Early Years of Bruce Lee*. Lee, 2006. ISBN: 1-58430-265-8. Gr K–3.

Myers, Christopher. *H.O.R.S.E.* Egmont USA, 2012. ISBN: 978-1-60684-218-8. Gr 3–6.

Myers, Walter Dean. *Muhammad Ali: The People's Champion*. HarperCollins, 2010. ISBN: 978-0-06-029131-0. Gr 1–3.

O'Brien, John. *The Beach Patrol*. Holt, 2004. ISBN: 0-8050-6911-9. Gr K–3.

Perdomo, Willie. *Clemente!* Henry Holt, 2010. ISBN: 978-0-8050-8774-1. Gr 1-3.

Robinson, Sharon. *Jackie's Gift: A True Story of Christmas, Hanukkah, and Jackie Robinson*. Viking, 2010. ISBN: 978-0-6700-1162-9. Gr K–3.

Rodriguez, Edel. *Sergio Saves the Game!* Little, 2009. ISBN: 978-0-316-06617-4. Gr K–3.

Salerno, Steven. *Brothers at Bat*. Clarion, 2012. ISBN: 978-0-5473-8557-0. Gr 1–3.

Shannon, David. *Jangles: A Big Fish Story*. Scholastic, 2012. ISBN: 978-0-545-14312-7. Gr K–3.

Smith Jr., Charles R. *Black Jack: The Ballad of Jack Johnson*. Roaring Brook Press, 2010. ISBN: 978-1-59643-473-8. Gr PK–1.

Tavares, Matt. *Henry Aaron's Dream*. Candlewick, 2010. ISBN: 978-0-7636-3224-3. Gr 2–4.

Tavares, Matt. *There Goes Ted Williams: The Greatest Hitter Who Ever Lived*. Candlewick, 2012. ISBN: 978-0-7636-2789-8. Gr 2–5.

Tavares, Matt. *Becoming Babe Ruth*. Candlewick, 2013. ISBN: 978-0-7636-5646-1. Gr K–3.

Vernick, Audrey. *Brothers at Bat: The True Story of an Amazing All-Brother Baseball Team*. Clarion, 2012. ISBN: 978-0-5473-8557-0. Gr PK–3.

Winter, Jonah. *You Never Heard of Sandy Koufax?!* Random. 2009. ISBN: 978-0-375-83738-8. Gr K–3.

Winter, Jonah. *You Never Heard of Willie Mays?!* Random, 2013. ISBN: 978-0-375-86844-3. Gr K–3.

Wise, Bill. *Silent Star: The Story of Deaf Major League William Hoy.* Lee, 2012. ISBN: 978-1-60060-411-9. Gr K–3.

Yolen, Jane. *All Star! Honus Wagner and the Most Famous Baseball Card Ever.* Philomel, 2010. ISBN: 978-0-399-24661-6. Gr 1–3.

Yoo, Paula. *Sixteen Years in Sixteen Seconds.* Lee, 2005. ISBN: 1-58430-247-X. Gr K–3.

## ANNOTATED BOOK FOR BOYS

Scieszka, Jon. *Guys Read: The Sports Pages.* Walden Pond Press, 2012.
  This book contains 10 stories by a variety of well-known authors. Selected by Jon Scieszka, they are guaranteed to put the reader in the ring, under the basket, and right behind home plate. Most of the activities that boys do turn into sports of one kind or another: rope swinging, speed pizza eating, apple war, bicycle polo, and Frisbee butt waterskiing.

# Chapter 20

# THRILLERS AND MYSTERY

Many boys welcome a good mystery packed with lots of clues, cliff-hangers, and intrigue. The idea of being a detective and figuring out who done it has a strong attraction for boys' imaginations. It offers them a fun way to dig for facts and mentally piece together puzzles. Boys also like chilling movies and stories about ghosts, vampires, and zombies because they can project how brave and fearless they can be—and the creepier the story the better. R. L. Stine's Goosebumps Series has proved to be good reads for boys; the covers are always scary and the stories are not all that bad. The Stine books for teens are much more frightening and menacing. Today, there are a number of entertaining thriller series for all ages that boys will love.

## FEATURED AUTHORS

Name: M. T. Anderson

Birth date: November 4, 1968

Place of Birth: Stowe, Massachusetts

Most popular book(s): Feed, Thirsty

About: Being a somewhat shy individual, Anderson has stated that he greatly prefers writing to speaking in a public persona. However, in his writings, he does not shy from taking on difficult questions and deeper, more mature concepts and themes. Unlike many other young adult authors, Anderson views the characters he creates simply as figures moving and acting on his terms.

Web site: http://www.mt-anderson.com

Name: James Preller

Birth date: February 1, 1961

Place of Birth: Wantagh, Long Island, New York

Most popular book(s): Scary Tales: Home Sweet Horror; Scary Tales: I Scream, You Scream

About: Preller still likes peanut butter and jelly sandwiches and still cares—deeply, foolishly, insanely—about the scores of professional baseball games. He is probably best known for writing the Jigsaw Jones mystery series.

Web site: http://www.jamespreller.com

## ANNOTATIONS

Anderson, M. T. *Thirsty*. Candlewick Press, 2003. ISBN: 0-7636-2014-9.
Chris is noticing some physical changes that he is struggling to control. He is having trouble sleeping and eating. One day, in the woods, he is separated from his friends and meets up with an Avatar of the Forces of Light known as Chet. He tells Chris what he already suspected: With the onset of puberty, Chris will change into a vampire within four months. In this society vampires are hunted and publicly executed. Chet offers to cure Chris of the "scourge of vampirism" if he will act as a spy among the vampires. Chet wants Chris to enter their den, take an object through the gates of the Vampire Lord, activate it, and then leave it behind. This object, the Arm of Moriator, will destroy the Vampire Lord if he tries to escape. Chris agrees to help Chet but he is not sure Chet is telling the truth. Is Chet a celestial being? Is he able to cure Chris?

Faryon, Cynthia J. *Real Justice: Guilty of Being Weird: The Story of Guy Paul Morin*. Lorimer, 2012. ISBN: 978-1-4594-0092-4.
Guy Paul went to the mall and the grocery store after work. He arrived home around 5:30 in the afternoon. In the meantime, his nine-year-old neighbor was abducted, raped, and murdered sometime before 4:10 when her mother and brother arrived home. In spite of the time difference, the police were guilty of tunnel vision and were convinced that Guy Paul, who was considered weird, was responsible for the little girl's death. After ten years and two trials, Guy Paul was declared innocent because of the just developed science of DNA. His thoughts later in an interview, "It is wonderful for you as much as it is for me, because what happened to me could happen to you, and I have been through an experience that I would not wish on anyone."

Lyga, Barry. *I Hunt Killers*. Little, Brown and Company, 2012. ISBN: 978-0-316-12584-0.
Jazz, fifteen years old, is the son of Billy Dent, a notorious serial killer who has been in jail for four years. Jazz has an insider view of the crimes: the trophies, thoughts, and manipulations of his "Dear old Dad's" prospects or victims. When several murders occur in his small town, Jazz wants to make some good use of what his father taught him to catch The Impressionist, a copycat serial killer. "If I catch killers, then maybe that means I am not a killer." The second of this series was published in 2013, a taut psychological thriller.

Owen, Ruth. *Zombies and Other Walking Dead*. Bearport Publishing, 2013. ISBN: 978-1-61772-4.
A zombie is a dead body that rises out of the grave in a trance. Several stories are related about people who were considered zombies; however, plausible explanations help to find the truth behind these terrifying tales.

Platt, Richard. *Crime Scene: The Ultimate Guide to Forensic Science.* DK Publishing, 2003. ISBN: 0-7894-8891-4. YA.

> Forensic science is a science as it relates to law but it must be combined with "the knowledge, experience, and intuition of detectives, uniformed police, and civilian experts, and administrators" to be effective. The chapters include: At the Crime Scene, The Victim, Human Identification, The Suspect, Analysis of Evidence, Lethal Agents, and Crimes without Corpses or White-Collar Crimes. Each chapter includes many visuals, compelling information, followed by an actual case study.

Preller, James. *Scary Tales: Home Sweet Horror.* Feiwel and Friends, 2013. ISBN: 978-1-250-01887-8.

> Liam's father, his sister Kelly, and the family dog move to upstate New York to start a new life after his mother dies. When they move into a haunted house and are threatened by "Bloody Mary," mom sends them a message that saves their lives. A chilling story for the younger reader.

Snead, Rebecca. *Liar & Spy.* Random, 2012. ISBN: 978-0-3857-3743-2.

> Georges's father loses his job, his mother works longer hours, and they move from their house to an apartment where he meets Safer, a boy his age and his younger sister, Candy. Through friendship Georges sees the big picture in this story about lies, spies, and bullies.

## READ ALOUD

MacLeod, Elizabeth. *Royal Murder: The Deadly Intrigue of Ten Sovereigns.* Annick Press, 2008. ISBN: 978-1-5545-1128-0.

O'Reilly, Bill. *Kennedy's Last Days: The Assassination that Defined a Generation.* Holt, 2013. ISBN: 978-0-8050-9802-0.

Sheinkin, Steve. *Bomb: The Race to Build—and Steal—the World's Most Dangerous Weapon.* Roaring Book, 2012. ISBN: 978-1-5964-3487-5.

## BIBLIOGRAPHY

### Thriller

Almond, David. *Clay.* Delacorte, 2006. ISBN: 0-385-73171-X. YA.

Anderson, M. T. *Zombie Mommy.* Beach Lane Books, 2011. ISBN: 978-1-4424-5440-8. Gr 5 and up.

Anderson, M. T. *The Suburb Beyond the Stars.* Scholastic, 2010. ISBN: 978-0-545-13882-6. Gr 4–6.

Augarde, Steve. *X Isle.* David Fickling Books, 2010. ISBN: 038-575193-1. Gr 7 and up.

Avi. *Seer of Shadows.* HarperCollins, 2008. ISBN: 978-0-06-000015-8. Gr 4–6.

Beaudoin, Sean. *The Infects.* Candlewick, 2012. ISBN: 978-0-7636-5947-9. YA.

Becker, Tom. *Lifeblood.* Scholastic, 2008. ISBN: 978-0-545-03742-6. YA.

Bick, Ilsa J. *Shadows.* Egmont, 2012. ISBN: 978-1-60684-176-1. YA.

Black, Holly. *Doll Bones.* Margaret K. McElderry Books, 2013. ISBN: 978-1-4169-6398-1. Gr 5 and up.

Brewer, Heather. *First Kill.* Dial, 2011. ISBN: 978-0-8037-3741-9. YA.

Brooks, Kevin. *The Road of the Dead.* Scholastic, 2006. ISBN: 0-439-78623-1. YA.

Bruchac, Joseph. *Bearwalker.* HarperCollins, 2007. ISBN: 978-0-0611-2311-5. Gr 4–6.

Buckingham, Royce. *The Dead Boys.* Putnam, 2010. ISBN: 978-0-399-25222-8. Gr 4–6.

Burgess, Melvin. *The Ghost Behind the Wall.* Holt, 2003. ISBN: 0-8050-7149-0. Gr 5–7.

Cabot, Meg. *Haunted.* HarperCollins, 2003. ISBN: 0-06-029471-X Gr. 7–10.

Carmody, Isobelle. *The Gathering.* Dial, 1996. ISBN: 0-8037-1716-4. YA.

Coville, Bruce. *Oddest of All.* Harcourt, 2008. ISBN: 978-0-15-205808-1. Gr 4–6.

Dakin, Glenn. *The Society of Unrelenting Vigilance.* Egmont, 2009. ISBN: 978-1-60684-015-3. Gr 4–6.

Del Negro, Janice M. *Passion and Poison: Tales of Shape-Shifters, Ghosts, and Spirited Women.* Cavendish, 2007. ISBN: 978-0-7614-5361-1. Gr 4–6.

Despeyroux, Denise. *Dark Graphic Tales by Edgar Allan Poe.* Enslow, 2012. ISBN: 978-0-7660-4086-1. Gr 4–6.

Doctorow, Cory. *Homeland.* Tor Teen, 2013. ISBN: 978-0-7653-3369-8. YA.

Fleming, Candace. *On the Day I Died: Stories from the Grave.* Schwartz & Wade, 2012. ISBN: 978-0-3758-6781-1. Gr 5 and up.

Gaiman, Neil. *The Graveyard Book.* HarperCollins Publishers, 2008. ISBN: 978-0-0605-3092-1. Gr 5 and up.

Gewirtz, Adina. *Zebra Forest.* Candlewick Press, 2013. ISBN: 978-0-7636-6041-3. YA.

Gilman, Charles. *Professor Gargoyle Tales from Lovecraft Middle School #1.* Quirk Books, 2012. ISBN: 978-1-59474-591-1. Gr 4–7.

Higgins, F.E. *The Eyeball Collector.* Feiwel, 2009. ISBN: 978-0-312-56681-4. Gr 4–6.

Higson, Charlie. *The Enemy.* Hyperion, 2010. ISBN: 978-1-4231-3175-5. YA.

Horowitz, Anthony. *Oblivion*. Scholastic Press, 2013. ISBN: 978-0-4396-8004-2. Gr 4–6. The Gatekeepers series.

Horowitz, Anthony. *Return to Groosham Grange: The Unholy Grail*. Philomel, 2009. ISBN: 978-0-399-25063-7. YA.

Jacobs, John Hornor. *The Twelve-Fingered Boy*. Carolrhoda Lab, 2013. ISBN: 978-0-7613-9007-7. YA.

Jinks, Catherine. *Evil Genius*. Graphia, 2011. ISBN: 978-0-1520-6185-2. Gr 7 and up.

MacHale, D. J. *Sylo*. Razorbill, 2013. ISBN: 978-1-5951-4665-6. YA.

McBride, Lish. *Hold Me Closer, Necromancer*. Macmillan Children's Book Group, 2010. ISBN: 978-0-8050-9098-7. Gr 8 and up.

McDonald, Megan. *Stink and the Midnight Zombie Walk*. Candlewick Press, 2012. ISBN: 978-0-7636-5692-8. Gr 1–4.

Poznanski, Ursula. *Erebos: It's a Game. It Watches You.* Annick Press, 2012. ISBN: 978-1-5545-1373-4. Gr 7 and up.

Rapp, Adam. *The Children and the Wolves*. Candlewick, 2012. ISBN: 978-0-7636-5337-8. Gr 9–12.

Rees, Douglas. *Vampire High*. Delacorte, 2003. ISBN: 0-385-73117-5. Gr 6–9.

Regan, Sally. *The Vampire Book*. DK Publishing, 2009. ISBN: 978-0-7566-5551-8. Gr 5 and up.

San Souci, Robert D. *Dare to Be Scared: Thirteen Stories to Chill and Thrill*. Cricket, 2003. ISBN: 0-8126-2688-5. Gr 4–8.

Schreiber, Joe. *Perry's Killer Playlist*. Houghton Mifflin, 2012. ISBN: 978-0-5476-0117-5. YA.

Scieszka, Jon. *Guys Read: Thriller*. Walden Pond, 2011. ISBN: 978-0-0619-6375-9. Gr 3 and up.

Scott, Kiernan. *Jungle Boy*. Delacorte, 2003. ISBN: 0-385-73113-2. Gr 6–9.

Shan, Darren. *Zom-B City*. Little, Brown, 2013. ISBN: 978-0-316-21436-0. Gr 7-10. Zom-B series.

Stine, R. L. *Goosebumps Most Wanted #3: How I Met My Monster*. Scholastic, 2013. ISBN: 978-0-5454-1800-3. Gr 3–7.

Thomas, Lex. *Quarantine: The Loners*. Egmont, 2012. ISBN: 978-1-6068-4329-1. Gr 10–12.

Valentine, Jenny. *Double*. Disney-Hyperion, 2012. ISBN: 978-1-4231-4714-5. Gr 7 and up.

Wells, Robinson. *Variant*. HarperTeen, 2011. ISBN 978-0-0620-2608-8. Gr 8 and up.

Wildavsky, Rachel. *The Secret of Rover*. Amulet Books, 2011. ISBN: 978-0-8109-9710-3. Gr 5 and up.

Wynne-Jones, Tim. *Blink & Caution*. Candlewick Press, 2011. ISBN: 978-0-7636-3983-9. Gr 9 and up.

Young, Suzanne. *The Program*. Simon Pulse, 2013. ISBN: 978-1-4424-4580-2. YA.

Zadoff, Allen. *Boy Nobody*. Little, Brown, 2013. ISBN: 978-0-31619968-1. YA.

## Mystery

Adam, Paul. *Max Cassidy: Escape from Shadow Islands*. HarperCollins, 2009. ISBN: 978-0-06-186323-3. Gr 5–9.

Avi. *Murder at Midnight*. Scholastic, 2009. ISBN: 978-0-545-08090-3. Gr 5–8.

Baccalario, Pierdomenico. *Star of Stone*. Random House, 2010. ISBN: 978-0-375-85896-3. Gr 5–9.

Balliett, Blue. *The Danger Box*. Scholastic, 2010. ISBN: 978-0-4398-5209-8. Gr 3–6.

Barnett, Mac. *The Ghostwriter Secret*. Simon & Schuster, 2010. ISBN: 978-1-4169-7817-6. Gr 3–6.

Barrett, Tracey. *The Case That Time Forgot*. Henry Holt, 2010. ISBN: 978-0-8050-8046-9. Gr 4–6. Sherlock Files series.

Bosch, Pseudonymous. *Write This Book: A Do-It-Yourself Mystery*. Little, Brown Books for Young Readers, 2013. ISBN: 978-0-3162-0781-2. Gr 4–7. Secret series.

Bowler, Tim. *Storm Catchers*. Simon & Schuster, 2003. ISBN: 0-689-84573-1. Gr 6–10.

Bray, Libba. *The Diviners*. Little, Brown Books for Young Readers, 2012. ISBN: 978-0-3161-2611-3. YA.

Brezenoff, Steve. *The Zoo With the Empty Cage*. Stone Arch, 2009. ISBN: 978-0-4342-1610-6. Gr 3–6.

Broach, Elise. *Missing on Superstition Mountain*. Henry Holt, 2011. ISBN: 978-0-8050-9047-5. Gr 3–5.

Brooks, Kevin. *Black Rabbit Summer*. Push; Reprint edition, 2009. ISBN: 978-0-5450-6089-9. Gr 9–12.

Buckley, Michael. *M Is for Mama's Boy*. Abrams, 2010. ISBN: 978-0-8109-8986-3. Gr 4–7.

Butler, Dori Hillestad. *The Case of the Fire Alarm*. Whitman, 2010. ISBN: 978-0-8075-0935-7. Gr 2–4.

Butler, Dori Hillestad. *The Case of the Lost Boy*. Whitman, 2010. ISBN: 978-0-8075-0910-4. Gr 1–3.

Cheshire, Simon. *Treasure of Dead Man's Lane and Other Case Files*. Roaring Brook, 2010. ISBN: 978-1-5964-3475-2. Gr 4–7.

Clements, Andrew. *Fear Itself*. Atheneum, 2011. ISBN: 978-1-4169-3887-3. Gr 4–6.

Conly, Jane Leslie. *Murder Afloat*. Hyperion, 2010. ISBN: 978-1-4231-0416-2. Gr 5–8.

Dickinson, Peter. *The Tears of the Salamander*. Random, 2003. ISBN: 0-385-73098-5. Gr 4–6.

Dixon, Franklin W. *The Tower Treasure*. Penguin Group, 1987. ISBN: 978-0-4480-8901-0. Gr 3 and up. Hardy Boys series.

Doyle, Sir Arthur Conan. *Adventures of Sherlock Holmes*. Avon Paper, 1981. ISBN: 0-380-78105-0. Gr 7–12. Classic.

Evans, Lissa. *Horten's Miraculous Mechanisms: Magic, Mystery, and a Very Strange Adventure*. Sterling Children's Books, 2012. ISBN: 978-1-4027-9806-1. Gr 3–6.

Gaiman, Neil et al. *Coraline*. HarperCollins Paper, 2004. ISBN: 0-06-057591-3. Gr 6–8.

Gibbs, Stuart. *Spy School*. Simon & Schuster, 2012. ISBN: 978-1-4424-2182-0. Gr 4–7.

Giles, Stephen M. *The Death (and Further Adventures) of Silas Winterbottom*. Sourcebooks, 2010. ISBN: 978-1-4022-4090-4. Gr 5–7.

Grabenstein, Chris. *The Smoky Corridor*. Random House, 2010. ISBN: 978-0-375-96511-1. Gr 5–8.

Grant, Katy. *Hide and Seek*. Peachtree, 2010. ISBN: 978-1-56145542-3. Gr 5–8.

Grisham, John. *Theodore Boone: The Activist*. Dutton Juvenile, 2013. ISBN: 978-0-5254-2577-9. Gr 3 and up.

Grisham, John. *Theodore Boone: The Accused*. Dutton Juvenile, 2012. ISBN: 978-0-5254-2576-1. Gr 3 and up.

Haddix, Margaret Peterson. *Into the Gauntlet*. Scholastic, Inc., 2010. ISBN: 978-0-5450-6050-9. Gr 3-7. The 39 Clues series.

Hahn, Mary Downing. *Closed for the Season*. Sandpiper; Reprint edition, 2010. ISBN: 978-0-5473-9853-2. Gr 5 and up.

Hiaasen, Carl. *Scat*. Knopf, 2009. ISBN: 978-0-3759-3486-5. Gr 5–8.

Higgins, Jack. *First Strike*. Putnam, 2010. ISBN: 978-0-3992-5240-2. Gr 5–8.

Horowitz, Anthony. *The Greek Who Stole Christmas*. Penguin Paper, 2008. ISBN: 978-0-1424-0375-4. Gr 4–7.

Irving, Washington. *The Legend of Sleepy Hollow*. Atheneum, 2007. ISBN: 978-1-4169-0625-4. Gr 4–6.

Jackson, Melanie. *The Big Dip*. Orca Paper, 2009. ISBN: 978-1-55469-178-4. Gr 4–7.

Kelly, Katy. *Melonhead and the Undercover Operation*. Delacorte, 2011. ISBN: 978-0-385-90618-0. Gr 3–-5.

Klise, Kate. *Till Death Do Us Bark*. Harcourt, 2011. ISBN: 978-0-5474-0036-5. Gr 3–6.

Krosoczka, Jarrett. *The Frog Who Croaked*. Walden Pond Press, 2013. ISBN: 9780-06-207165-4. Gr 3–7.

Krulik, Nancy. *Jack Gets a Clue: The Case of the Beagle Burglar*. Scholastic Inc., 2011. ISBN: 978-0-545-26654-3. Gr 2–5.

Lacey, Josh. *Island of Thieves*. Houghton Mifflin, 2012. ISBN: 978-0-5477-6327-9. Gr 4–7.

Lawrence, Caroline. *P. K. Pinkerton and the Petrified Man*. Putnam Juvenile, 2013. ISBN: 978-0-3992-5634-9. Gr 3 and up.

Lawrence, Caroline. *The Case of the Deadly Desperados*. G. P. Putnam's Sons, 2012. ISBN: 978-0-3992-5633-2. Gr 3–7.

Legrand, Claire. *The Cavendish Home for Boys and Girls*. Simon & Schuster, 2013. ISBN: 978-1-4424-4292-4. Gr 5–8.

Lerangis, Peter. *The Sword Thief*. Scholastic, 2009. ISBN: 978-0-5450-6043-1. Gr 3–7. The 39 Clues series.

MacDonald, Bailey. *The Secret of the Sealed Room: A Mystery of Young Benjamin Franklin*. Simon & Schuster, 2010. ISBN: 978-1-4169-9760-3. Gr 5–8.

Mone, Gregory. *Fish*. Scholastic, 2010. ISBN: 978-0-545-11632-9. Gr 3–5.

Mulligan, Andy. *Trash*. David Fickling Books, 2010. ISBN: 978-0-3857-5214-5. Gr 7 and up.

Newsome Richard. *The Billionaire's Curse*. HarperCollins, 2010. ISBN: 978-0-06-194490-1. Gr 4–6.

Nixon, Joan Lowry. *Ghost Town*. Delacorte, 2000. ISBN: 0-385-32681-5. Gr 4–7 .

Norriss, Andrew. *I Don't Believe It, Archie!* Random, 2012. ISBN: 978-0-385-75251-0. Gr 1–3.

Oates, Joyce Carol. *Freaky Green Eyes*. HarperCollins, 2003. ISBN: 0-06-623759-9. YA.

Osborne, Mary Pope. *Blizzard of the Blue Moon*. Random, 2006. ISBN: 0-375-83037-5. Gr 1–3.

Pullman, Philip. *Two Crafty Criminals! And How They Were Captured by the Daring Detectives of the New Cut Gang*. Knopf, 2012. ISBN: 978-0-3758-7029-3. Gr 3–6.

Roy, Ron. *Turkey Trouble on the National Mall*. Random House, 2012. ISBN: 978-0-307-93220-4. Gr 1–4. Capital Mysteries series (14).

Roy, Ron. *January Joker*. Random House, 2009. ISBN: 978-0-375-95661-4. Gr 1–3. Calendar Mysteries series.

Sachar, Louis. *Holes*. Dell Yearling, 2000. ISBN: 978-0-4404-1480-3. Gr 3–7.

Seidler, Tor. *Brainboy and the Deathmaster*. HarperCollins, 2003. ISBN: 0-06-029181-8. Gr 4–7.

Shan, Darren. *Trials of Death*. Little, Brown, 2003. ISBN: 0-316-60637-8. YA.

Sharman, Marjorie Weinman. *Nate the Great and the Hungry Book Club*. Delacorte, 2009. ISBN: 978-0-385-73695-4. Gr 1–3.

Silvey, Craig. *Jasper Jones*. Ember; Reprint edition, 2012. ISBN: 978-0-3758-6627-2. Gr 7 and up.

Skurzynski, Gloria and Alane Ferguson. *Buried Alive*. National Geographic, 2003. ISBN: 0-7922-6966-7. Gr 4–7.

Smith, Roland. *I. Q.* Sleeping Bear Paper, 2008. ISBN: 978-1-5853-6325-4. Gr 5–8.

Snicket, Lemony. *"Who Could That Be at This Hour?" (All the Wrong Questions)*. Little, Brown Books for Young Readers, 2012. ISBN: 978-0-3161-2308-2. Gr 4–7.

Sobol, Donald J. *Encyclopedia Brown, Super Sleuth*. Dutton, 2009. ISBN: 978-0-5254-2100-9. Gr 3–6.

Springer, Nancy. *Blood Trail*. Holiday House, 2003. ISBN: 0-8234-1723-9. YA.

Stewart, Trenton Lee. *The Extraordinary Education of Nicholas Benedict.* Little, Brown, 2012. ISBN: 978-0-3161-7619-4. Gr 4–6.

Tharp, Tim. *Mojo.* Knopf Books for Young Readers, 2013. ISBN: 978-0-3758-6445-2. Gr 7 and up.

Turnage, Sheila. *Three Times Lucky.* Dial, 2012. ISBN: 978-0-8037-3670-2. Gr 4–6.

Van Draanen, Wendelin. *Sammy Keyes and the Night of Skulls.* Knopf, 2011. ISBN: 978-0-3758-6108-6. Gr 5–8.

Van Draanen, Wendelin. *Sinister Substitute.* Knopf, 2010. ISBN: 978-0-3758-4378-5. Gr 3–5.

Warner, Gertrude Chandler. *The Spy in the Bleachers.* Whitman, 2010. ISBN: 978-0-8075-7606-9. Gr 2–5. Boxcar Children series.

Watson, Jude. *In Too Deep.* Scholastic, 2009. ISBN: 978-0-5450-6046-2. Gr 4–7. 39 Clues series.

Zindel, Paul. *The Gourmet Zombie.* Hyperion Paper, 2002. ISBN: 0-7868-1590-6. Gr 6–9.

Zindel, Paul. *The Phantom of 86th Street.* Hyperion/Volo Paper, 2002. ISBN: 0-7868-1591-4. Gr 6–9.

Zindel, Paul. *The Square Root of Mystery.* Hyperion Paper, 2002. ISBN: 0-7868-1388-4. Gr 5–7.

## INFORMATIONAL

Arnosky, Jim. *Monster Hunt: Exploring Mysterious Creatures with Jim Arnosky.* Hyperion, 2011. ISBN: 978-1-4231-3028-4. Gr 2–5.

Blackwood, Gary. *Mysterious Messages: A History of Codes and Ciphers.* Dutton Juvenile, 2009. ISBN: 978-0-5254-7960-4. Gr 4 and up.

Boyer, Crispin. *That's Gross!* National Geographic, 2012. ISBN: 978-1-4263-1127-7. Gr 3–7.

Bragg, Georgia. *How They Croaked: The Awful Ends of the Awfully Famous.* Walker & Company, 2012. ISBN: 978-0-8027-2794-7. Gr 5 and up.

Clark, Jerome. *Unexplained! Strange Sightings, Incredible Occurrences and Puzzling Physical Phenomena.* Visible Ink, 2012. ISBN: 978-1-5785-9344-6. YA.

Cooper, Chris. *Forensic Science.* DK Publishing, 2008. ISBN: 978-0-7566-3383-7. Gr 3–7.

Doft, Tony. *Nostradamus*. Children's Press, 2011. ISBN: 978-1-6001-4584-1. Gr 3–6.

Dunkleberger, Amy. *Write a Mystery in 5 Simple Steps*. Enslow, 2012. ISBN: 978-0-7660-3835-6. Gr 4–5.

Erickson, Justin. *Alien Abductions*. Children's Press, 2011. ISBN: 978-1-6001-4582-7. Gr 3–6. Unexplained series.

Everett, J. H. *Haunted Histories: Creepy Castles, Dark Dungeons, and Powerful Palaces*. Holt, 2012. ISBN: 978-0-8050-8971-4. Gr 4–6.

Fletcher, Ralph. *Guy Write: What Every Guy Writer Needs to Know*. Holt, 2012. ISBN: 978-0-8050-9404-6. Gr 4–6.

Friedlander, Mark P., Jr., and Terry M. Phillips. *When Objects Talk: Solving a Crime with Science*. Lerner, 2001. ISBN: 0-8225-0649-1. Gr 5–8.

Hirschmann, Kris. *Demons*. Reference-Point, 2011. ISBN: 978-1-6015-2147-7. Gr 5–8. Monsters and Mythical Creatures series.

Innes, Brian. *Forensic Science*. Mason Crest, 2003. ISBN: 1-59084-373-8. Gr 6–12.

Jackson, Donna M. *The Bone Detectives: How Forensic Anthropologists Solve Crimes and Uncover Mysteries of the Dead*. Little, Brown, 1996. ISBN: 0-316-82935-8. Gr 5–9.

Kline, Suzy. *Horrible Harry and the Dead Letters*. Viking, 2008. ISBN: 978-0-670-06346-8. Gr 1–3.

Murphy, Glenn. *Stuff That Scares Your Pants Off! A Book of Scary Things (and How to Avoid Them)*. Roaring Brook Paper, 2011. ISBN: 978-1-59643-633-6. Gr 4–8.

Murray, Elizabeth A. *Putting a Name and Face on Death*. Twenty-First Century Books, 2012. ISBN: 978-0-7613-6696-6. Gr 6–12.

Owens, David. *Police Lab Show Forensic Science Tracks Down and Convicts Criminals*. Firefly, 2002. ISBN: 1-55297-620-3. Gr 6–12.

Pearce, Q. L. *Ghost Hunters*. Kidhaven, 2011. ISBN: 978-0-7377-5290-8. Gr 5–7.

Steiger, Brad. *Real Ghosts, Restless Spirits and Haunted Places*. Visible Ink Press, 2003. ISBN: 9789-1-5785-9146-6. YA.

Tibballa, Geoff. *Ripley's Believe It or Not! Enter If You Dare!* Ripley Entertainment, 2011. ISBN: 978-1-8939-5163-1. Gr 5–7.

Valentino, Serena. *Undead: Everything the Modern Zombie Needs to Know*. Welson Owen Inc., 2012. ISBN: 978-1-61628-397-1. YA.

Walker, Sally M. *Written in Bone: Buried Lives of Jamestown and Colonial Maryland.* Carolrhoda Books, 2009. ISBN: 978-0-8225-7135-3. Gr 5 and up.

Williams, Dinah. *Monstrous Morgues of the Past.* Bearport, 2011. ISBN: 978-1-6177-2149-6. Gr 4–6. Scary Places series.

Yeatts, Tabatha. *Forensics: Solving the Crime.* Enslow, 2001. ISBN: 1-881508-75-7 Gr. 6–9.

## PICTURE BOOKS

Adler, David. *Bones and the Roller Coaster Mystery.* Viking, 2009. ISBN: 978-0-670-06340-6. Gr K–3.

Adler, David. *Young Cam Jansen and the 100th Day of School Mystery.* Viking, 2009. ISBN: 978-0-670-06172-3. Gr K–3.

Base, Graeme. *Enigma: A Magical Mystery.* Abrams, 2008. ISBN: 978-0-8109-7245-2. Gr K–3.

Bauer, Marion Dane. *The Green Ghost.* Random, 2008. ISBN: 978-0-375-84043-8. Gr 1–3.

Beaumont, Karen. *Where's My T-R-U-C-K?* Dial, 2011. ISBN: 978-0-8037-3222-3. Gr K–3.

Butler, Dori Hillestad. *The Case of the Library Monster.* Whitman, 2010. ISBN: 978-0-8075-0914-2. Gr 1–3.

Butler, Dori Hillestad. *The Case of the School Ghost.* Whitman, 2012. ISBN: 978-0-8075-0915-9. Gr 1–3.

Christelow, Eileen. *Where's the Big Bad Wolf?* Scholastic, 2005. ISBN: 978-0-4396-8487-3. Gr K–2.

Fleischman, Paul. *The Dunderheads Behind Bars.* Candlewick, 2012. ISBN: 978-0-7636-4543-4. Gr 1–3.

Gorpog, Judith. *In a Creepy, Creepy Place and Other Scary Stories.* HarperCollins, 1997. ISBN: 0-06-025-32-8. Gr 1–3.

Jacobson, Jennifer Richard. *Andy Shane and the Barn Sale Mystery.* Candlewick, 2009. ISBN: 978-0-7636-3599-2. Gr 1–3.

Kelly, David A. *The Fenway Foul-Up.* Random, 2011. ISBN: 978-0-375-96703-0. Gr 1–3.

Krensky, Stephen. *The Three Blind Mice Mystery.* Delacorte, 1995. ISBN: 0-440-41082-7. Gr 1–3.

Logan, Claudia. *The 5,000-Year-Old Puzzle: Solving a Mystery of Ancient Egypt*. Farrar, 2002. ISBN: 0-374-32335-6. Gr 1–3.

Michelson, Richard. *Did You Say Ghosts?* Simon & Schuster, 1998. ISBN: 0-02-766915-7. Gr 1 and up.

O'Connor, Jane. *Eek! Stories to Make You Shriek*. Penguin Young Readers, 1992. ISBN: 0-448-40382-3. Gr 2–4.

Reynolds, Aaron. *Creepy Carrots*. Simon & Schuster Books for Young Readers, 2012. ISBN: 978-1-4424-0297-3. Gr PK–3.

Schwartz, Alvin. *More Scary Stories to Tell in the Dark*. HarperCollins, 2010. ISBN: 978-0-06-083521. Gr K–3.

Stevenson, James. *The Mud Flat Mystery*. Little, Brown for Young Readers; First Edition reprint, 2013. ISBN: 978-0-3161-8748-0. Gr 1–3.

Van Allsburg, Chris. *The Mysteries of Harris Burdick*. Houghton Mifflin, 1984. ISBN: 0-395-35393-9. Gr K–3.

Wild, Margaret. Woolvs in the Sitee. Front, 2007. ISBN: 978-1-59078-500-3. Gr 6–9.

## ANNOTATED PROFESSIONAL BOOK

Scieszka, Jon. *Guys Read: Thriller*. Walden Pond Press, 2011.
   This book contains 10 stories by a variety of well-known authors. They are selected by Jon Scieszka and are the best thriller authors around. The writers deliver a wild mix of detectives, spooks, cryptids, snakes, pirates, smugglers, a body on the tracks, and one terribly powerful serving of fried pudding.

# Appendix A

# APPS

## READING

*A Story Before Bed:* More than 300 stories in this app's library for an interactive read-along experience with your child. Record video of storytime so that your little one can watch it again in the morning while paging through and following along! *iPad, iPhone, iPod Touch; $10 per month.*

*ABC Phonics Animals* offers several sections of activities to teach kids phonics while learning to identify animals. The app costs $1.99, and a free lite version is also available. One caveat: kid headphones may be needed with this app as the carnival-like sounds could become annoying.

*abc PocketPhonics,* priced at $2.99, teaches children more than 170 frequently used words. This app plays a recording of a letter and then asks the child to find the letter out of a group of about eight letters. When the child selects the correct letter, he or she receives a thumbs up and moves on. Additionally, it demonstrates how to write each letter by allowing children to trace the letter with their fingers. http://computer.howstuffworks.com/tablets/10-ipad-apps-for-teaching-kids-to-read.htm

*Blio* offers all the same features of any basic e-reader, and also a few things that make it unique. Through synchronized highlighting and a serial presentation view, the app helps those with reading disabilities make sense of the text, something many other similar apps do not offer.

*BOB Books #1* (free version).

*BOB Books* ($3.99 for the iPad or $1.99 for iPhone/iPod Touch).

*Bookster:* Young readers can find new literary faves with helpful narration from kids their age. Kids will also learn new vocabulary words and can record themselves reading the books when they've finished! *iPad, iPhone, iPod Touch, Android; free with first e-book.*

*Dragon Dictation:* Dragon Dictation works in reverse of the two apps we just listed. Instead of reading text out loud, the application writes down spoken text. For students who struggle with writing, it can be a great way for them to jot down ideas or get help learning.

*Flashcards for iPad:* This app makes it easy to study words, spelling, and other things that young and LD readers might need help with.

*iDiary for Kids Lite:* Although this isn't technically a reading app—reading and writing go hand-in-hand—it is a great diary option for young writers.

*iWrite Words,* priced at $2.99, focuses on handwriting and writing words. Once a child has written all of the letters in a line correctly, a drawing appears. The child then slides the letters onto a rotating hole to get to the next level. The app offers 70 levels of both upper- and lowercase letters, 20 levels of numbers and 26 levels of individual letter tracings for both upper- and lowercase letters. There is a free version as well.

*Jumbline:* If you are looking to make reading, writing, and spelling into a game, this app can help. It's full of word games that ask players to use speed, smarts, pattern recognition, and spelling skills to win.

*Learn to Read!:* Priced at $1.99, it is a technologically advanced spin on traditional flashcards. The app includes words from the Dolch Word List.

*Marbleminds:* Phonics (designed for both iPhone and iPad—$2.99).

*MeeGenius:* Highlight words for review and use the MeeGenius audio playback and a child can substitute his or her own name for that of a favorite character in the book! *iPad, iPhone, Android, Google TV; free with book selection.*

*Montessori Crosswords* (designed for both iPhone and iPad—$2.99).

*Question Builder* (iPad only—$5.99).

*Read 2 Me:* For those who have difficulty reading, apps like Read 2 Me can be a godsend. The app comes complete with an entire library of texts, all of which can be read out loud.

*Read Me Stories:* This *free* app features a new book every day!

*Reading Eggs Sight Words* (free version): Similar to the Paid Version, but with some restrictions.

*Reading Eggs Sight Words* (iPad only or get the version compatible with iPhones and iPod Touch here—$2.99).

*Reading Raven* (compatible with iPhone and iPad—$2.99, or get the HD iPad version—$3.99).

*Rock 'n Learn Phonics Easy Reader,* priced at $1.99, helps children develop their reading skills through three phonics stories. The stories can be read to the child or she can sound out the words and read the story. If the child needs some extra help with figuring out a word, she can click on the word for assistance. In the Read to Me section, a story is read aloud to the child. As the story is read, words are highlighted on the screen so that kids can read along.

*Sentence Builder:* Through this application, elementary school children will learn how to build grammatically correct sentences, with a special focus on using connector words.

*Speak It!* is a great text-to-speech solution that can allow students with reading disabilities to get a little help with reading when they need it.

*Speech with Milo: Sequencing* (Designed for both iPhone and iPad—$2.99).

*Spelling Bee Challenge:* Kids can have fun taking part in a mock spelling bee using this application that boosts both spelling and vocab skills.

*Story Builder:* After kids are done learning how to build sentences, they can move onto this app, which combines those sentences into one coherent story, complete with illustrations.

*Tales2Go:* A Parents' Choice Gold Award-winner that streams on-demand, unlimited access to more than 1,000 stories. Scroll through and sort by reader age, genre, and more. Bookmark and build a favorites list for easy return visits! *iPad, iPhone, iPod Touch; $10 per month.*

*The Land of Me—Story Time* (iPad only—$2.99).

*The Monster at the End of This Book:* This is a high-tech update of the original 1971 hardcover published by Golden Books. Sesame Street's Grover reads the title of the book and instantly becomes frightened about discovering the monster at the end of the story. The book is narrated by Grover, and the words are highlighted on the page so that children can follow along. This app, costing $3.99, is particularly fun for kids because they feel that they are interacting with Grover and playing a part in the completion of the story while they are learning reading and listening skills.

*The Writing Machine:* By correlating pictures and words, reading text, and sounding out letters, this tool helps students develop early literacy abilities with greater ease.

*Tikatok StorySpark:* From Barnes & Noble, kids write and illustrate their own books, using a catalog of art or their own photos or digital drawings for the backgrounds. When it's ready, books are "published" under a chosen pen name and posted online at Tikatok.com. *iPad, iPhone, iPod Touch, Android; app is free, books are $3 each.*

*TouchyBooks:* Quirky sounds, animation, and flip-book usability offer a realistic experience and a touch of magic for toddlers and tweens. *iPad, iPhone, iPod Touch, Android, Windows Phone; free with two free books.*

*Word Magic* is a spelling app that shows kids a picture of an object and gives them some of the letters of the word for it. They have to choose the letters that are missing by touching the screen. Based on the child's level, the missing letters can come from the beginning, middle, or end of the word. Priced at $.99.

*WordLadder:* This highly challenging word game will get older readers thinking about how words are spelled and how they can be connected and changed to form new words.

*Writing Prompts:* Having trouble thinking of things for students to write about? This app removes that roadblock and offers up numerous ideas for short writing assignments.

## GAMES

*Blox*
Available for: Android or iPhone
Download at: https://market.android.com/ or www.itunes.com
Cognitive skills: visual processing, processing speed, planning, strategy
Inspired by Tetris and Bubble Blast, this game lets you tilt and touch to play.


*Bubble Blast 2*
Available for: Android or iPhone
Download at: http://m.androlib.com/ or www.itunes.com
Cognitive skills: planning, visual processing, strategy
Burst the different colored bubbles and launch chain reactions to eliminate groups of bubbles.


*Hangman Free*
Available for: Android or iPhone
Download at: http://www.optimesoftware.com/ or www.itunes.com
Cognitive skills: logic and reasoning, visual processing, segmenting
This classic vocabulary game allows you to play against the machine or a friend.


*Kids Preschool Puzzle FREE*
Available for: Android or iPhone
Download at: https://market.android.com/ or www.itunes.com
Cognitive skills: visual processing, planning
This highly rated game offers 20 free puzzles and lots of positive reinforcement.


*Memory Matches*
Available for: Android or iPhone

Download at: https://market.android.com/ or www.itunes.com
Cognitive skills: working memory, short-term memory
Tough enough for grown-ups but easy enough for young children, this classic card-matching game can help anyone strengthen their memory.


*Motion Math Zoom*
Available for: Android and iPhone
Download at: https://market.android.com/ or www.itunes.com
Cognitive skills: numerical fluency, processing speed, visual processing
This fun math game has different levels to work for ages 4 through 12.


*Simon Says*
Available for: Android or iPhone
Download at: https://market.android.com/ or www.itunes.com
Cognitive skills: auditory processing, processing speed, visual processing, attention
The simple-but-not-easy famous game is back!


*Soduko Free*
Available for: Android or iPhone
Download at: http://www.Genina.com
Cognitive skills: strategy, visual processing, logic, and reasoning
Your favorite numbers game from the Sunday paper is now available for your phone!


*Tangram*
Available for: Android or iPhone
Download at: http://m.androlib.com/ or www.itunes.com
Cognitive skills: spatial reasoning, visual processing, planning
Invented in China, this game requires that users form specific shapes with seven puzzle pieces. Master the game through the Arcade mode and you can advance to the 1,000-puzzle challenge mode.


*Tetris Free*
Available for: Android
Download at: http://www.eamobile.com/home/
Cognitive skills: planning, visual processing, processing speed
Slide, rotate, and drop shaped pieces into place at a fast pace.


*Train Conductor 2 Lite*
Available for: Android

Download at: http://trainconductorusa.com/
Cognitive skills: strategy, planning, processing speed
Voted "Best Mobile Game of 2010" by the Independent Game Festival of China, the lite version of this game requires quick decision-making skills to guide trains to their destination while avoiding disastrous collisions.


*WordSearch Unlimited*
Available for: Android or iPhone
Download at: http://jiuzhangtech.com/ or www.itunes.com
Cognitive skills: visual processing, strategy
With three levels and your choice of themes, each puzzle is unique.

# Appendix B

# AUTHORS JUST FOR BOYS

Joseph Bruchac
http://www.josephbruchac.com

Bruce Coville
http://www.brucecoville.com/

Chris Crutcher
http://www.chriscrutcher.com/

Carl Deuker
http://members.authorsguild.net/carldeuker/bio.htm

Margaret Peterson Haddix
http://haddixbooks.com/home.html

S. E. Hinton
http://www.sehinton.com

Brian Jacques
http://www.redwall.org/

Gordon Korman
http://gordonkorman.com/

Julius Lester
http://members.authorsguild.net/juliuslester/

David Lubar
http://www.davidlubar.com

Garth Nix
http://www.garthnix.com/

Gary Paulsen
http://www.randomhouse.com/features/garypaulsen/

Rodman Philbrick
http://www.rodmanphilbrick.com/

Philip Pullman
http://www.philip-pullman.com

J. K. Rowling
http://www.jkrowling.com

Louis Sachar
http://www.louissachar.com/

Graham Salisbury
http://www.grahamsalisbury.com

Jon Scieszka
http://www.guysread.com

Darren Shan (Darren O'Shaughnessy)
http://www.darrenshan.com

Neal Shusterman
http://www.storyman.com/

Lemony Snicket (Daniel Handler)
http://www.lemonysnicket.com

Jerry Spinelli
http://www.jerryspinelli.com

Todd Strasser
http://www.toddstrasser.com

Theodore Taylor
http://www.theodoretaylor.com

Jacqueline Woodson
http://www.jacquelinewoodson.com

Jane Yolen
http://www.janeyolen.com

# Appendix C

# BOOKS MADE INTO FILM

*A Day with Wilbur Robinson* by William Joyce

*A Series of Unfortunate Events* by Lemony Snicket

*A Wrinkle in Time* by Madeline L'Engle

*Airborne* by Kenneth Oppel

*Alice in Wonderland* by Lewis Carroll

*Because of Winn-Dixie* by Kate DiCamillo

*Beezus and Ramona* by Beverly Cleary

*Bridge to Terabithia* by Katherine Paterson

*Charlie and the Chocolate Factory* by Roald Dahl

*Charlotte's Web* by E. B. White

*Chronicles of Narnia Series* by C. S. Lewis

*Cirque Du Freak* by Darren Shan

*Clifford the Big Red Dog* by Norman Bridwell

*Cloudy with a Chance of Meatballs* by Judi Barrett

*Confessions of a Teenage Drama Queen* by Dyan Sheldon

*Coraline* by Neil Gaiman

*Curious George* by H. A. Rey

*Diary of a Wimpy Kid Series* by Jeff Kinney

*Ender's Game* by Orson Scott Card

*Eragon* by Christopher Paolini

*Ethel and Ernest* by Raymond Briggs

*Ever After: A Cinderella Story* by Wendy Loggia

*Fantastic Mr. Fox* by Roald Dahl

*Flipped* by Wendelin Van Draanen

*Freak the Mighty* by Rodman Philbrick

*Freaky Friday* by Mary Rodgers

*Harry Potter Series* by J. K. Rowling

*Hatchet* by Gary Paulsen

*Headhunters* by Jules Bass

*Holes* by Louis Sachar

*Hoot* by Carl Hiaasen

*Horton Hears a Who!* by Dr. Seuss

*Hotel for Dogs* by Lois Duncan

*How the Grinch Stole Christmas* by Dr. Seuss

*How to Eat Fried Worms* by Thomas Rockwell

*How to Train Your Dragon* by Cressida Cowell

*Indian in the Cupboard* by Lynne Reid Banks

*Inkheart* by Cornelia Funke

*James and the Giant Peach* by Roald Dahl

*Jeremy Fink and the Meaning of Life* by Wendy Mass

*Judy Moody* by Megan McDonald

*Jumanji* by Chris Van Allsburg

*Legends of the Guardians: The Owls of Ga'Hoolea* by Kathryn Lasky

*Lemonade Mouth* by Mark Peter Hughes

*Mars Needs Moms!* by Berkeley Breathed

*Matilda* by Roald Dahl

*Millions* by Frank Cottrell Boyce

*Mr. Popper's Penguins* by Richard and Florence Atwater

*Nim's Island* by Wendy Orr

*Nurse Matilda: The Collected Tales* by Christianna Brand

*Percy Jackson Series* by Rick Riordin

*Peter Pan* by J. M. Barrie

*Shrek* by William Steig

*Stardust* by Neil Gaiman

*Stormbreaker* by Anthony Horwitz

*Stuart Little* by E. B. White

*The Alchemyst: The Secrets of the Immortal Nicholas Flamel* by Michael Scott

*The Ant Bully* by John Nickle

*The Secret World of Arrietty,* a Disney remake of *The Borrowers* by Mary Norton

*The Boy in the Striped Pajamas* by John Boyne

*The Cat in the Hat* by Dr. Seuss

*The City of Ember* by Jeanne DuPrau

*The Girl with the Dragon Tattoo* by Stieg Larsson

*The Golden Compass* by Philip Pullman

*The Gruffalo* by Julia Donaldson

*The Hitchhikers Guide to the Galaxy* by Douglas Adams

*The Hobbit* by J. R. R. Tolkien

*The Hunger Games Trilogy* by Suzanne Collins

*The Invention of Hugo Cabret* by Brian Selznick

*The Life of Pi* by Yann Martel

*The Little Engine That Could* by Watty Piper

*The Lorax* by Dr. Seuss

*The Many Adverntures of Winnie the Pooh* by A. A. Milne

*The Mortal Instruments: City of Bones* by Cassandra Clare

*The Neverending Story* by Michael Ende and Ralph Manheim

*The Night at the Museum* by Milan Trenc

*The Perks of Being a Wallflower* by Stephen Chobsky

*The Seventh Son* by Joseph Delaney

*The Spectacular Now* by Tim Tharp

*The Spiderwick Chronicles* by Holly Black and Tony DiTerlizzi

*The Tale of Despereaux: Being the Story of a Mouse, a Princess, Some Soup and a Spool of Thread* by Kate DiCamillo

*The Wonderful Wizard of Oz* by L. Frank Baum

*Tuck Everlasting* by Natalie Babbitt

*War Horse* by Michael Morpurgy

*Where the Wild Things Are* by Maurice Sendak

*Where's Wally* by Martin Hanford

# Appendix D

# MAGAZINES FOR BOYS

*Adventure Box*—Each issue includes a 40-page chapter story illustrated in full color, with sections on animals and science, games, jokes, and cartoons about two madcap siblings for ages 6–8.

*Appleseeds*—Filled with nonfiction reading and social studies topics for kids ages 7–9.

*Ask*—Cartoons, contests, projects, Web experiments, games and puzzles for kids ages 6–9.

*Boys Quest*—Adventure and educational entertainment for boys ages 6–14.

*Boys' Life*—News, nature, sports, science, and comics for boys ages 7–14.

*Bumples*—www.bumples.com—interactive story magazine for ages 4–10.

*Calliope*—A passport to world history for ages 9–14.

*Chickadee*—A discovery magazine designed to educate and entertain ages 6–9.

*Children's Web Magazine*—www.childrenswebmagazine.com—A fun and informative online magazine for ages 8 and up.

*Cicada*—A fiction and poetry magazine for teens and young adults age 14 and up.

*Click*—Opens up a universe of wonder by introducing kids ages 3–7 to the world.

*Cobblestone*—Award-winning American history magazine for ages 9 and up.

*Cricket*—Feeds the minds and imaginations of readers ages 9–14.

*Dig*—Mummies, pyramids, and new discoveries about ancient civilizations for ages 9–14.

*Faces*—Understanding how people in other countries and cultures live for ages 9–14.

*Fun for Kidz* —Fun activities, no advertising, and no teen material for ages 5–13.

*Highlights for Children*—The world's best loved magazine with fun for a purpose for ages 6–12.

*Humpty Dumpty*—Stories, poems, cartoons, puzzles, games, recipes, and crafts are designed for emergent readers ages 5–7.

*Jack & Jill*—Keeps kids entertained with engaging stories, challenging games, colorful comics, kid-centered interviews, recipes, and crafts for ages 7–12.

*Junior Baseball*—Covers baseball skills, profiles of outstanding youth teams and players, tournaments, new equipment, profiles of Major League stars, nutrition, injury prevention, skills clinics, baseball cards, and autographs for ages 7–17.

*Kids Discover*—Investigates a single science or social studies topic in each issue for ages 6–12.

*KIND News*—Published by the Humane Society of the United States profiles of amazing kids, features about rescued animals, pet care tips, and how-tos on helping backyard wildlife. Available in three reading levels: Primary Edition (grades K–2), Junior Edition (grades 3–4), and Senior Edition (grades 5–6).

*Ladybug*—Opens the door to reading for ages 2–6.

*Muse*—Stimulates, delights, and challenges every curious child ages 9–14.

*National Geographic Kids*—Fact-filled, fast-paced magazine with photos, facts, and fun created especially for ages 6 and up.

*National Geographic Little Kids*—An innovative new magazine full of learning and fun for preschoolers with lively photographs, engaging stories, and interactive picture games.

*New York Times Upfront*—A news magazine for teenagers published biweekly during the school year by The New York Times and Scholastic Inc.

*Odyssey*—An award-winning science magazine for ages 10 and up.

*Owl*—Challenges kids with articles on science, technology, and the natural world for ages 9–13.

*Preschool Friends*—Combines learning, laughter, playtime, and fun with Curious George, Scooby Doo, Clifford Puppy Days, Super Why, Wow! Wow! Wubbzy, and other favorite friends.

*Popular Science*—For ages 12 and up.

*Ranger Rick*—Packed with amazing facts, stunning photos, and outdoor adventures that help kids sharpen reading skills and develop a deeper appreciation for nature for ages 7 and up.

*Ranger Rick Jr.*—Fun activities, simple stories, and wild animals for ages 3–7.

*Scooby-Doo!*—Stories, a collectible poster, and a workbook full of fun educational activities ages 4–9.

*Skipping Stones*—Multicultural literary magazine for ages 8–17.

*Spider*—Stories, poems, nonfiction articles, riddles and games for ages 6–9.

*Sports Illustrated*—For ages 12 and up.

*Sports Illustrated KIDS*—Excitement, passion, and fun of sports to kids, tweens, and young teens in an action-oriented, authentic and interactive style.

*Stone Soup*—Stories, poems, and art by children for ages 8–13.

*Teen Ink*—A national teen literary magazine devoted entirely to teenage writing, art, photos, and forums for ages 13–19.

*Thomas & Friends*—Charming stories, a collectible poster, and a workbook filled with fun and educational activities for ages 3–8.

*Time for Kids*—A classroom magazine that engages students while presenting them with high-quality nonfiction writing to build reading and critical thinking skills. Each issue covers a variety of themes, topics and current events. The magazine has four grade-level targeted editions that help fit the needs of different K–6 classrooms.

*TransWorld Skateboarding*—Showcasing the best photography, creative direction, and storytelling in skateboarding for ages 12 and up.

*Turtle*—Fun for preschoolers ages 3–5.

*Weekly Reader and Scholastic News*—Classroom magazines—elementary magazines explore grade-appropriate nonfiction content and news stories, middle and high school magazines provide subject-specific articles about science, current events, health, and literature.

*WWE Kids*—Topics range from fitness and nutrition to geography and esteem building for ages 6–13.

*Yum Food & Fun for Kids*—Fun, fresh, quick, and effortless recipes.

*Zoobies*—Beautiful photographs, adorable illustrations, poems, and fingerplays for ages 0–3.

*Zoobooks*—Each issue "captures" one of sixty different animals through magnificent photography, illustrations, diagrams, descriptions, and includes interactive activity pages for ages 6–12.

*Zootles Magazine*—Wildlife photography, stories, activities and puzzles, a featured letter and number, and fascinating animal facts for ages 2–6.

# Appendix E

# WEB SITES

## GENERAL SCHOOL SITES

Boy Friendly Schools—Helping Boys Succeed in School Today - www.boy friendlyschools.com

Mike McQueen: We are a community-based blog for parents, librarians, and teachers. We provide information and support through articles, videos, interviews, and our forum - http://www.gettingboystoread.com

Physics Problems and Solutions for Real World Applications - http://www.real -world-physics-problems.com

*National Geographic Kids*—Creature features, games, homework help, and kids news sections - http://kids.nationalgeographic.com/kids/

Exploratorium Museum of Science, Art and Human Perception - http://www .exploratorium.edu/

The Rock and Roll Hall of Fame and Museum - http://www.rockhall.com/education/

Social Media Technology and Learning - www.worldwideworkshop.org

The Perfect Music for Brain-Based Learning - www.jensenlearning.com/news/the -perfect-music-for-brain-based-learning/brain-based-learning

Rhythm Rhyme Results - www.educationalrap.com

Songs for Teaching and Learning - www.songsforteaching.com

Study Skills and Test Taking Tips - http://testtakingtips.com

Study Guides and Strategies - http://studygs.net

## GRAPHICS, ANIMATION, AND GRAPHIC NOVELS

Fastest Way to Create Comic Strips - www.toondoo.com

Make a Comic - www.stripcreator.com/make.php

Animation Software – www.toonboom.com

Learn to Design Video Games - www.gamestarmechanic.com

Comics in Education - www.humblecomics.com/comicsedu/index.html

Comics in the Classroom - www.comicsintheclassroom.blogspot.com

Graphic Novel Reporter - www.graphicnovelreporter.com

Graphic Novel Resources - www.graphicnovelresources.blogspot.com

Great Graphic Novels for Teens - www.ala.org/yalsa/ggnt

Librarian's Guide to Anime and Manga - www.koyagi.com/Libguide.html

No Flying No Tights - www.noflyingnotights.com

Reading with Pictures - www.readingwithpictures.org

Getting to Know Graphic Novels - http://www.ala.org/aasl/aaslpubsandjournals/knowledgequest/archive/v41no3

## READING

Share What You Are Reading - http://teacher.scholastic.com/activities/swyar

Spotlighting Great Books for Kids and Teens - www.booktrailersforreaders.com

Books That Boys Love to Read - https://www.Facebook.com/GreatBooksForBoys

Jon Scieszka - www.guysread.com

Teach with Picture Books - http://teachwithpicturebooks.blogspot.com/

Best Books for Boys - http://www.boysread.org/books.html

James Patterson's Web site for Kids' Books – www.readkiddoread.com

I Hated to Read til I Read This—Book List for Boys - http://www.readkiddoread.com/uploads/ihatedtoreadtilireadthisbooksforboys.php

Wall of Books: 140+ Books for the Boys of YA - http://www.thereadventurer.com/1/post/2012/11/wall-of-books-140-books-for-the-boys-of-ya.html

Books Guys Dig - http://yaloveblog.com/books-guys-dig/

Eight YA Authors Recommended for Teenage Guys - http://www.thereadventurer.com/1/post/2012/11/eight-ya-authors-recommend-books-for-teenage-guys.html

Reading and Writing Help - http://livethewritinglife.blogspot.com/

Ralph Fletcher's site - http://www.ralphfletcher.com

## GAMES AND FUN

http://www.kidswb.com - This site is filled with games featuring the WB's great kid's shows.

http://disney.com/ - Fun and games of all things Disney contains a family fun section plus educational games.

http://www.harrypotterwizardscollection.com/ - The official site of *Harry Potter*. Filled with fun, games, and information about Harry Potter.

http://www.billsgames.com/ - Bill's Games—Filled with fun and games for the whole family.

http://www.lego.com/en-us/ - Legos games to play, your own Lego webpage and Lego building, a community section, and a free magazine subscription.

http://www.nick.com/ - Nickelodeon.

http://pbskids.org/ - Educational Games and Videos.

http://www.nickjr.com/ - Family Shows.

http://www.cartoonnetwork.com/ - Cartoon Network.

http://www.poptropica.com/ - A virtual world for kids to travel, play games, compete in head-to-head competition, and communicate safely.

http://www.moshimonsters.com/welcome - Adopt Your Own Pet Monster.

http://www.funbrain.com/ - Fun Brain.

http://www.coolmath-games.com/ - Free Online Math Games.

# Appendix F

# ANNOTATED PROFESSIONAL RESOURCES

## RESOURCES ABOUT BOYS

King, Kelley. *Writing the Playbook: A Practitioner's Guide to Creating a Boy-Friendly School.* Corwin Press, 2013.

>   This is one of the best books I have read about educating boys. The author is a master trainer for the Gurian Institute and actually put all of the book's strategies to use in a Colorado school in 2005 and obtained spectacular results. It is puzzling that because this model is a documented success it has not been replicated in other schools and was discontinued at her school when she left. The entire playbook is filled with excellent ideas and strategies. The important factor is taking what we have in front of us in the classroom/school situation and working to improve the education of all students, not just boys.

Reichert, Michael and Richard Hawley. *Teaching Boys Reaching Boys: Strategies That Work and Why.* Jossey-Bass, 2010.

>   The authors discuss the importance of creating specific games or adapting existing games for academic purposes. Games can be used to reinforce foundational skills, to review difficult operations, to help with skill retention, and strengthen problem-solving skills. Most all boys love gaming. Motor activity is important for boys as in role-playing, teamwork, and competition. They are especially attentive and more easily engaged when teachers really know their subjects. Boys can sense and profit from a teacher's personal enjoyment of the subject they are teaching. They are also especially eager for a solid teacher-student relationship where the teacher actually shows interest in a student's extracurricular activities.

Sullivan, Michael. *Connecting Boys with Books 2: Closing the Reading Gap.* American Library Association, 2009.

> The author is a media specialist. When we talk about the problem of boys and reading, we usually focus on boys who struggle with reading. Becoming better and more avid readers would certainly help boys in general. An important thing to remember is that boys often see reading as just a required subject in school. It is important to change that perception by exposing boys to stories. This goal can be accomplished by reading aloud to boys. Another often overlooked opportunity to build interest is to allow boys to choose the books they would like to read. It is also important to understand how critical the beginning years at home are with regard to learning to read.

Tyre, Peg. *The Trouble with Boys: A Surprising Report Card on Our Sons, Their Problems at School and What Parents and Educators Must Do.* Three Rivers Press, 2008.

> For nearly a decade now, the evidence has been accumulating that boys, in general, are doing less well in school than girls. And slowly, parents, teachers, and school administrators are waking up to the fact that they are going to need to do something about it. Boys get expelled from preschool nearly five times more often than girls. In elementary school, they're diagnosed with learning disorders four times as often. By eighth grade, huge numbers are reading below basic level. Perhaps most alarming, boys now account for less than 43 percent of those enrolled in college. The author explains just why and how the educational system is failing our sons, from the banning of recess and the lack of male teachers as role models to the demands of the school curriculum. The author proposes changes that we must undertake right away if we hope to salvage our boys' educational futures.

## GENERAL PROFESSIONAL RESOURCES

Jensen, Eric and Carole Snider. *Turnaround Tools for the Teenage Brain: Helping Underperforming Students Become Lifelong Learners.* Jossey-Bass, 2013.

> Jensen, a long-time favorite of mine in the field of applying brain research in education, discusses the teenage brain and ways to identify and help underperforming students. The chapters cover attitude, cognitive capacity, student effort, and empowering all exceptional learners. He also provides information on strengthening the body, mind, and soul as well as helping students to focus on attainable goals.

## COMMON CORE PROFESSIONAL RESOURCES

Bellanca, James and Robin Fogarty, Brian Pete. *How to Teach Thinking Skills within the Common Core: 7 Key Student Proficiencies of the New National Standards.* Solution Tree, 2012.

> The seven key student proficiencies include: critical thinking, creative thinking, complex thinking, comprehensive thinking, collaborative thinking, communicative thinking, and cognitive transfer. Each area has key skills that are necessary to use to develop these proficiencies. Critical thinking skills include: analyze, evaluate, and problem solve. Creative thinking skills include: generate, associate, and hypothesize. Complex thinking skills include: clarify, interpret, and determine. Comprehensive thinking skills include: understand, infer, and compare and contrast. Collaborative thinking skills include: explain, develop, and decide. Communicative thinking skills include: reason, connect, and represent. Cognitive transfer skills include: synthesize, generalize, and apply.

The authors also include an interesting teaching model: talk through, walk through, and drive through.

Calkins, Lucy, Mary Ehrenworth, and Christopher Lehman. *Pathways to the Common Core: Accelerating Achievement.* Heinemann, 2012.

Lucy Calkins, the reading-writing workshop guru from Teachers College at Columbia University, is the lead organizer-writer for this book on the English Language Arts Common Core. The first two chapters provide an overview of the standards. Next is a complete discussion of text complexity and reading literature and informational text. The next section thoroughly evaluates all aspects of the writing program, covering the three types of writing. The last two chapters highlight speaking and listening and effective ways to implement the English Language Arts Common Core Program school wide.

Eliot, Lise. *Pink Brain Blue Brain: How Small Differences Grow into Troublesome Gaps—and What We Can Do About It.* Harcourt Houghton Mifflin, 2009.

The author, a neuroscientist, calls on years of exhaustive research and her own work in the field of neural plasticity and argues that infant brains are so malleable that small differences in birth become amplified over time, as parents, teachers, peers, and the culture at large, unwittingly reinforce gender stereotypes. She zeros in on the exact differences between boys and girls retracting harmful stereotypes. Boys are not in fact better at math but in certain kinds of spatial reasoning. Girls are not naturally more empathetic than boys, they are just allowed to express their feelings more. Social factors such as how we speak to our sons and daughters and whether we encourage their physical adventurousness are proving to be far more powerful than we previously realized. We need our boys to be emotionally intelligent and our girls to be technologically savvy. By appreciating how sex differences emerge, rather than assuming them to be fixed biological facts, we can help all children reach their fullest potential, close the troubling gaps between boys and girls, and ultimately and the gender wars that currently divide us (from http://www.rosalindfranklin.edu/faculty/Eliot_Lise/publications/Book1/Synopsis.aspx).

Fisher, Douglas and Nancy Frey, Diane Lapp. *Teaching Students to Read Like Detectives: Comprehending, Analyzing, and Discussing Text.* Solution Tree, 2011.

Literacy is an access skill to understanding, not an end unto itself. Literacy must be part of all content areas. David Coleman, project editor for Common Core English Language Arts Standards, said, "We want students to read like detectives and write like reporters." The authors elaborate on the need for proficient readers to actively and reciprocally draw on their experiences to compare, contrast, validate, and extend what they are reading. There is an implied importance of background knowledge and possibly the importance of major use of informational text from a very young age. The authors also share how important academic talk and text-based conversations will be when teaching students to read like detectives.

Frey, Nancy and Diane Lapp, Douglas Fisher. *Text Complexity: Raising Rigor in Reading.* International Reading Association, 2012.

The authors share thoughts on the newfound importance of text complexity, by thoroughly describing it and highlighting the importance of struggling a bit in the quest to be a more efficient reader and tempering that with ample strategies for assisting readers. They provide information on readability and say that quantitative measure should only be the first step. The authors fully develop the concept of the qualitative measures of text complexity: considerate texts, structure, coherence, and audience. They also discuss the importance of matching text to readers and emphasize that not all students need to read the same text at the same time. In close reading, the teacher should not give away the meaning of the text or of the vocabulary.

Glass, Kathy Tuchman. *Mapping Comprehensive Units to the ELA Common Core Standards: K–5.* Corwin, 2012.

The author begins by talking about standards and knowledge, understanding informational text, and different text types. The second chapter tells about essential understandings and guiding questions. This chapter includes examples of essential units and lesson guiding questions. The next two chapters provide unit templates with examples and culminating assessments along with rubrics and checklists. A chapter incorporates skills, activities, formative assessments, and resources. There is also a chapter about differentiated instruction with content, process, and product. There is a chapter on lesson design, and the book concludes with a resource section on English Language Arts Common Core Standards.

McEwan-Adkins, Elaine and Allyson Burnett. *20 Literacy Strategies to Meet the Common Core: Increasing Rigor in Middle & High School Classrooms.* Solution Tree Press, 2013.

The authors provide clear and easy-to-follow strategies for the English Language Arts Common Core Standards grouped by the four main categories: key ideas and details, craft and structure, knowledge and ideas, and text complexity.

Tovani, Cris. *Do I Really Have To Teach Reading? Content Comprehension, Grades 6–12.* Stenhouse Publishers, 2004.

This text was published in 2004 but it is especially timely today when English Language Arts Common Core Standards are required of all content area middle and high school teachers to effectively teach reading. Tovani shares strategies used by good readers, fix-up strategies, and what works. The author also shares special principles for reading math textbooks and samples for using mental modeling. She also describes the need for sharing the instructional purpose for reading text and then strategies for marking texts, and for getting "unstuck" as well as the importance of group work. The appendix includes an excellent silent reading response sheet and a template for a reading response log.

# WORKS CITED

Anderson, Julie. "To Encourage Boys Reading, Look To Book Clubs." http://www.omaha.com/article/20130520/NEWS/705209952. Accessed May 2013.

Aronson, Marc, Kathleen Odean, Myra Zarnowski, and Sue Bartle. "The Uncommon Core: Champions of Nonfiction Literature for Children and Young Adult." http://nonfictionandthecommoncore.blogspot.com

Aronson, Marc. Nonfiction Matters. School Library Journal Blog. http://www.blogs.slj.com/nonfictionmatters

Aronson, Marc. "The Road Ahead: Common Core Insights: Consider the Source." http://www.slj.com/2013/05/opinion/consider-the-source/the-road-ahead-common-core-insights-consider-the-source/. Accessed May 29, 2013.

Benjamin, Amy. *Big Skills for the Common Core*. Eye on Education, 2012.

Binns, Barbara and James Klise. "Attracting Reluctant Male Readers." *American Library Association Annual Conference* (June 2013).

Boyd, Fenice. "The Common Core State Standards and Diversity: Unpacking the Text Exemplars Presented in Appendix B." *Reading Today* 30:3 (2013): 10–11.

Boyles, Nancy. "Closing in on Close Reading." *Education Leadership* 70:4 (2012–2013): 36–41.

Bradley, Linda Golson and Carol Donovan. "Information Book Read-Alouds as Models for Second-Grade Authors." *Reading Teacher* 64:4 (2010–2011): 246–260.

Ciardiello, A. Vincent. "Did You Ask a Good Common Core Question Today? The Cognitive and Metacognitive Dimensions of Enhanced Inquiry Skills." *Reading Today* 30:3 (2013): 14–16.

Claiborne, Ron and Hanna Siegel. "New Study Shows Boys Lagging Behind Girls in Reading: Boys Are Struggling With Reading in All 50 States." http://abcnews.go.com/WN/study-shows-boys-lagging-girls-reading/story?id=10128586#.UdX5cW3W-4I. Accessed March 2010.

Corsaro, Julie. "Common Core: It's Not Happening without the Librarian." *Kids & Book News* (September 2012).

Cummins, Sunday and Cate Stallmeyer-Gerard. "Teaching for Synthesis of Informational Texts with Read-Alouds." *Reading Teacher* 64:6 (2011): 394–405.

Daniels, Harvey, S. Zemelman, and A. Hyde. *Best Practice: Bringing Standards to Life in America's Classrooms.* Heinemann, 2012.

Day, Lori. "Why Boys Are Failing in an Educational System Stacked Against Them." http://www.huffingtonpost.com/lori-day/why-boys-are-failing-in-a_b_884262.html. Accessed June 2011.

DeCost, Sally. "Exemplar Read Aloud Texts for Common Core." www.elementarymatters.com. September 2012.

Dobler, Elizabeth. "Authentic Reasons for Close Reading: How to Motivate Students to Take Another Look." *Reading Teacher* 30:6 (2013): 13.

Duke, Nell, and V. Susan Bennett-Armistead. *Reading & Writing Informational Text in the Primary Grades: Research-Based Practices.* Scholastic, 2003.

Eliot, Lise. "The Myth of Pink and Blue Brains." *Best of Educational Leadership* 68 (2010–2011): 32–36.

Everette, Meghan. "Common Core: Key Shifts in English Language Arts." http://www.scholastic.com/teachers/top-teaching/2013/02/common-core-key-shifts-english-language-arts. Accessed February 22, 2013.

Finn, Chester. "Standards, Reading Lists, and Censorship." *The Education Gadfly* 13:36 (2013).

Firth, Shannon. "Five Ways To Get Boys To Read." http://www.findingdulcinea.com/news/education/2010/april/5-Ways-to-Get-Boys-to-Read.html. Accessed June 28, 2011.

Fisher, Douglas, Nancy Frey, and Diane Lapp. *Teaching Students to Read Like Detectives: Comprehending, Analyzing, and Discussing Text.* Solution Tree Press, 2012.

Gewertz, Catherine. "Common Core Thrusts Librarians into Leadership Role." *Education Week* 32:3 (2012): 1, 18–19.

Gewertz, Catherine. "Common Standards Ignite Debate Over Student Prereading." *Education Week* 31:29 (2012): 1, 22–23.

Hiebert, Elfrieda. "CCSS Text Exemplars: Understanding Their Aims and Use in Text Selection." *Reading Today* 30:3 (2013): 6–7.

Hiebert, Elfrieda. "Looking 'Within' the Lexile for More Guidance: Word Frequency and Sentence Length." www.textproject.org. January 2011.

Hiebert, Elfrieda. "Read-Aloud Favorites: A Source for Enriching Students' Knowledge of the World and of Language." www.textproject.org. March 2013.

Hiebert, Elfrieda. "Seven Actions That Teachers Can Take Right Now: Text Complexity." www.textproject.org/text-matters. 2012.

Hiebert, Elfrieda and P. David Pearson. "What Happens to the Basics?" *Educational Leadership* 70:4 (2012–2013): 48–53.

Hill, Rebecca. "All Aboard!: Implementing Common Core Offers School Librarians an Opportunity to Take the Lead." *School Library Journal Archive Content* (March 16, 2012).

Hoyt, Linda. "Igniting a Sense of Wonder: Helping Students Find Joy in Informational Texts." www.heinemann.com/pd/journal. 2013.

Hunt, Jonathan. "The Amorphous Genre." *Hornbook.* http://www.hbook.com/2013/05/choosing-books/horn-book-magazine/the-amorphous-genre/. Accessed May 2013.

Jaeger, Paige. "Balancing Readability and Reading Fluency: On Common Core." http://www.slj.com/2013/03/standards/common-core/readability-and-reading-fluency-students-need-to-enjoy-what-they-choose-for-independent-reading-on-common-core/. Accessed March 12, 2013.

Jaeger, Paige. "Vulcanizing Vocabulary: Librarians Lead Path to Achievement." *School Library Journal.* http://www.slj.com/2013/06/opinion/on-common-core/vulcanizing-vocabulary-a-research-scientist-charts-a-pah-to-achievement/. Accessed June 25, 2013.

Kimmel, Michael. "Solving the Boy Crisis in School." http://www.huffingtonpost.com/michael-kimmel/solving-the-boy-crisis-in_b_3126379.html. Accessed April 2013.

King, Kelley, Michael Gurian, and Kathy Stevens. "Gender-Friendly Schools." *Educational Leadership* 68:3 (2010): 38–42.

Kleinfeld, Judy. "Schools Find Ways to Help Boys Learn." http://www.newsminer.com/opinion/community_perspectives/schools-find-ways-to-help-boys-learn/article_683a66d8-a8c8-11e2-89da-0019bb30f31a.html. Accessed April 2013.

Knowles, Elizabeth and Martha Smith. *Boys and Literacy: Practical Strategies for Librarians, Teachers, and Parents.* Libraries Unlimited, 2005.

Lahey, Jessica. "Stop Penalizing Boys for Not Being Able to Sit Still at School." *The Atlantic* (June 2013).

Lehman, Christopher. *Energize Research Reading and Writing: Fresh Strategies to Spark Interest, Develop Independence, and Meet Key Common Core Standards, Grades 4–8.* Heinemann, 2012.

Lipsyte, Robert. "Boys and Reading: Is There Any Hope?" http://www.nytimes.com/2011/08/21/books/review/boys-and-reading-is-there-any-hope.html?pagewanted=all&_r=0. Accessed August 2011.

McLaughlin, Maureen and Brenda Overturf. "The Hunger Games and the Common Core: Determining the Complexity of Contemporary Texts." December 2012/January 2013. *Reading Today* 30:3 (2013): 8–9.

McLaughlin, Maureen and Douglas Fisher. "Teaching Students to Meet the Common Core Standards in Grades 6–12? Analyze This!" *Reading Today* 30:3 (2013): 12–13.

McQueen, Mike. "An Interview with Ralph Fletcher." http://gettingboystoread.com/content/interview-ralph-fletcher/. Accessed 2011.

McTighe, Jay and Grant Wiggins. "Common Core Standards to Curriculum: Five Big Ideas." Privately Published Paper, 2012.

Nelson, Daryl. "Girls Are Thrashing Boys in Academic Achievement. How Come?" http://www.newstribune.com/news/2013/apr/21/girls-are-thrashing-boys-academic-achievement-how-/. Accessed April 2013.

Ohio State University (February 25, 2013). "Boys' lack of effort in school tied to college gender gap." *ScienceDaily.* Retrieved September 26, 2013.

Overturf, Brenda and Timothy Shanahan. "Literacy Implementation Guidance for the ELA Common Core Stater Standards." *International Reading Association Common Core State Standards Committee.* 2012.

Phillips, Vicki and Carina Wong. "Teaching to the Common Core by Design: Not by Accident." *Phi Delta Kappa International.* Published online: April 6, 2012.

Reichert, Michael and Richard Hawley. "Relationships Play a Primary Role in Boys' Learning." *Phi Delta Kappan* 94 (2013): 49–53.

Rothman, Robert. *Something in Common: The Common Core Standards and the Next Chapter in American Education.* Harvard Education Press, 2011.

Rothstein, Dan and Luz Santana. *Make Just One Change: Teach Students To Ask Their Own Questions.* Harvard Education Press, 2011.

Sacks, Glenn. "Boys: The New Underclass in American Schools." http://www.glennsacks.com/column.php?id=40. Accessed April 2002.

Schmoker, Mike and Carol Jago. "Simplifying the ELA Common Core: Demystifying Curriculum." *Phi Delta Kappa Record.* Published online: April 29, 2013.

Sellers, John. "BEA 2013: The Boy Readers Are All Right." http://www.publishers weekly.com/pw/by-topic/childrens/childrens-industry-news/article/57688-bea-2013-the -boy-readers-are-all-right.html. Accessed June 2013.

Senn, Gary, Deborah McMurtrie, and Bridget Coleman. "RAFTing with Raptors: Connecting Science, English Language Arts, and the Common Core State Standards." *Middle School Journal.* January 2013.

Serafini, Frank. "Supporting Boys as Readers." *Reading Teacher* 67:1 (2013): 40–42.

Shanahan, Timothy. "CCSS Allows More than Lexiles." http://www.shanahanon literacy.com. September 2012.

Smith, Brett. "Study Examines Why Girls Do Better than Boys in School." http:// www.redorbit.com/news/science/1112757027/girls-do-better-in-school-than-boys -010313/. May 4, 2013.

Smith, Michael, Jeffrey Wilhelm, and James Fredricksen. "The Common Core: New Standards, New Teaching." *Phi Delta Kappan* 94:8 (2013): 45–48.

Snow, Catherine. "Cold Versus Warm Close Reading: Building Students' Stamina for Struggling with Text." *Reading Today* 30:6 (2013): 18–19.

Tyre, Peg, "It's Time to Worry: Boys are Rapidly Falling Behind Girls in School." http:// www.takepart.com/article/2013/02/14/boys-fall-behind-girls-school. Accessed February 2013.

Weeks, Matt. "New UGA Research Helps Explain Why Girls Do Better in School." http:// news.uga.edu/releases/article/why-girls-do-better-in-school-010212/. Accessed January 2013.

Wessling, Sarah Brown. "My 10 Greatest 'Ah-Ha' Moments in Working with the Common Core." www.theteachingchannel.com. August 7, 2012.

Wood, Summer and Robin Jocius. "Combating 'I Hate This Stupid Book!' Black Males and Critical Literacy." *Reading Teacher* 66:8 (2013): 661–669.

Zehr, Mary Ann. "Authors Share Tips on Getting Boys to Read." *Education Week* 28:36 (2009): 9.

Zimbardo, Philip and Nikita Duncan. *The Demise of Guys: Why Boys Are Struggling and What We Can Do About It.* TED e-book: May 2012.

# AUTHOR INDEX

# TITLE INDEX

## About the Authors

LIZ KNOWLES, EdD, is owner of Cognitive Advantage, a one-on-one cognitive coaching business. She is a former elementary teacher for grades K–6 and was adjunct professor, teaching graduate courses in reading, at Florida Atlantic University. Knowles has been the director of professional development and curriculum at Pine Crest School in Boca Raton and Fort Lauderdale, FL. Knowles received an undergraduate degree in elementary education from Central Connecticut State University; a master's degree in reading from Nova Southeastern University in Fort Lauderdale, FL; and a doctoral degree in curriculum development and systemic change, also from Nova Southeastern University.

MARTHA SMITH has been a media specialist for more than 30 years in the pre-K through 8th grade setting. She recently served as library media specialist at Pine Crest School, Boca Raton, FL. Smith received an undergraduate degree in library science from Eastern Michigan University and a **and a master of arts in library and information science** from the University of South Florida.